"With Meltdown, Sarah Boon evokes landscapes of intense vulnerability and power, inviting her readers on a journey that is both a daring adventure and a poetic meditation on seeking meaning in a precarious world."
—KATIE IVES, author of Imaginary Peaks

"In Meltdown, Sarah Boon's riveting account of breaking from her courageous, exacting life as an Arctic researcher is also a hope-filled map to making it as a world-class writer."
—REBECCA LAWTON, author of The Oasis This Time

"Boon's work can be compared to Rachel Carson's Silent Spring in its ability to channel scientific and human storytelling about our world at an extraordinary juncture of change and transformation. Boon is a writer who can observe field work like Aldo Leopold in A Sand County Almanac, convey anguish like Patricia Van Tighem in The Bear's Embrace, and open up silences like Maria Coffey in Where the Mountain Casts Its Shadow."
—PEARLANN REICHWEIN, author of Climber's Paradise

"Meltdown is a deeply personal narrative that reveals the hidden challenges of academic careers, including physical struggles, mental health issues, and the complexities of identity and impostor syndrome. Through candid accounts of fieldwork, interactions with colleagues, and the pursuit of work-life balance, Sarah Boon offers an unflinching look at the highs and lows of a career set against the backdrop of Arctic expeditions and a passion for nature and science."
—MELODY SANDELLS, Northumbria University

"Meltdown skillfully draws readers into a fast-changing world of snow and ice, glaciers and grizzlies. With unflinching honesty, Sarah Boon illuminates the hidden cracks and pitfalls in the life of a field scientist, even while her deep love of the natural world shines on every page."
—MELISSA L. SEVIGNY, author of Brave the Wild River

"A raw and honest look at the challenges of being a woman in academia, of the simultaneously competing and complementary aspects of science and art, and of the beauty, power, and fragility of icy worlds."
—JOSEPH SHEA, University of Northern British Columbia

"*Meltdown* is a real-life science thriller with a narrative as richly braided and unexpected as the glacial stream systems Sarah Boon studies. It's a clear-eyed, courageous look at the costs of being female in field science, suffused with deep love for the wild places where glaciers live."
—SUSAN J. TWEIT, field botanist and author of Bless the Birds

"Sarah Boon brings us along on her expeditions as she seeks to understand the precious, disappearing glaciers of northern Canada. *Meltdown* shows us in beautiful, open-hearted prose what it takes to build up a scientist over many years of trial, error, and determination... and how paradoxically fragile that balance can be."
—ERIN ZIMMERMAN, author of Unrooted

MELTDOWN

MELTDOWN

THE MAKING AND BREAKING OF A FIELD SCIENTIST

SARAH BOON

UNIVERSITY *of* ALBERTA PRESS

Published by

University of Alberta Press
1-16 Rutherford Library South
11204 89 Avenue NW
Edmonton, Alberta, Canada T6G 2J4
amiskwaciwâskahikan | Treaty 6 |
Métis Territory
ualbertapress.ca | uapress@ualberta.ca

Copyright © 2025 Sarah Boon

**Library and Archives Canada
Cataloguing in Publication**

Title: Meltdown : the making and breaking of a field scientist / Sarah Boon.
Names: Boon, Sarah, 1977– author.
Description: Includes bibliographical references.
Identifiers: Canadiana (print) 20240480732 | Canadiana (ebook) 20240481127 | ISBN 9781772127911 (softcover) | ISBN 9781772128024 (EPUB) | ISBN 9781772128031 (PDF)
Subjects: LCSH: Boon, Sarah, 1977- | LCSH: Women scientists—Canada—Biography. | LCSH: Scientists—Canada—Biography. | LCGFT: Autobiographies.
Classification: LCC Q143.B66 A3 2025 | DDC 509.2—dc23

First edition, first printing, 2025.
First printed and bound in Canada by Houghton Boston Printers, Saskatoon, Saskatchewan..
Copyediting by Mary Lou Roy.
Proofreading by Kay Rollans.
Maps by Dave Lewis.

All rights reserved. No part of this publication may be reproduced, stored in a retrieval system, or transmitted in any form or by any means (electronic, mechanical, photocopying, recording, generative artificial intelligence [AI] training, or otherwise) without prior written consent. Contact University of Alberta Press for further details.

University of Alberta Press supports copyright. Copyright fuels creativity, encourages diverse voices, promotes free speech, and creates a vibrant culture. Thank you for buying an authorized edition of this book and for complying with the copyright laws by not reproducing, scanning, or distributing any part of it in any form without permission. You are supporting writers and allowing University of Alberta Press to continue to publish books for every reader.

GPSR: Easy Access System Europe |
Mustamäe tee 50, 10621 Tallinn, Estonia |
gpsr.requests@easproject.com

University of Alberta Press gratefully acknowledges the support received for its publishing program from the Government of Canada, the Canada Council for the Arts, and the Government of Alberta through the Alberta Media Fund.

For Pappie, who loved fieldwork but never got to do enough of it.

Tell me, what is it you plan to do
With your one wild and precious life?
   —Mary Oliver, "The Summer Day"

This book is a work of creative nonfiction and is thus heavily reliant on my memory. To ensure the veracity of that memory, I have used personal journals, field notebooks, photos, blog posts, emails, university transcripts, and more, including conversations with people who were there with me. I have used pseudonyms for some people and changed some identifying details. In some instances, I have recreated dialogue and setting to maintain a cohesive narrative. As best as my memory allows, this book is a true account of my experience.

CONTENTS

PROLOGUE xv
MAPS xxiii

1 | VIEW FROM THE TOP 1
2 | HISTORY AROUND THE CORNER 29
3 | PREPARING FOR TAKEOFF 55
4 | TWENTY-FOUR-HOUR DAYLIGHT 77
5 | STAYING THE ARCTIC COURSE 107
6 | GOODBYE TO THE ARCTIC 137
7 | NOT "PAYING ATTENTION" 167
8 | INTO THE FOREST 191
9 | WOMEN IN SCIENCE 219
10 | OUTSIDE SCIENCE 249

EPILOGUE 271
ACKNOWLEDGEMENTS 275
NOTES 277
BIBLIOGRAPHY 279

PROLOGUE

"I DON'T WANT TO DIE, I DON'T WANT TO DIE," Derek moaned, huddled on the ice in a foil blanket from our first aid kit, freezing cold and soaking wet from the waist down.

It was June 2008. My grad student Derek and I had been up-glacier checking equipment installations until late in the evening, and were finally heading back to camp. We didn't get far before we realized we had a serious problem. A massive melt event had occurred on the lower glacier while we were away, and the previously safe snow surface we travelled on had become supersaturated and unstable, resulting in deep, fast-flowing, and almost impassable slushy streams. We were on the Devon Island Ice Cap in the Canadian Arctic, just off the west coast of Greenland, and were completely cut off from our tents, food, and gear. One saving grace was that, with the twenty-four-hour daylight, it didn't get cold at night.

Derek had decided to try to cross the first stream we encountered. The slush was like quicksand, and his legs got sucked into it. "Spread your weight!" I yelled, as he crawled onto the ice on the opposite side, pulling his legs out and using his arms to shuffle forward. Once across, he discovered that there was yet another slush flow blocking

(Top) On-ice field camp at Belcher Glacier, Nunavut, June 2008. (Photo by the author.)
(Bottom) Recording observations near a surface lake on Belcher Glacier.
(Photo by Derek, used with permission.)

his path to camp. He was effectively trapped on an island. I couldn't reach him, and he was starting to panic. We had to raise our voices to be heard over the raging, slushy stream. I was terrified that he was going to lose it, and I wasn't sure I could calm him down from a distance. On top of that, I had blown my bad knee by wading through deep snow all day. It was painful, swollen, and hard to bend. Even if I'd wanted to cross the slush flow to get to him, I couldn't. It was now 10:00 p.m. We didn't have to worry about being stuck in the dark, but Derek was freaking out. We were in trouble, and we needed help. Now.

I pulled the satellite phone out of my pack with shaky hands, my heart racing as I punched in the number for the research base in Resolute, some four hundred kilometres southwest of us. When the night crew answered, my first aid training kicked in. My heart rate slowed, I took a deep breath, and calm descended over me. I described our situation as best I could, including Derek's failing mental state, and pushed away the feeling of wanting to just yell at them to get us the hell out of there. Instead, I levelly asked for their suggestions as to what we should do. They decided that we needed to be evacuated immediately by helicopter and brought back to the base to be assessed by the nurse. We'd figure out what to do about our camp—and the rest of the field season—later.

The helicopter was several hours away. Not ideal, but manageable given the constant summer daylight. The dance of light and shadows accentuated different parts of the cliffs around us than it did during the day, a 180-degree shift in perspective from what we were used to. Was it strange to notice a touch of beauty in the middle of a live-action nightmare? I needed to keep Derek calm and alert so that he would focus on something other than his plight. To pass the time, we talked about the students who were camped higher on the glacier, the weather, where he lived, and what he did for fun. I tried everything in my repertoire to distract him from the position we were in.

Every hour or so the base would call back to check on us and I'd ask them questions: Should Derek take off his wet clothes? (No.) How long until the chopper arrives? (Two more hours.) They also had questions for me: How's the weather for flying? (Still great.) Where can the chopper land? (Not on the slush.)

Finally, around two in the morning, the *whoomph whoomph* of the chopper reached us as the aircraft crested the distant mountains and headed down-glacier. I was instantly relieved to know that we were going to be safe, that this ordeal would soon be over. Since Derek was the priority to evacuate, the pilot touched down close to him but the landing skids immediately started to get pulled into a slush flow. His eyes widened briefly before he quickly repositioned the helicopter on solid ice. He got Derek, still wet and cold, and his gear safely into the chopper then flew over to me; I threw in my pack and climbed aboard. We made a brief stop at our camp to grab essential personal effects, then buckled up, put on our headsets, and lifted off to return to base. I was exhausted and numb, not only from being awake for eighteen hours but from managing an emergency. I hardly noticed the rugged Arctic landscape pass below us on our three-hour flight; instead I dozed fitfully for the entire trip.

We arrived at the base at 5:00 a.m. and were immediately sent to see the nurse as protocol required. In three years of doing research out of the Resolute base, I'd never seen the place so quiet. Everyone was asleep, and even the kitchen crew wasn't up yet. The nurse gave me some anti-inflammatories and an ice pack for my knee and gave Derek some Ativan for anxiety. Once our medical check was done, I limped to my room and tried to sleep for an hour before the designated 7:00 a.m. check-in time, when I would have to tell the other field team on the glacier what had happened. I wasn't sure if they'd heard the chopper in the middle of the night, but they were definitely in for a surprise.

After our morning check-in, I emailed our team's principal investigator back in Alberta to fill him in. Apparently, he'd already been briefed by base staff and was glad that we were both in one piece. We drew up a plan of what to do next, which included dismantling our abandoned camp, sending our food to the two students who were camped on the upper glacier, and bringing the rest of the equipment and personal gear back to base.

Because of our adventure, however, Derek was adamant that he'd never set foot on a glacier again. So it was just me with my bad knee and the chopper pilot who went back to camp two days later. I hobbled around and packed up with the pilot's help—this wasn't his job but it was greatly appreciated. We shuttled the food to the upper camp, and then headed back to Resolute with the remaining gear. We flew over newly formed ice-surface stream channels with mounds of slush piled metres high on either side; they were flowing clear with meltwater now, running wide, fast, and deep. Derek and I were lucky to have survived what could have been a disaster. Now, the only disaster we faced was a five-week field season that had ended after just five days.

It was a beautiful day for a flight, though, sunny with blue skies. Staring out the window watching the Devon Island Ice Cap go by, I was lost in thought. Should I have become a writer as I had originally intended, instead of a scientist? Hard to say. Would this be my last stint in the Arctic? Probably, but not my last field season ever. I longed for female mentors to discuss this recent setback with, as I was afraid that speaking with a male mentor would raise questions about my competence in the field. Unfortunately, like in most sciences, women were scarce in glaciology. I knew of Dr. Bea Alt, a Canadian scientist who had worked on the Meighen Ice Cap as part of her PhD research in the 1960s and 1970s. The issues she faced as the only woman on her field research team required that she tread carefully to avoid being considered a "problem." There were two other female glaciologists in Canada at the time who were closer to my age, but I was intimidated by one of them and underwhelmed by the other—neither scenario would make for a good relationship.

* Scientific fieldwork is an integral part of research in many disciplines, including geology, geography, forestry, ecology, and others. Researchers use the outdoors as a natural laboratory, measuring snowpack and glacier movement, tree growth and wildfire spread, and everything in between. When anthropologist Jane Goodall studied chimpanzees in Tanzania, she was doing fieldwork. When

Parks Canada archaeologists worked with Inuit in Canada's Arctic to find the wreck of one of Sir John Franklin's ships, the HMS *Erebus*, they were doing fieldwork. When University of Alberta glaciologist Dr. Alison Criscitiello collected an ice core from the summit of Mount Logan, Canada's highest peak, she was doing fieldwork.

But it's not just research scientists who do fieldwork. The average person can participate through community science, which involves working on a local research project run by scientists who rely on volunteers to collect more data points than they could on their own. North America's longest running community science project started in 1900: the annual Christmas Bird Count. On a single day between December 14 and January 5, birders come out in droves to observe and count birds in a twenty-four-kilometre diameter circle in their region—the same circle every year. They submit their findings to the national coordinator who collates their results. Another example of ecologically focused community science is the BioBlitz, a concept that started in 1996 and involves volunteers in an intensive one-day inventory of all species in a defined area.

What all fieldwork projects have in common is that they require working outside, whether that's in your own neighbourhood or on a remote glacier. For community science projects, there's a leader who explains what data you have to collect and what methods to use. For your own field research, you have to decide what needs to be measured and how. Both require flexibility and patience, and sometimes dealing with the discomfort of bad weather, insects, heavy backpacks, malfunctioning equipment, and even boredom. Remote fieldwork, in particular, requires tackling a range of mental, physical, and logistical challenges. Field researchers thrive on a specific set of skills and attributes: resilience, self-reliance, creative problem-solving, and the ability to focus on the moment to decide what needs to be done.

In a short story by Jorge Luis Borges, cartographers were so exacting about their science that they ended up creating a map at the same scale as the world itself.[1] We can't do that. If we could measure everything, we'd have reams of data but not enough human power or computer power to analyze it. In environmental science, field research is often used to measure small-scale processes and then scale them up using numerical models (computer models that use field data as input) or remote sensing (satellite data analysis, lidar measurements). Field research can also be used in the opposite direction: to ground-truth the output from numerical models and remote sensing analyses. Small-scale research provides a sense of how larger-scale processes work, which are much more difficult to measure. Researchers set up experiments in natural systems by first identifying what their research questions are. The trick lies in determining the best variables to measure or monitor in order to answer those questions.

In many university programs, attending a field school is a required part of earning a degree, especially in geology, forestry, archaeology, and geography. Students are immersed in the outdoors for a short, intensive period, during which they learn field skills applicable to their discipline, like how to measure river flow or tree growth. Everyone learns the same things in the same environment and works together to complete their field projects. Students also live together in field camps for up to ten days at a time. They eat meals together, conduct their research together, and socialize in the evenings—either doing homework or hanging out around a campfire.

This combination of working and living together creates a camaraderie that forges strong bonds of friendship and belonging, and can be especially important for the success of historically marginalized people in academia. Studies have shown that students who participate in field schools have higher graduation rates and higher graduating GPAs, suggesting that these experiences could be a way to enhance diversity in science by increasing access for women and other underrepresented groups.[2] For me, field school changed my career trajectory: I went from potentially dropping out of university to sticking around for a fun and interesting outdoors course.

In remote field camps, you rely on your camp-mates not only for company but, in many cases, for safety. In our glacier camp, we travelled roped together during the spring season to reduce the risk of losing someone in a crevasse, as these hazards were often covered by rotten, unstable spring snow. If someone did fall in, it was up to our entire crew to get them out. In a geology camp where ATVs are used to access field sites, camp-mates help when an ATV gets stuck or when a driver can't make it up a particularly tricky hill.

Fieldwork is not without its downsides, however, notably for women. A 2014 study in anthropology found that 64 per cent of field participants experienced sexual harassment, while 22 per cent experienced sexual assault; only in rare cases were these events reported.[3] In 2017, three women stepped forward to accuse Boston University glacial geologist Dave Marchant of sexual harassment in Antarctica. The stories of their experiences are harrowing, including having rocks thrown at them while urinating in the field, being called demeaning names, and being urged to have sex with Marchant's brother, who was also in the field.[4] In a *New York Times* article, Hope Jahren wrote about being sexually assaulted while she was doing fieldwork in Turkey in 1996, and how it led her to change her research field from geology to plant biology.[5] Why? Because in plant biology you're in a lab, which is safer than being in the field. Harassment, assault, and abuse can stop excellent students from taking on research topics where fieldwork is required; in the Marchant case, one of the complainants left academia entirely. Marchant was ultimately fired from Boston University in 2019.[6]

Fieldwork may be fun and rewarding, but it's tempered by these and other challenges facing women and other marginalized groups. So, why do we pursue such opportunities? Though I was always interested in writing and being a writer, I enjoyed the outdoors and assumed the right type of degree, perhaps in geography, would give me the opportunity to work outside regularly. Field science was also a good backup plan, something that would make me more employable than writing. But the longer I stayed in academia, the less time I spent outdoors. After more than a decade, I was in the field for just a few days each year.

Fieldwork played a big part in making me who I am today. This is the story of my time as a female field scientist at research sites ranging from glaciers to beetle-chewed forests. I explore the challenge of juggling writing and science, and how the two can complement each other. I champion the women who went before me and those who came afterwards, in both field science and outdoor exploration, and prove that remote field research doesn't always require exceptional outdoor prowess (though it can help). I recount my experiences with the precarities and sometimes hidden pitfalls of the academic career path—especially for women—and describe my struggle with a serious mental health diagnosis, losing my identity as an academic scientist, and finding the right work–life balance to sustain my creativity. Join me on my journeys around western Canada and the Arctic, as I fly in Twin Otters and helicopters, traverse glaciers, and scare away grizzly bears to study snow, ice, and climate change.

MAPS

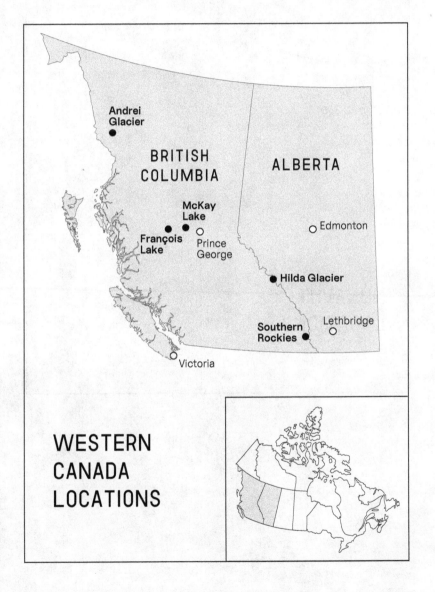

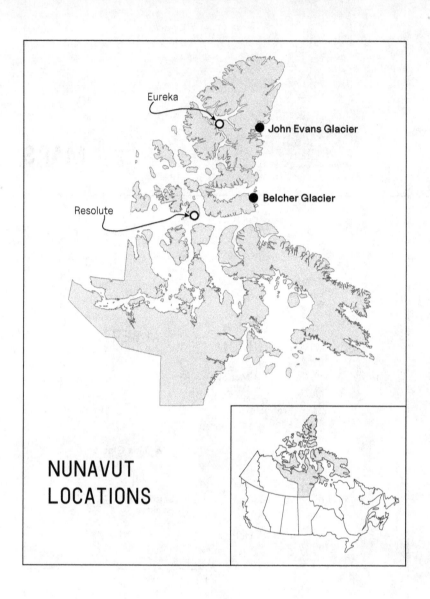

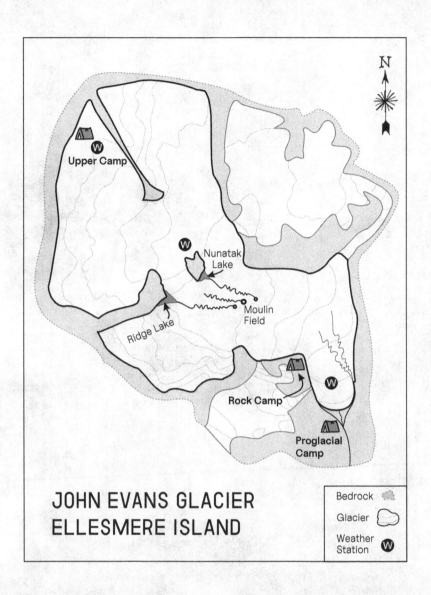

1
VIEW FROM THE TOP

WHEN I WAS A CHILD, my family went on numerous camping trips west to the Canadian Rocky Mountain national parks, as we lived within a four-hour drive of our favourite camping spots. I was always the first person awake, thrilled to be in the mountains again and unable to sleep in like my parents and sister. I would sneak down from my bed in the pop-up top of our beige 1978 VW camper van and slide out the side door into the cool mountain air. The whisky jacks would screech while the crows burbled and cawed, and the rich scent of pine was almost overwhelming. I'd play quietly around the campsite, savouring the tranquility of nature and the time to myself before the rest of my family got up and the campground got too busy. Somewhere there is a picture of two-year-old me standing on the Athabasca Glacier: a glacier lover from an early age and a sign of things to come.

The only problem with our camping trips was my earth-scientist dad's in-depth lectures on local geology. Whenever he saw something he thought was interesting, he'd expound on it with a long lecture and I'd immediately tune out. I'd watch an ant struggle

Learning to ski in Fort Saskatchewan, Alberta, December 1980. Notice the "skis" are plastic planks, and the poles lie in the snow behind me. (Inset) In a stroller at Lake Louise, Alberta, with my grandmother and older sister, September 1978. (Photos by J. Boon, author's personal collection.)

with a breadcrumb across the splintered picnic table. I'd imagine exploring the mountain valley across the road, its contours shaped by a zipper of conifers. I'd watch other kids playing in the river a short distance away, or fantasize about getting an ice cream cone to beat the heat—a treat that was doled out sparingly. One morning, my dad pointed to a nearby mountain and described how it had been pushed up by terranes—individual pieces of continental crust—that slammed into the west coast and crumpled the landscape ahead of them, forming anticlines and synclines, terms I didn't understand. His words flowed over me like water as he talked *at* me instead of with me, dissecting the physical landscape around us. I was just a kid who wanted to play in and explore that landscape, not learn its technical details. I vowed then and there I'd never become a scientist like him.

Instead, I developed an inordinate love of the written word, and even created a home lending library so the rest of my family could check out my Ramona Quimby books and *Harriet the Spy*. I also had a passion for writing, fancying myself a journalist as I typed up a "newspaper" on my dad's old manual typewriter, pounding hard on the keys to get the letters on the page, covering news events like the space shuttle *Challenger* disaster. Later I dabbled in poetry, and in junior high was highly embarrassed but also proud that my Remembrance Day poem was selected to be read over the school intercom. In high school, I published a couple of not-so-bad poems in *The Claremont Review*, and a research paper on Canadian soldiers in World War I in *The Concord Review*, outlets that showcased the work of secondary students. Based on my experience, science was dry and boring whereas writing was intoxicating and would take you to worlds you could never imagine. It seemed obvious that I was destined to write for a living.

But how? I never believed that I could only be a writer—I was convinced I needed something more practical to fall back on. I couldn't afford to fail, as my family expected me to succeed at whatever I did. Which is how I ended up, thirteen years after that Rocky Mountain morning and three years into a geography degree at the

University of Victoria in British Columbia, studying the landscape of the Canadian Rockies. Maybe I wasn't that removed from my dad's geology lectures after all.

✳ On a beautiful day in autumn 1997, eleven of my classmates and I unfolded ourselves from our travel van and stretched our legs. It had been a long drive from Vancouver Island to the Rockies, from the ocean to the mountains in the span of forty-eight hours. I was thrilled to be back in the mountain landscape I'd visited throughout my childhood: snow-capped peaks, glaciers, and tree-flanked mountain slopes. Ahead of us was a three-kilometre trail that switchbacked up to the top of Parker Ridge. The trail meandered from the alpine forest of the crowded parking lot to the ridge above the treeline, where shrubs and small scrubby plants replaced the trees. The summit promised a panoramic view of the surrounding landscape from almost 2,300 metres above sea level. This was the first hike on our week-long stay for this fourth-year field school, and it started with a lung-busting bang.

Early September is the perfect time of year for a Rockies field school: the nights get cold and the mornings can be frosty, but the days are still warm enough for shorts. The bugs are minimal thanks to the cold nights, and the foliage is just starting to shift to autumn colours. I arrived dressed in coastal clothes: shorts and a T-shirt, plus a sweater to ward off the slight chill in the air. We set out on the trail, happy to not need our backpacks for such a short hike, as we were tired and stiff and didn't want to have to carry extra weight up the steep slope. Our minds were ready for the mountains, but our bodies were still used to being at oxygen-rich sea level. Our group spread out along the trail, everyone going at their own pace. Enjoying the scenery as I climbed the ridge, I spotted a rogue yellow larch on a distant hillside, surrounded by a forest of green, in a hurry to put on its fall coat ahead of its brethren. A slight breeze carried the chatter of late-season tourists, eager to gawk at Canada's famous mountains and picture-postcard glaciers.

⁎ Parker Ridge was our outdoor classroom for the day, named for journalist Elizabeth Parker, a co-founder of the Alpine Club of Canada (ACC). She had spent eighteen months in the Rockies around 1904, "taking the waters" at the Banff hot springs and exploring the region extensively in the hopes of improving her poor health.

The American Alpine Club was established in 1902. In early discussions, members proposed forming a Canadian chapter as part of their national organization. Inaugural club president Charles Fay mentioned this idea to Arthur O. Wheeler, a land surveyor who charted the Alberta–British Columbia border. An enthusiastic Wheeler wrote letters to Canadian national newspapers in support of this proposition. Parker responded, voicing her fierce opposition to this notion in her columns in the *Manitoba Free Press*. She believed, rightly, that Canada had enough people interested in mountains to form its own alpine club. That belief saw fruition with the formation of the ACC in 1906, with Parker as its first secretary and female member.

Parker and Wheeler held the club's first meeting in Winnipeg, the centre of the country and also Parker's home. They invited key players, including the head of the Canadian Pacific Railway, who donated rail passes for potential members to attend. Though it was on short notice, Parker and Wheeler agreed to run the first ACC summer camp in Yoho National Park that year. Ironically, Parker herself wasn't a mountaineer like many other ACC members, and her prairie home was a long train ride from the Rockies. However, she enjoyed the mountain scenery and the company of like-minded mountain enthusiasts, and played an integral role in setting up that first 1906 camp. The camp hosted one hundred people, including at least fifteen women, who summited a mountain known as The Vice President, in the nearby Emerald Lake area—in full Victorian dress and hobnailed boots.[1] In subsequent years, the club decided that men and women would share the same dress code, thus allowing women to wear pants for climbing and greatly increasing the ease of ascent. By 1917, fully half of the ACC's membership was female.[2] However, a century later, in 2017, the membership of the ACC was only about 30 per cent female.[3]

Parker saw the ACC as a protector of the environment against the ills of society, "a national trust for the defense of our mountain solitudes against the intrusion of steam and electricity…for keeping free from the grind of commerce, the wooded passes and valleys and alplands of the wilderness." She wrote, "it is the people's right to have primitive access to the remote places of safest retreat from the fever and the fret of the market place and the beaten tracks of life."[4] Parker and Wheeler also saw the club not just as a way for outdoorspeople to recreate in the mountains, but as an organization that would support mountain science and art. To me, Parker was a kindred spirit: not a serious mountaineer, but a writer who simply loved being in the mountains.

✻ As we made our way up the winding, steep trail to Parker Ridge, I gasped for breath and my leg muscles tensed; it felt like I was dragging a piano behind me. I was grateful to get a break partway up, as our professor, Dr. Dan Smith, stopped to examine an interesting formation on the trail: a damp area with little pillars of ice, each with a piece of soil atop them, like small toadstools.

"Anyone know what this is?" Dan asked. We all tiredly shook our heads. "Needle ice!" he said, exasperated with our inability to remember what we'd learned in his geomorphology class the previous term. "It forms overnight when wet soil freezes into vertical ice 'needles' that push soil up as they grow," he explained. The crystals tinkled as I walked over them, falling against one another and breaking into shards like tiny glass spindles. This was a perfect example of the way Dan wanted us to experience the mountains: examining and understanding the landscape instead of just passing through it.

Dan was a quintessential mountain man, having done his master's and PhD theses on alpine geomorphology in the Canadian Rockies. He had taught the subject for years, including previous field schools in the Rocky Mountains. His big white beard complemented a tanned and weathered face, and he was most comfortable in jeans and a button-up shirt, his receding hairline covered by a well-worn ball cap. While my early introduction to earth science consisted of my dad's one-sided geology lectures, Dan's teaching style involved hiking, observing, and discussion. Dan saw field school as an immersive learning experience for all students, regardless of whether they planned to pursue a geography degree. The intent was that students learn to "see" a landscape and understand what was happening or had happened there. To be able to tell the story of what forces had acted on it and why it looked the way it did.

He took a more process-based, natural-history approach to science, rather than a measuring, analytical approach. We didn't need notebooks because Dan didn't lecture—he showed and discussed, as with the needle ice, and was keen on everyone having a positive outdoor experience. Rather than taking copious notes and memorizing them, we had to focus on listening and looking as Dan taught us how to interpret the landscape around us. Our field school would involve a lot of hiking and observing. Only two projects required us to collect data and write about what it revealed: one where the entire group learned to collaborate and share data, and a second where we worked in smaller breakout groups.

✳ At the top of Parker Ridge, near the edge of the treeline, I was rewarded for my perseverance with some epic 360-degree views. I wandered slowly around the summit, resting my legs and lungs, wishing for a water bottle, and gaping at the rows of mountain ranges fading into the horizon.

The feature that stood out the most from this perch was the once-mighty Saskatchewan Glacier in the valley to the south, a glacier that has retreated more than two kilometres since the early 1900s and thinned significantly. A line halfway up the valley walls indicated where the glacier once sat. Now there was only bare rock beneath the line and a carpet of trees above it; more trees would eventually grow lower on the exposed cliff face. The scale of that long-ago glacier was awe-inspiring, well beyond what I could realistically imagine. The valley floor in front of the glacier was now crisscrossed with boulders and braided stream channels draining from the melting ice, their surfaces glittering in the morning sunlight. One of our hikes for this field school would be right along this valley and up onto the glacier itself, so it was a treat to preview it from above. This was part of Dan's approach—having us observe a natural process from several different angles to gain a better understanding of how that process worked.

The Saskatchewan Glacier is the largest outlet glacier of the Columbia Icefield. The Columbia is a mass of ice that feeds one of the two hydrologic apexes in North America: Snow Dome. Snow Dome is a massive bedrock hump, on top of which sits Dome Glacier, which is fed by the Columbia Icefield. A drop of water that falls on Snow Dome can flow one of three ways: down the Columbia Glacier to the Columbia River and west to the Pacific Ocean; down the Athabasca Glacier to the Athabasca River and north to the Arctic Ocean; or down the Saskatchewan Glacier to the North Saskatchewan River and east to Hudson Bay. From high on Parker Ridge, I was looking at the source of the North Saskatchewan River, the very same river that flows next to the city where I grew up.

✷ My hometown of Fort Saskatchewan, Alberta, is defined by the North Saskatchewan River. When the river finally reaches the city, about thirty kilometres northeast of Edmonton, it has passed through six hundred kilometres of mountains and foothills into what's called the aspen parkland: not as flat as the true prairie, but a land of small rolling hills and pockets of shimmering aspen forest. The parkland marks the transition between boreal forest to the north and prairie to the south, a welcoming and open landscape that shares aspects of both ecozones.

The North Saskatchewan River fills a wide floodplain with meandering channels near its source in the Rocky Mountains. Once it reaches Edmonton and beyond, however, it has picked up flow from numerous tributaries and become a broad, well-defined channel with average summer flows more than three times greater than where it began in the mountains. This is the muddy river of my youth, whose banks I explored endlessly and whose restless flows captured my young imagination.

As a ten-year-old, I would often cycle down an asphalt path to reach my favourite part of town: the steep road down to the river valley. After racing down the hill, hair streaming out behind me, I would join another asphalt path that travelled parallel to the shore of the North Saskatchewan. At a break in the bushes, I'd hop off my bike and push through the riverside vegetation to reach a finger of land that poked out into the river itself. The water was like chocolate milk, and farther across than I could swim, despite all the swimming badges I'd earned during a childhood spent in the pool. The river seemed alive, and I was fascinated by thoughts of where it came from and where it was going. In my ten-year-old world, I was an explorer in the wilderness. And like any good explorer, I carried a peanut-butter-and-jam snack with me so that I could take a much-deserved break on a dry log, daydreaming about past and future expeditions.

Unfortunately, climate change in the North Saskatchewan headwaters has begun to slow the mighty river in summer, as there's less winter snowpack in the mountains and spring snowmelt occurs earlier than it once did. Also, the major shrinkage of the Saskatchewan Glacier in both length and thickness has reduced late-summer flows; high-elevation tributaries to the North Saskatchewan are experiencing the same problem. These drastic shifts make it all the more important to study the water produced by glaciers and the impacts of climate change on downstream flows.

✳ Early European exploration in the headwaters of the North Saskatchewan River started in 1805. British explorer David Thompson, a North West Company employee, created a trade route from Rocky Mountain House, in the western foothills of what is now Alberta, into the Columbia River valley in what is now British Columbia. He and his men, plus a few horses, followed the North Saskatchewan to Howse Pass, located one ridge north of the North Saskatchewan headwaters and one of the few places where they could cross the Rocky Mountains. It was too snowy for horse travel in the pass, so Thompson and his men camped in the "lap of the

Rockies, in a broad bowl ringed with craggy peaks and glacial headwalls."[5] Once the snow melted enough, they headed up and over Howse Pass and into the Columbia River watershed.

Much later, once the fur trade had largely collapsed and local Indigenous Peoples like the Stoney Nakoda were ravaged by settler-borne disease and starvation and forced onto reservations, British mountaineers Norman Collie, Hugh Stutfield, and Herman Woolley came to the Canadian Rockies. In 1898, they were some of the first white climbers to reach the icefield area. They noted that many of the trails they encountered were overgrown, and they didn't meet anyone on their travels. They assumed the region had been abandoned for at least half a century.

After days of bushwacking and crossing rivers swollen with summer melt, they finally reached the Continental Divide, where they camped near the headwaters of the North Saskatchewan and Athabasca Rivers. "Immediately opposite our camp…rose a noble snow-crowned peak, about 12,000 feet in height, with splendid rock precipices and hanging glaciers," Collie and Stutfield wrote.[6] They named it Athabasca Peak, and the glacier flowing from it Athabasca Glacier. A few days later they climbed Athabasca Peak and saw the Columbia Icefield and the surrounding mountains. From their viewpoint, "a new world was spread at [their] feet; to the westward stretched a vast ice-field…surrounded by entirely unknown, unnamed, and unclimbed peaks. From its vast expanse of snows the Saskatchewan glacier takes its rise, and [the icefield] also supplies the head-waters of the Athabasca; while far away to the west…the level snows…finally melt and flow down more than one channel into the Columbia River, and thence to the Pacific Ocean."[7] Several prominent landforms in the area are now named after these mountaineers, including Stutfield and Woolley Glaciers.

My hometown was originally built near the confluence of the North Saskatchewan and Sturgeon Rivers in 1875, as an outpost for the North West Mounted Police. Then called Sturgeon Creek Post, it was renamed Fort (on the) Saskatchewan and was incorporated as a town in 1904. The railway arrived in 1905, making the town accessible to the outside world. Fort Saskatchewan had transitioned from an isolated outpost to a thriving hamlet in the span of just thirty years.

How fitting, then, that the North Saskatchewan would play a role in my introduction to field science, taking my passion for the outdoors to the headwaters of the river I loved so much as a kid.

✽ Back on Parker Ridge, Dan pointed out the prominent Hilda Peak to the west that hosts a small glacier, appropriately named Hilda Glacier. This glacier is tucked up against the valley wall behind the Hilda Creek hostel, and is so small that it was hard to see from where we stood; it could almost be mistaken for an avalanche chute. Given the proximity to the hostel, the trail to Hilda Glacier was well used by hostel visitors. As we would soon find out, part of the region in front of the glacier was covered in a singular type of backcountry graffiti: rocks laid out in the silt to spell names and dates such as "Pete wuz here 1997" or "AW + TD" enclosed in a heart.

To our north was the Brazeau region, a well-known backpacking area immortalized in *The Canadian Rockies Trail Guide* as the Brazeau Lake–Poboktan Pass–Jonas Pass loop, a world-class backcountry destination. My first backpacking trip as a teenager in 1993 was on this trail. It was organized by a faith-based group, and though I wasn't a believer I saw it as a good opportunity to be outdoors in the mountains. I had injured my knee playing basketball the night before we left, so I hiked awkwardly and painfully with a walking stick in one hand, weighed down by my heavy pack and wishing my fabric Hi-Tec hiking boots were made of more supportive leather. Despite my injury, I loved that trip, especially the designated quiet time we had each morning to sit in our own piece of the wilderness and collect our thoughts for the day. I realized the mountains were my church, and nature my religion.

✽ From Parker Ridge, Dan also pointed out the location of the "Big Bend" to the southeast, a landmark hairpin curve in the highway that wraps in a tight loop below towering peaks. The bend marks the beginning of the climb onto the high points of the Icefields Parkway that we were looking down on. Many glaciers can be accessed on foot from this stretch of high-elevation highway through the heart of icefield country. Hikers can reach the toe of the Saskatchewan, Hilda, and Athabasca Glaciers. They can also do day hikes in to Stutfield and Woolley Glaciers, which are a little farther northeast. The forefield of each glacier is a pared-down landscape of rock, ice, and water, with small bunches of willow growing tenaciously in sparse pockets of soil. This is one of my favourite landscapes to visit: it contains only the essentials, but, far from being monochromatic, it reveals a complex interplay of light and shadow as the day wears on and the sun angle shifts.

Unfortunately, since Elizabeth Parker's time, Canada's mountain parks have been invaded by roads, buses, and hordes of tourists, so her wish to keep the area "free of the grind of commerce" is a lost cause. But the landscape is a refuge that we still have access to, a retreat from the "beaten tracks of life." I have spent my time in the Rockies marvelling that I can lace up my boots, throw on a pack, and step off the roadside onto trails that take me into the high country and beyond. These are places that most people never see because they stick to the highway and only stop at each designated viewpoint. I suspect it's also because most visitors are uncomfortable in the wilderness; they'd rather take pictures and get back in their tour bus than visit remote valleys and glaciers. I've enjoyed many hikes in the icefield region where I've had the trail to myself. Even on the well-trodden Hilda Glacier trail, which I've travelled many times, I've encountered people only once, and have explored the glacier valley in peace every time I've visited.

✶ The trip up Parker Ridge was a challenging introduction to the region where we would spend the next week, in a natural classroom. We would hike, observe, and measure the relationships between glaciers, trees, and water through hands-on alpine research projects. We'd learn to be field scientists in the splendour of the mountains. After drinking in the scenery from the ridgetop, we headed down the trail and jammed ourselves back into the van to return to our accommodations.

At the time, I was a twenty-year-old undergraduate, two-thirds of the way through a geography degree, who had felt at home in the outdoors since childhood. I was excited about the week ahead and the opportunity to apply my geography knowledge in a field setting, though I was intimidated by the vastness of the landscape we'd be exploring. I liked Dan's approach to field science, but was a bit worried about learning to think critically and academically about our surroundings. I was also intrigued by the hazel eyes that were watching me in the van's rear-view mirror. They were those of a graduate student, along for the trip to help shuttle and supervise Dan's rowdy field school crew. With his dark hair and goatee, Dave was more mature than anyone I'd met on campus, and I sensed we'd be more than good friends.

* Two years before this field school, I had begun to dislike university. My first year at the University of Victoria wasn't the cerebral meeting of the minds that I had imagined it would be. It felt like I was going through the motions, jumping through the required hoops to pass my courses. I wanted to do something completely different, like travel, work abroad, and feed my soul by writing about it. In the spring of 1995, I filled in the paperwork for a student work abroad program but, since I wasn't yet eighteen, I needed my parents' signature to apply. "Please, sign this form so I can go to Australia," I begged. Their response was a firm no. "It's better if you try a second year of university and see how it goes," they said.

Instead of heading south to Australia, I headed east to Alberta. I'd been hired by a mining company in Edmonton to do geological mapping in the subarctic for the summer. Though I'd sworn I wouldn't end up a geologist like my dad, the chance to be outside and do fieldwork won me over. However, just a few weeks into our trip preparations, the company ran out of money. All of the students they had hired were laid off immediately, so there would be no visit to the subarctic for me.

I was devastated. I managed to find a job doing mind-numbing data entry for another mining company, where I played Tetris when work was slow. The office radio was tuned to a country music station all day, with songs so sad they made me want to cry. I had been stymied again in my search for outdoor adventure, and poured my disappointment into the journal I wrote in religiously.

After a discouraging first year of university and a summer of thwarted field jobs, I reconsidered my options. For my second year of university, I decided to switch from a bachelor of arts to a bachelor of science—I thought it would give me a better chance of taking outdoors-focused courses. I also enrolled in the geography department's co-op program, which sends students out on job placements for four to eight months at a time, between semesters of coursework. I was convinced I'd have my pick of jobs offering an outdoor field experience.

Boy, was I wrong! As it turned out, I switched to a BSc just as undergraduate class sizes exploded. I didn't get enough hands-on experience in fieldwork because my physical geography classes were so big that our professors couldn't take us all into the field. This meant that I always got stuck with office-based co-op jobs, thanks to my cursed skills in geographic information systems (GIS): a mapping program designed to analyze the relationships between data in space and time.

During one co-op work term, I sat in the cubicle that I shared with a government employee, mostly trying not to listen in on his phone conversations. I spent days writing code to automatically analyze the watershed datasets that made up the backbone of the GIS project I was working on. Ironically, I was calculating aspects of a terrain feature I'd much prefer to be exploring in person. Instead, I was trapped in front of a monitor for eight hours a day, antsy in my chair and breathing recycled air under buzzing fluorescent lights.

In the autumn of 1996, I took my first geomorphology class with Dan Smith, the professor who would eventually take me to field school in the Rockies. Our very first class of the term was held on top of Mount Tolmie, a scenic 120-metre hill not far from the

University of Victoria. The autumn rains hadn't yet started and the day felt almost summery: there wasn't a cloud in the sky and a light breeze rustled the pages of my notebook. Dan talked about the glaciation of the local area and the landforms it created. My classmates and I touched the scratch marks, or striations, on the rocks we were sitting on, marks that showed the direction in which ice sheets had flowed. From our viewpoint over the city, we imagined what Victoria would have looked like during the last glaciation. Dan's hands-on, observational approach brought the landscape to life, and fuelled my desire for fieldwork. I started to feel that a science degree might actually be interesting after all.

I was focused on more than just fieldwork, however. In reorganizing my university degree I had also added English classes in essay writing and modern poetry. I relished the opportunity to analyze others' writing and do some writing of my own. My friends and I immersed ourselves in Victoria's rich literary scene, attending book launches and poetry readings. We wrote our own poetry and critiqued each other's work, helping improve each poem's content and structure to emulate the poets we were studying in class. I knew that I wanted to create a life that combined writing with working outdoors, even though I'd been striking out on the latter front. But how to reconcile the two worlds?

* Here I was, in a van on the Icefields Parkway, finally about to do some fieldwork. I'd done my time, with three years of being stuck behind a desk and offered only tantalizing glimpses of an outdoor life. I was now jumping with both feet into the world of a field scientist, in a stunning environment. I hadn't given up on writing, however; I faithfully documented our activities in my journal each evening.

After our time on Parker Ridge, we drove north along the Icefields Parkway to the turnoff for Parks Canada's Tangle Creek bunkhouse. This was to be our home for the week, one that we would share with Parks staff who worked in the area. It was a series of industrial trailers that had been converted to double-occupancy dorm rooms with fake wood panelling on the walls, communal men's and women's washrooms that could have used a good cleaning, and a commercial-sized kitchen with a giant walk-in fridge. We were divided into groups for kitchen duty; each group was responsible for cooking a shared dinner and cleaning up afterwards. As for breakfast and packed lunches, we were on our own.

The day after our Parker Ridge hike, we went to see the famous Athabasca Glacier, the most visited glacier in North America at more than a million people each year. The glacier has retreated six hundred metres and thinned an average of sixty metres since the 1960s, with retreat accelerating recently—up to five metres annually.[8] It's a popular and accessible tourist attraction: visitors can reach the glacier terminus on foot, walking past a series of markers along the way that show where the terminus was at different dates over the past 175 years. They can see how the moving glacier has shaped the proglacial zone, by scouring and depositing debris and shifting stream channels. Repeat visitors will notice that the parking lot has moved significantly over the years, getting farther from the highway as the glacier retreats. Visitors can also pay to ride a snow coach, sort of like an all-terrain bus, onto the middle of the glacier itself. There they can get out and stand on the ice to experience its sounds and smells and touch its surface, something few people get to do.

We hiked to the Athabasca Glacier snout with the rest of the tourist crowd, up to where the ice front slopes down to the ground, making it tempting to step onto despite the warning signs cautioning people not to do so. The sound of running water was constant, and in the distance we could see the snow coach turnaround point, situated well below the glacier's crevasse field. We scouted the ice margin for a discreet site to place our project equipment, out of the way of curious tourist eyes. Once we reached a stream channel flowing out of the far north side of the glacier, we set up a stream and weather station to monitor the stream for the duration of our stay. We visited the station every morning and evening, and a different group was responsible for collecting data each day.

The goal of our project was to measure how water flow from the glacier changed throughout the day and over the week, depending on weather. But we were using vintage equipment that Dan had amassed during his many years of teaching field schools, so we had to pay close attention to our own observations of the stream system to supplement our data collection.

One piece of equipment we set up was a water level sensor. It consisted of a plastic garbage bin with the bottom cut off, and an aluminum float that moved up and down on the water surface as the water level fluctuated. The float was attached by a wire to a piece of graph paper and a stylus; as the water level changed, the stylus recorded the movement on the paper. To gauge streamflow, someone would stand in the freezing water in hip waders and use a current meter, which was a small propeller attached to a metal pole that spun in the stream current. A group member on shore recorded the measurements, and we then matched these measurements to the water level data from the water level sensor. We also had a bi-metal sensor to measure air temperature: it contracted and expanded with changes in temperature, and was connected to a stylus and a piece of graph paper to record maximum, minimum, and average air temperature, similar to how the water level sensor worked. At each visit we checked the graph papers to make sure everything was working. We also installed a rain gauge like the ones sold at garden stores: a plastic tube with a pointed end to stake it in the ground, and gradations to mark the amount of collected rainfall. We recorded the volume of rain and emptied the gauge at each visit.

It was often chilly, not only in the morning before the sun had a chance to warm things up but also in the late afternoon and evening when the sun moved lower on the horizon and the heat of the day slowly leached out of the landscape. I recorded our measurements in my field notebook with a pencil because pens don't work when it's raining or too cold. Since our groups were relatively small, I was able to try my hand at all the measurement techniques, including stream gauging. Despite the hip waders, my feet and legs were frozen by the time I'd finished. But I was hooked. I felt like I was moving towards being a real field scientist—taking measurements while bundled up in a fleece jacket and a toque, reading out and recording numbers, and watching the stream respond to changes in weather. This was the hands-on work that had been missing from my undergraduate experience thus far.

At the end of the field school, we pooled our water and weather data for the week into a communal package. It was a challenge to collate the daily notes from the stream and weather station: every group had a different data-recording protocol—and sometimes hard-to-decipher handwriting. We worked together to synthesize and interpret our environmental data and determine the relationship between streamflow, air temperature, and precipitation. I was thrilled to realize that I could understand how environmental systems work by collecting the right data and extracting a story from those data. That was something I wanted to do more of. The dry science I had originally disliked as a child began to seem more exciting and invigorating, a possible career path that would allow me to be outdoors in some breathtaking environments.

The data for our class project showed that streamflow increased during the day as the sun came out and the glacier began to melt. It decreased again in the evening as the glacier stopped melting from lack of sunlight and colder air temperatures. When it rained, streamflow increased quickly, suggesting that the rainfall was making its way directly to the stream instead of being filtered through the glacier. This is a microcosm of what happens to runoff from glaciers on a larger watershed scale: melt peaks in spring during snowmelt, then shifts from snowmelt to ice melt. In August and September, when most streams are otherwise at their lowest, glacier melt maintains streamflow. But this usually coincides with peak water demand from urban and agricultural users—so as climate change causes glaciers to shrink, critical water supplies are lost. Our experience showed that small research projects can provide insight into larger processes happening on the landscape.

✴ During field school, we spent a lot of our time hiking the local trails. One of our hikes was up the Saskatchewan Glacier valley to the glacier itself, the same one we had looked down on from Parker Ridge. We parked at a pullout at the beginning of the Big Bend hairpin turn, then hiked a few kilometres through the woods, ensuring we made enough noise to scare away any bears. We were on an old military road; the US military had conducted exercises on the Saskatchewan Glacier in the 1930s to test winter equipment. Pieces of vehicles can still be found here and there along the road, along with the remains of wooden structures they'd built in their time there.

The scent of pine and spruce and the sound of rushing water filled the air as we emerged from the woods into the proglacial zone, the area that the glacier had once covered before it gradually retreated several kilometres up-valley. It seemed an awfully long way to walk, to get to the glacier—we couldn't even see its snout from our vantage point. I spent some of that walk with the hazel-eyed graduate student, Dave, who was over six feet tall and wore a ball cap over his dark hair. "This is my first trip to the Rockies," he said, shyly. "It feels like home." Dave was born and raised in Victoria, British Columbia; I saw the landscape through his eyes and realized how spectacular it really was. I was surprised to learn that he hadn't been to the area before, given that I'd visited pretty much every year of my life and knew a lot of the landmarks quite well. "You'd love it in winter," I said as I adjusted my backpack. "There's so much to do, like cross-country skiing and snowshoeing."

The proglacial valley was flat and wide and covered with braided streams that we had to cross to reach the glacier itself. The rocks underfoot were rounded, both from being ground beneath a glacier and from tumbling in rivers, making for relatively easy walking. As we walked and talked, I learned that Dave was doing a master's degree in dendroglaciology: the study of trees pushed over by glaciers. His research sites were some of the last glaciers remaining on Vancouver Island, which are shrinking rapidly due to climate change.

The Saskatchewan Glacier valley was hemmed in by high mountain ridges, including Parker Ridge and the peaks around Hilda Glacier. I spotted the same trim line on the valley walls that I'd seen from the top of Parker Ridge, only now I looked up—*way* up—at it, marvelling at how thick the ice must have been right where we were standing. Even though I felt awkward and nervous around Dave, the time flew by as we chatted, and I was surprised to realize that we'd already made it more than halfway to the glacier snout.

Along the way, our group stopped to examine a series of parallel longitudinal ridges that looked like snakes with rock heads. They were half a metre high and had an n-shaped profile on top of the rounded rocks of the valley floor. Dan asked us if we knew what they were but, as with the needle ice, we had no clue. They were called flutes, and they form when a glacier flows over a large boulder that it can't move, creating a hollow arch on the underside of the glacier ice. As the glacier continues to flow downstream, the arch flows past the stationary boulder, while the rest of the ice pushes into the ground, squeezing rocky till from under the glacier into the space beneath the arch. When the glacier melts away, these features remain on the landscape. Standing next to one of the flutes, I was astonished by how extensive and thick the Saskatchewan Glacier had to have been to produce these hundred-metre-long "snakes." The boulders that made up their heads were rounded and had parallel scratches on them, showing that the glacier had flowed down-valley, over and around them.

After a two-hour-long hike, we reached the glacier. Directly in front of it stood a tall, lonely chunk of dirty ice, about the size of a large truck, covered in rocky debris. Dan explained that this ice was insulated from melting by its debris cover, whereas the glacier itself melted faster because it was debris-free. This lump had been left behind as the glacier retreated.

We walked up onto the lower part of the glacier, feeling the strong, cool wind blowing down-glacier and the ice's pebbly texture underfoot. The sound of streams burbling all over the ice surface mixed with the sound of the wind. Some of the streams disappeared into deep holes in the ice called moulins, and we leaped across these streams as we traversed higher up-glacier. Before each leap I checked my footing carefully, afraid of falling into the water and vanishing down a moulin. Unfortunately, we didn't have crampons and couldn't travel too far in just our boots, but it was an adventure nonetheless. I had never been up close and personal with a glacier and the landforms it had created; I felt incredibly fortunate to be there. The rushing water and the excitement of being on the ice resonated with me, and I vowed to find a way to regularly return to this environment.

✳ Not only did each field school group collect data at the Athabasca Glacier stream station, we also designed team projects to do at Hilda Glacier—a location that provided lots of questions to answer, and gave each group something different to work on.

Following our Saskatchewan Glacier visit, we hiked in to Hilda Glacier along a well-beaten path that followed a fast-moving proglacial stream. This channel meandered through a coniferous forest, with handmade footbridges spanning some of its reaches. About a kilometre in, we were confronted with a wall of rocky debris as high as a double-decker bus. This was the terminal moraine of Hilda Glacier, a pile of rocks that had been pushed up by the glacier likely as it advanced during the Little Ice Age, which ended around 1850. Mountain glaciers have shrunk significantly since then, leaving behind terminal moraines as markers of their former extent. The proglacial stream we'd been following, Hilda Creek, flowed out of this moraine.

We skirted to the right of the terminal moraine and followed a steep path to the top of another rocky moraine. This one had been pushed up along the side of the ice—an ice-marginal moraine. From there we could look down into the natural amphitheatre below: a broad, flat, and silty proglacial zone surrounded by piles of morainal debris. A string of narrow, cathedral-like peaks lined the far side of the amphitheatre, with avalanche chutes that brought snow and rocks down to the proglacial zone. Hilda Glacier itself was a small triangle of ice plastered up against headwall of the valley to the north—a long way from our viewpoint atop the ice-marginal moraine.

After an hour of exploring our surroundings, we broke into groups to select our projects. It was tough to come up with a project in a region that we weren't familiar with, but this was what field school was all about. Dan walked with us around the proglacial zone, identifying geomorphological events at different locations. He suggested we examine the proglacial zone like researchers, thinking about the features we saw, how they might have been formed, and how we could study them within a short time frame. He suggested potential projects around the terminal moraine and proglacial zone, and a different group volunteered to take on each one.

One group chose to study the terminal moraine. They found six buried trees that the glacier had pushed over as it advanced and, dating these trees using tree rings, they discovered that the moraine actually had an ice core. This meant the moraine was flowing like a rock glacier rather than remaining static. It had been slowly flowing down-valley since 1856 at a rate of about one centimetre per year, for a total movement of 1.4 metres by the time we were there in 1997.[9]

Dave helped another group use tree rings to measure shifts in alpine treeline. He guided them on the techniques they could use to sample trees at different elevations: first to find out how old they were, then to calculate how long after glacier retreat it had taken those trees to start growing at higher elevations. They observed that the smaller trees on top of the moraine were much younger than the larger trees on the ground beside the moraine. Tree colonization took longer at the top because the moraine had to stabilize before trees could grow on it, and their growth was limited by cold temperatures from being close to the glacier prior to its retreat. This group's results were an analogue for how treeline around the world will shift with climate change: as it gets warmer, treeline will move up in elevation, invading alpine meadows and changing ecosystems.

My group had a hard time picking a project until Dan said "What about these?" pointing to what looked like a jumble of broken rocks on the far side of the proglacial zone, about one hundred metres up from the terminal moraine. At first, the rocks seemed wholly unremarkable. But viewing them in the right light revealed a pattern of arc-shaped ripples running parallel to the terminal moraine, spaced a metre or so apart. It was all a matter of perspective and of doing what Dan was famous for: observing things from different angles. My group decided that our project would be to figure out what these ripples were and how they had formed.

The area with the ripples was covered in blocky, angular rocks, each about half the size of a shoebox, that we needed to clamber over to do our work; we had to be careful not to twist an ankle or a knee. Protected from the midday mountain winds by the tall ridges surrounding the Hilda Glacier valley, we warmed up quickly as the sun's heat radiated from the rocks. We worked as a team, using only a tape measure and a set of calipers.

"Pull the tape tight!" I yelled, hot, dusty, and mildly irritated with fellow group member Mike for daydreaming while we had work to do. Mike pulled his end of the tape measure so it aligned with the ripple and called out "One hundred, forty-nine metres!" to Chris, who was recording the measurements in his field notebook. We walked to the next ripple and followed the same procedure: pull the tape tight, call out the number, and move on. "Let's see how far apart they are," Mike said. We scrambled up and down the glacier forefield, measuring the distance between the ripples at various points along their length, mapping them all.

Last, we measured rock shape. Chris grabbed the calipers and we randomly selected rocks from within each ripple, measuring their thickness, length, and width while continuing to record our results in Chris's field notebook. By the time we were done, it seemed as though we'd walked a hundred kilometres over sharp and tumbled boulders. It was exciting to take our measurements, record our observations, and discuss our ideas of what these ripples might be.

Once we'd gathered all our data and started deciphering it back at the bunkhouse, we concluded that the ripples were what are called push moraines. They formed when the glacier was in overall retreat, but was still moving forward a bit during the winter months as it accumulated snow and ice. Because the rocks we sampled were more angular than rounded, we determined that they'd fallen onto the ice surface—and the ground in front of it—from the adjacent cliffs. They were then pushed up in winter by the advancing glacier, forming a small rock ridge. The glacier then melted back slightly during summer, and advanced a bit again the next winter, pushing forward another line of angular rocks. This back-and-forth movement created a curved, nested set of arcuate rock ridges.

The ripples were a record of annual variations in glacier extent from back when the glacier was much larger, waxing and waning with the seasons. Also, since the ripples weren't too far from the terminal moraine, it's likely that they formed not long after the Little Ice Age, as the glacier retreated from its maximum extent. These days, though glaciers still advance in winter, they melt significantly more in summer and the position of the glacier snout shifts dramatically each year. As a result, today's push moraines are not as obvious; they don't create the adjacent ripple complexes we measured.

Given the basic equipment we used for our project, we had to rely heavily on field observations. We weren't able to collect a lot of high-tech quantitative data, kind of like at our Athabasca Glacier stream station. This forced me to pay more attention to what I was doing and seeing within the larger landscape, rather than depending on a piece of equipment to do the seeing for me. I wouldn't have even noticed the push moraines if Dan hadn't pointed them out. This lesson in observation stuck with me and informed my approach to fieldwork in the future. I had to read the landscape like a book. But that felt right to me, like something I not only *could* do but something I *wanted* to do.

Later in my career, I'd see science change. It would shift from including fieldwork and hands-on experiments to focusing more on remotely sensed data, biogeochemistry, and numerically modelled predictions, with limited real-life observations. At a job interview years after these field school projects, I was asked why I didn't use more high-tech gadgets in my research. Feeling a bit nervous that my opinion might be unpopular, I replied that high-tech gadgets are, of course, valid research tools. However, there's no substitute for recording on-site observations in tandem with remote datasets or numerical modelling, as opposed to relying solely on the latter two. While I understand the value of technology, it's complementary to, rather than a replacement for, basic field observations and data collection. Ground-truthing—using field-based monitoring to verify and directly understand what's happening in an environmental system—is a key component of remotely sensed or numerical modelling research.

There is beauty in observing the functioning of an ecosystem while measuring it, as opposed to gathering data remotely and moving on to the next project. I'm particularly a fan of long-term field data collection, where I can witness a field site change over the seasons and the years. For example, I can measure a glacier's size and extent using satellite imagery, and I can measure glacier movement by looking at a time series of images that show how crevasse fields shift with glacier flow. But what about the depth of the ice? Can an image show how the glacier towers above me as I stand at the snout and look up? Can it show when the base of the snowpack on the ice becomes so saturated that I have to walk step by dripping step across the glacier surface? Can it tell me how the glacier wind feels on my face as I squint in the sunlight reflected off the wet snow?

Aerial photography and satellite data can't tell me how much water is entering the glacier through moulins and crevasses, or leaving the glacier at the snout through the proglacial river. Unless I find the perfectly timed image, there's no way to tell when the melt season has ended and the proglacial river has slowed to a trickle.

Remote images can tell me if the river has changed course, but they can't tell me if the river is moving more water than in previous years. Multiple years of in-person observation and data collection are needed to measure such things. I can't tell the complete story of glacier change without being there to see it for myself, in real time.

✳ That week in the Rockies in 1997 was spent taking in the scenery and being immersed in the outdoors. After long days out in the field, we unwound by sitting around a campfire, talking and playing guitar. I learned a lot about my companions, including Dave, during these relaxed chats.

One evening we drove an hour and a half north to the town of Jasper to get groceries and go to the pub. On the way back it was pitch black, the road lit only by starlight. We drove below the speed limit to avoid running into an elk or a bighorn sheep, as we couldn't afford to have an accident. The van was quiet and smelled vaguely of beer; everyone except Dave, our driver, had enjoyed quite a night. Most of us were close to sleep. Suddenly there was a bang and a commotion as the rear door flew open.

"Stop the van!" Chris yelled. "Cam's fallen out!"

Cam had decided he needed to throw up, but since we didn't have side windows he cracked open the back door. Being a big guy—well over six feet tall and 220 pounds—he leaned too far over the back seat, past his point of equilibrium, and tumbled onto the road. Dave screeched to a halt and we got Cam back inside in one piece. It was one of those bonding moments that united us—not to mention a great story to tell, even though it's sometimes said that "what happens in the field, stays in the field."

Spending so much time together resulted in a close-knit group that collaborated even when we returned to the university. We'd become familiar with one another's company and were happy to keep working together in our other courses. The field school experience taught me that fieldwork isn't necessarily a solo effort: it can be a group activity and relationship-builder all in one. Even for introverts like me.

Soon after we got back, our group put together our first-ever conference presentation about the push moraine project, and presented it at a regional conference that strongly supported student research. I started to think more and more that I could get paid to work outside, like Dan—someone who had been to the mountains every year for three decades. Dan's field school had formed the landscape of my future career. But, as a geographer, I knew how easily a landscape could change.

2
HISTORY AROUND THE CORNER

IT WAS THE SUMMER OF 1998 in Alberta's aspen parkland, and every afternoon like clockwork a thunderstorm rolled in. In the windowless clean lab where I worked, I could tell a storm was underway when the scent of rain wafted through the ventilation system: petrichor and ozone. It wasn't until I traded my lab coat and gloves for my pullover sweater and backpack at the end of the day that I saw the traces of these storms. They left large puddles on the sidewalk and blew leaves from the trees, scattering them along the path to the LRT station.

Just a few months previously, in May, I had moved to Nelson, BC, excited about a co-op job with the BC Ministry of Forests. It promised fieldwork in new terrain: the Monashee Mountains of the province's Kootenay region. The person I was going to work with was known not only for his research on mountain hydrology but for the amazing landscape photographs he took during helicopter flights to and from field sites. I was stoked that I'd be working outdoors, and excited to become part of a broader community of researchers within the provincial government. These connections would build my career and give me future opportunities—exactly

(Top) Measuring electrical conductivity in the proglacial stream at Hilda Glacier, Canadian Rockies, July 1998. (Bottom) Making field notes below a stagnant ice bank at Hilda Glacier. (Photos by D. Lewis, used with permission.)

what the University of Victoria's geography co-op program was meant to do.

Dave from field school was now my partner, and we lived together in a small apartment in Victoria. We drove the 750 kilometres from Victoria to Nelson and stayed with the parents of one of our field school friends. Our hosts fed us homemade buckwheat pancakes in the morning, gave us a key to their house, and regaled us with stories of their extensive travels. I spent a couple of days looking for furnished rental accommodations, which were scarce in such a desirable mountain town. However, I eventually found a quirky one-bedroom apartment in a downtown heritage building, the type of building Nelson is known for. The apartment came with a futon and a couple of wooden chairs, but not much else. Dave's father had passed away recently, so we drove the 650 kilometres back to Vancouver to get some of his household items to furnish it. We then turned around to make the same trip back to Nelson.

We were getting used to driving this stretch of road, winding our way east on Highway 3 along Canada's southern border with the United States, and turning north onto Highway 3A at Castlegar. We grew familiar with the landmarks along the way, like the Manning Park signs just east of Hope; the fruit and vegetable stands in Keremeos; and the community of Greenwood, an old mining town full of slag heaps, touting the best drinking water in the world. We crossed all the ecozones of the province: from the coastal rainforest, through the interior sagebrush desert near Osoyoos, and into the Monashee and Purcell Mountains as we entered the Kootenays. We had favourite stops along the way, including the café in Greenwood where we could get a hot chocolate and a cinnamon bun or hazelnut cake, or the A&W in Castlegar where we could stop for a late meal. Of course we also got a speeding ticket on the big downhill stretch near Castlegar, an unwelcome road-trip memento.

Dave had to stay in Victoria that summer to work on his master's thesis, and part of me looked forward to living without a roommate for once. It felt like things were falling into place: a field-based job, living in the mountains, a new life for the summer. However, I was also daunted by the prospect of being on my own, not sure I would fit into the local community. Was I too much of a word nerd? I definitely wasn't a cool outdoors person like the people who populated the steep streets of Nelson. I was worried about making friends in a town where even the kids had expensive mountain bikes, and where marijuana culture was prevalent.

After Dave helped me set up my apartment, we drove to the Ministry of Forests office so I could introduce myself and meet the person I'd be working with. I couldn't wait to find out what projects I'd be part of, and how soon we would get out into the field. When I checked in at the front desk, the administrative assistant was visibly confused. "Didn't you get the message?" she asked. "We contacted your co-op coordinator and let her know that we've cancelled all summer jobs due to budget cuts."

I struggled to fight back tears. Why had the co-op coordinator not told me what was going on? This was meant to be my first real outdoor job; I was finally getting away from doing GIS work. Living in a mountain town was a dream come true, an opportunity to explore new landscapes and write about my adventures. But that dream fell apart in an instant, all because of the government's budget shortfall and someone's failure to communicate.

What was I going to do, now that I had no summer job? I scrambled to undo all the plans I had in place for staying in Nelson. I was kindly allowed to leave a lot of my stuff in my field-school friend's parents' garage, and I begged my landlady to let me out of my four-month lease. She relented, but she wasn't happy about it. I submitted a claim to the Ministry of Forests to reimburse my travel costs, and they grudgingly paid some of my expenses. Dave and I met up with my would-be supervisor at the pub the next night, and he grumbled about government cutbacks and serious mismanagement. He was genuinely apologetic about the way things had turned out, even though it was out of his hands.

Regardless, I needed to change gears quickly and find another job, so I contacted Dr. Martin Sharp, a glacier researcher at the University of Alberta in Edmonton. I had talked to him previously about his work on glaciers and water, as my field school experience had me thinking about a master's degree. He had even offered me a summer job analyzing ice-core chemistry, but I turned him down because of this amazing field job in Nelson. Fortunately, he still had the funds to support a summer student and work for me to do, so I would be heading back home, to the banks of the muddy North Saskatchewan, for the summer.

I packed up my Nelson apartment with a heavy heart, and Dave and I traversed British Columbia for the fourth time in two weeks, the now-familiar landmarks passing by outside the window. I was listless and defeated; life wasn't at all happening as I'd planned. Back at our Victoria apartment, I put together a few stacks of books, some clothes, swimming gear, my bicycle, my stereo, and CDs—everything I'd need for a summer back in the aspen parkland. Then I took the Greyhound bus east to Fort Saskatchewan where I would live with my parents and commute to Edmonton to work at the university. I felt like a failure with my cancelled co-op job, retreating to the familiarity of home with my head hung low.

✽ Martin Sharp was a tall, relatively young British researcher with sandy hair and a quirky sense of humour. He favoured jeans and sweaters and walked with a slight stoop, as though he was uncomfortable with his height. He had come to Canada in the early 1990s after several years of intensive research in Switzerland, on the Haut Glacier d'Arolla. Even though he'd earned a master's degree studying UK seabirds, he'd done his PhD in glaciology and was well-regarded in the field by the time he arrived in Edmonton. He had a research group full of students who were measuring and modelling all sorts of things: glacier flow, snow and ice hydrology, water quality, and microbes in extreme environments, such as under glaciers and in ice cores. Most of his students were studying a glacier in the Canadian Arctic, around which he had built an extensive research program. One student was working in Banff National Park, at the iconic Bow Lake and Bow Glacier along the Icefields Parkway.

Martin taught me to run an ion chromatograph, an imposing beige machine that filled one side of a clean lab with tubes and chambers. It whirred and clicked while it measured the number of positively and negatively charged atoms in a water sample. That summer, I would use it to analyze snow and ice samples collected by Martin's students at their field sites. It was made clear to me that even a small amount of contamination could mess up the whole process, because snow and ice have such low ion concentrations. For the first week or so, my hands shook a bit and I held my breath as I checked and rechecked every step. Once you put a sample in the chromatograph that's it; there often isn't enough sample left over to redo an analysis if something goes wrong—either with sample preparation or with the machine itself.

After a few weeks I got into a groove and had sample preparation down pat. I could do each task without thinking too hard about it. The chromatograph used a lot of solvent, so I was also kept busy making more to exacting standards while prepping samples to analyze. The machine was extremely finicky and sometimes glitchy, giving odd results for no reason, or failing to work at all. A large part of my job was troubleshooting problems with the system itself. I'd also been tasked with writing a how-to manual for the machine, so that anyone coming after me could get up to speed in a hurry about how it worked.

My days began with a predictable routine. I unlocked the door to the clean lab, tuned the radio to the CBC, and put on my white lab coat and gloves. I turned on the chromatograph and set out my samples for the day on the counter next to the sink: Ziploc bags full of either snow or a piece of ice core, each labelled according to the date and location at which it was collected. As the bags' contents melted, I cleaned fresh analysis bottles with deionized water. I'd fill each bottle with a melted sample and feed them into the chromatograph.

Once in the machine, the liquid sample flowed over resin tubes that worked like magnets to pull out the specific ions they were attracted to. For example, one resin tube pulled out sulphate ions while another picked out sodium ions. Then the tubes were flushed by a solvent and the chromatograph measured the concentration of ions washed off each tube. After that, the machine printed a graph and a table showing the concentration of each ion in a sample. Each sample had a unique code that I matched to the data output when the analysis was done.

The ion results revealed where the weather at each sample site came from; they were a record of what ions had been deposited over the winter season. Ions such as sodium and chlorine come from what's called wet deposition, when weather systems originating over the ocean move over land and dump "salty" snow. Ions also come from weather events that blow dry materials onto the snow surface, like pollution (sulphate) or dust (potassium, calcium, and magnesium). For example, sulphate pollution from vehicle emissions in North America lands on glaciers in Svalbard, Norway, while dust on Greenland often comes from storms in the Sahara. When ions such as these melt out of snow and ice, they flow into proglacial streams and lakes, affecting water quality—which was what Martin's student was studying at Bow Lake and Bow Glacier.

When I wasn't working in the clean lab I worked on ice cores in the department's walk-in freezer, bundled up against the chill in an oversized down jacket left hanging by the door exactly for that purpose. The temperature inside was minus twenty-five degrees Celsius, and exhaust fans hummed in the background like a white-noise machine, making it easy to zone out and not even notice if someone else entered the space.

Ice cores are just what they sound like: long cylinders of ice, drilled or "cored" from glaciers in different regions to analyze the weather and atmospheric conditions that were present when the ice in the core was formed. Arctic and Antarctic cores have annual layers of ice that identify each summer season. Some contain layers of ash from long-ago volcanic eruptions, while others contain layers of sediment, indicating dust storms. A record-breaking ice core from Antarctica provides an annual record of climate over the past 2.7 million years.

The freezer at the University of Alberta housed cores from all parts of the Canadian Arctic, sheathed in heavy plastic wrap and laid out on metal shelving, waiting to be analyzed. They had been collected over many field seasons, and provided data for several research projects. I would open up an ice core's plastic covering and run a sensor with two diodes down the side of it. This sent a current through the core that allowed me to automatically record the density of the ice with depth. These data helped determine whether each layer represented a warm or a cool year: warm years have more melt events and are denser; cool years are the opposite.

While I was grateful for the job, it was disheartening to be working indoors again, analyzing samples for field researchers instead of doing field research myself. I spent my mornings in the clean lab listening to the CBC or in the freezer listening to the exhaust fans, my lunch hours sitting outside and working on my writing, and my afternoons waiting for the scent of rain. It was solitary work, as not many people were in the building that summer: A group of Martin's students was in the Arctic doing field research. Another student was finishing his master's thesis so he spent long hours in his office writing. The student at Bow Glacier came back infrequently to collect more supplies. It was a far cry from the work I had thought I'd be doing that summer, namely studying forest hydrology in the Monashees around the funky town of Nelson. A field-based co-op job just wasn't in the cards for me.

✶ Because I was living in Fort Saskatchewan for the summer, I commuted the thirty kilometres to Edmonton daily in my dad's old VW van, the same one we'd used for so many family trips to the Rockies. The stick shift was a bit tricky and I had to really stomp on the clutch to get it to engage, but otherwise it was an easy drive on an almost empty highway across the vast, open landscape. The van swayed a bit in the wind—much more so in a crosswind—but it got me to the closest LRT station. Once aboard the train, I settled into its rhythm as it clicked and clacked along the tracks from the northeast end of the city, through the city centre, to University

Station, which at that time was the end of the line. I daydreamed as the familiar stops were called out along the way: "Stadium Station, Stadium," for—you guessed it—the local stadium, or "Central Station, Central" for the heart of downtown. I would have never imagined that I'd be part of the commuter crowd. The only saving grace was that the time on the LRT provided a welcome period of decompression from work.

Unfortunately, living at home had its downsides—I'd been used to living independently at university and I chafed at the constraints of being under my parents' roof again. It was strange to sleep in my childhood bedroom now that I was no longer a child. I spent my evenings out of the house, cycling the rural gravel roads near our small town like I had in high school, pedalling into a headwind with mosquitoes and other bugs whirling past my ears and over my helmet. I also swam at the local pool, thinking only of slicing through the water like a blade, arms pulling and mouth breathing, then baked in the sauna afterwards. It was a lonely existence. I had no friends in my hometown anymore and hadn't made any friends at my new job. Not living in the city, it was hard to go for drinks after work or participate in other social events. I spent a lot of time writing in my journal, calling or writing letters to Dave and some of my Victoria friends, and counting down the days until Dave came to visit.

Dave finally arrived in early June 1998, and I took a weekend off from boring lab work so we could go camping in the Alberta badlands northeast of Calgary. When we arrived at our campsite we set up the VW van's pop-up roof, cooked dinner on our Coleman stove at the picnic table, and enjoyed the view of the surrounding hills and the pervasive scent of sagebrush. That night we were serenaded by a storm that went on for hours. Thunder rolled around the silty hills that surrounded us as lightning flashed between rumbles. The rain pounded on the van roof, and I worried that the canvas sides would be sopping wet in the morning. Unlike my clean-lab afternoons when I could only smell a thunderstorm, this was a full sensory experience: the thunder shook the ground and the shafts of lightning left stars in my eyes.

The next day dawned blue and sunny, the only evidence of the night's tumult being the wet ground. We visited the famous Royal Tyrrell Museum of Palaeontology to see the dinosaur bones and watch the paleontologists work on new skeletal finds. Then we wandered the local landscape to absorb the otherworldly nature of the badlands and their hoodoos: pillars of sandstone, each with a rock cap that prevents the pillar from eroding away entirely. The hoodoos were large, surreal mushrooms on the landscape, surrounded by muddy ground from the recent rains. And it was sticky mud—it caked onto our shoes, forming thick platforms that had to be scraped off so that we could walk.

After Dave's visit, I went back to the clean lab for a few weeks. I was freed once again when I took another ten days off in July to work on a directed studies project at Hilda Glacier, the same glacier I'd visited during field school. My project would be supervised from afar by Dan Smith.

At the end of our field school, and with help from Dan, I had written and submitted a research proposal to the Royal Canadian Geographical Society requesting funds to study glacier hydrology at Hilda Glacier. That spring, they awarded me some funding to cover the cost of travel and accommodations. My goal was to better understand how water flowed out of the glacier itself, what path it took through the proglacial zone and along the terminal moraine, and how water flow was affected by the weather. Dave would be joining me and, thanks to Parks Canada, we would stay at the Tangle Creek bunkhouse, the same place we'd stayed during field school. We'd travel twenty minutes south daily to my research site.

I was eager to apply my knowledge from field school to a new project at Hilda Glacier, but this time I was on my own—there would be no professor on site to answer my questions, or to help me figure out the processes occurring there within my short ten-day window. It was a daunting project, but I was ready to get started.

✽ In early July, Dave made yet another trip across BC, returning to Fort Saskatchewan with all the hydrological field gear from Dan's lab. He picked me up and we headed southwest to the Rockies. We settled in at the Parks Canada bunkhouse and inspected the gear to make sure it was all there and in working order. I was excited to spend time with Dave doing our favourite thing: fieldwork in the mountains.

We brought the same research equipment that we'd used for our field school stream station—the simple rain gauges, the water level sensor, and the temperature sensor—along with a different type of current meter. On our first day, we'd have to carry all of this gear in fully loaded backpacks, and wished we had walking sticks to help take some of the strain off our legs. The water level sensor with its cut-off garbage bin would be strapped to Dave's large pack, and I would carry the rain gauges, temperature sensor, and an electrical conductivity probe. We'd fit the current meter inside Dave's pack and attach the metal rod to the outside of it. Of course, we'd also bring lunches and all-important snacks, plus rain gear, as mountain weather can change in an instant.

We parked in the driveway of the Hilda Creek hostel, which gave us a more direct route to the glacier than parking in the usual lot across the Icefields Parkway. We shouldered our packs, tightening our hip belts to take most of the weight, then started down the same trail we'd taken during field school, alongside Hilda Creek. The path was flanked by kinnikinnik growing low to the ground, and was blocked in a couple of places by large, fallen trees that we had to scramble over. The one-kilometre walk to the terminal moraine seemed longer this time, with our heavy packs. Once we reached it, we again skirted to the right of this imposing wall and climbed the steep, rocky trail to the top of the ice-marginal moraine, where previous hikers had built a cairn to mark the route. From the cairn, we looked down into the bowl of Hilda Glacier's proglacial zone. Our way into the valley would be over a steep slope of jagged, jumbled rocks—tough to navigate in our top-heavy state. We spotted a faint trail that previous hikers had taken, but it was nothing like the beaten trail to the cairn.

As glaciers around the world shrink because of climate change, their proglacial zones get relatively larger and more hydrologically complicated. In some regions, stagnant, debris-covered ice blocks slowly melt out while new stream systems develop, some of them underground. These changes affect when, and how much, water arrives in down-valley streams and lakes. The situation is especially serious for communities in places that rely on glacier melt for drinking water, irrigation, electricity generation, or all of the above—including the Himalayas and South America, and also parts of Canada. The city of Calgary, in particular, relies on water from the Bow River, which is fed by the Bow Glacier. This study, my first solo science project as a physical geography undergraduate, was meant to represent those glaciers and how their complex water systems might respond to changing weather.

We stood at the cairn and surveyed the landscape, trying to decide how and where to set up the equipment. Viewing the proglacial zone from above gave us the perfect perspective on the site, allowing us to take it all in at once. To our left was the terminal moraine, which made up the outer boundary of the proglacial zone. Opposite the ice-marginal moraine on which we were standing were a series of ice banks. The proglacial stream rushed along the far wall of the valley. Directly below us was a flat, silty area that formed an almost circular feature at the end of the proglacial zone. The glacier itself loomed a kilometre above us to our right, snug against the valley wall.

At many glaciers, ice melts and runs into streams that form channels in the proglacial zone. At Hilda Glacier, however, meltwater travelled alongside the stretch of stagnant ice banks that lined the valley wall. This ice was once part of the glacier, but as the glacier retreated it was left behind, much like the freestanding chunk of dirty ice we'd seen at the Saskatchewan Glacier during field school. The ice banks had layers of sediment that showed how the ice used to flow and where the glacier surface used to be. They echoed with the sound of melt; most harboured caves with intricately sculpted roofs, formed when the water level was higher. Working close to them was tricky, as there was always the danger of falling ice, or rocks tumbling off the steep ice surface—debris from the cliffs above.

The proglacial stream wound in and out of the stagnant ice and into the gravel beside it. As it flowed through the proglacial zone from the glacier snout towards the terminal moraine, it collected gravel and clay that had been exposed as the glacier retreated, getting muddier as it went farther down-valley. The stream then disappeared underground, only to reappear outside the terminal moraine as the crystal-clear Hilda Creek.

I had so many unanswered questions, as this proglacial hydrological system was far more complex than I'd first thought. How did the proglacial stream develop? Why was Hilda Creek so clear compared to the muddy proglacial stream? And what was the significance of the silty flat area that made up a large part of the proglacial zone? Did it have to do with flow in the proglacial stream?

I wanted to tell Hilda Glacier's story so that other people could understand it, too.

✳ I decided I would put my rain gauges at four key locations: one on the silty flats of the proglacial zone, to see if they were affected by rainfall; one at the end of the proglacial stream channel, just before it drained into the ground; and one at the edge of the glacier itself, where the weather was influenced by the proximity of the ice. The last one would go outside the terminal moraine to catch rainfall near Hilda Creek.

I installed the water level sensor in the same spot as one of the rain gauges, at the end of the proglacial stream channel. This way, I could use its data in combination with streamflow measurements to figure out how much water was leaving the proglacial area. I installed the temperature sensor near the ice-marginal moraine, to see how glacier streamflow responded to air temperature. As always happens during fieldwork, however, something broke—in this case the temperature sensor. I had to use an ancient net radiometer instead, a device that recorded incoming sunlight on graph paper. Set up near an ice bank, the radiometer was a crucial part of the bigger picture. In landlocked regions, radiation is a good indicator of air temperature: generally, the more radiation, the warmer the air.

This felt much different from my field school project. Now I had to make major project decisions on my own without the benefit of a more knowledgeable supervisor for advice. Dave had experience with designing experiments, so he was able to help somewhat. But I didn't just have to decide *where* to install each piece of equipment, I had to have a good reason *why* it was being set up there. It forced me to think hard about the processes happening in Hilda Glacier's proglacial stream system, and how to best capture the data I needed.

It was taxing to clamber over the hummocky, rocky ground with delicate instruments in hand, hoping that they would work properly and collect good data. Not only that, I had to navigate that same brutal terrain every day, a full kilometre up to the edge of the glacier and back. I checked and emptied the rain gauges after recording how much water was in them, checked the graph paper on the water level sensor and the net radiometer to make sure they were still working, gauged streamflow, collected water samples, and sketched the ever-shifting proglacial stream channel in my field notebook. But I was happy to be doing real fieldwork again, despite the challenges.

✻ On day two of the field season it was pouring rain. We were gauging streamflow in Hilda Creek, our waterproof hoods tied up tight around our heads. The mosquitoes were oblivious to rain, so we alternated between swatting, swearing, and measuring. The creek itself was loud: all we could hear was rushing water and the raindrops battering our hoods. No one in their right mind would be out in these conditions, yet we had the weird feeling that we were being watched.

"Weigh down the tape measure!" Dave shouted, as we prepared to stretch it across the stream channel. I put one end under a rock and he unspooled the rest to reach the other side of the stream, winding it around a tree to hold it tight. Dave, wearing hip waders, stood in the water with a handheld stream gauge called a pygmy meter, a smaller version of the standard current meter we used at field school. It consisted of a metal rod with a ring of metal cups tipped on their sides at its bottom, which turned like a windmill in the current. The recording device, which was attached to it by a cable, calculated the speed of water flow based on the number of times the ring rotated, and the metal rod was marked with numbers to measure water depth. Dave plunged the pygmy meter into the water at a set point along the tape measure and yelled, "Fifteen centimetres deep at ten centimetres across the stream!" I wrote the numbers down in my field notebook as he angled the recording device towards his face and, after a few seconds, yelled, "Five metres per second!" We continued measuring in this fashion until we had collected data every ten centimetres across the stream. That evening I would use the measurements we'd recorded from each section of the stream to calculate the total flow rate in Hilda Creek.

When we arrived at our home base at the end of that wet day, Parks Canada staff told us about a grizzly sow who had been seen regularly making the trek from nearby Parker Ridge, right across our study area, then up and over the valley wall. I imagine she was keeping an eye on us as we worked, which would explain why we felt we weren't alone. Perhaps she was wondering what we were doing and what the point of it was.

During our ten days in the field, we gauged streamflow in the proglacial stream and in Hilda Creek, one of us standing in hip waders in the water while the other stood on shore recording numbers as they came in. We did this in all weather and sometimes twice a day, to make sure we caught a range of streamflow values. It was harder to gauge the proglacial stream: the channel shape was constantly shifting as the gravel banks collapsed or the water flowed down a different pathway. This made it difficult to compare measurements between days. We had no such problems in Hilda Creek, however, where the channel was well established and surrounded by shrubby willows and small trees.

I measured the electrical conductivity (EC; a substitute for ion concentrations) in both the proglacial stream and Hilda Creek with a handheld EC meter. High EC values indicated lots of ions, suggesting that the water had been in contact with sediment for longer than water with low EC values. This data would give me insight into where the water was coming from. At each of fifteen set locations along both streams, I collected a water sample using a measuring cup, plopped in the EC meter, and recorded the numbers it provided. I did this daily, walking from the edge of the glacier snout down to the terminal moraine, trying to determine whether the EC changed with weather, time of day, or streamflow.

At the same fifteen locations where I measured EC, I spent two separate days collecting and hand-filtering water samples. The goal was to measure how much sediment was in the water, and then to run each sample through the ion chromatograph—once I got back to campus—to compare the results with the EC data. Hand-filtering was a tedious process that took at least half an hour for each sample, and yielded a filter paper full of sediment and fifty millilitres of filtered water to pour into a clean sample bottle for analysis. I labelled the hard plastic filter case and the sample bottle, noting the name, time, and location for each in my field notebook, and moved on to the next sample. There was a reason I took only two sets of water samples!

The samples I collected from the proglacial stream contained lots of sediments. These were picked up from the debris-rich, formerly glaciated terrain through which the stream flowed, with the amount of sediment increasing as the water got muddier farther downstream. Conversely, the samples from Hilda Creek were pretty much sediment-free, and the water was clear. However, the EC measurements were the opposite of what I had expected: the samples with more dirt in them had lower EC values than the clear samples from Hilda Creek. These results suggested that the proglacial stream water didn't touch the sediment long enough to pick up ions. The water in Hilda Creek, however, was in much longer contact with sediment as it flowed underground from the end of the proglacial stream channel out to the terminal moraine.

As I measured Hilda Glacier's proglacial hydrology, I realized I'd bitten off far more than I could chew. "There's no way I can figure out such a complex system with such basic tools," I said to Dave. He agreed. It was an ambitious project that wasn't necessarily doomed to fail, but was limited by my antiquated gear, my limited knowledge, and the short time frame I had to study the site.

In hindsight, I could have used a real weather station that more accurately measured rainfall and air temperature, and also measured wind speed and relative humidity, all of which are factors in glacier melt. It would also have been helpful to have an automated water sampler in Hilda Creek, so I could put a harmless dye into the proglacial stream, then trace its movement to the creek. That would help me understand what was happening to the water in the space between the stream sinking into the ground and it re-emerging outside the terminal moraine as Hilda Creek. And, of course, a summer-long field season would have been ideal to capture hydrologic change under a range of weather conditions.

But I was doing science on a tiny budget and, as a research neophyte, I didn't find out until a few years later that the equipment I just described even existed, let alone where to get it or how to use it. As with our field school project on push moraines, I had to rely heavily on detailed field notes and my own ideas of what was occurring rather than just empirical data. This required a combination of close observation of the local hydrology and the art of storytelling.

Field science is like writing, in that it involves communicating a story. You collect and analyze data to explain what's happening in a specific environmental system. Many scientists would be horrified to think of their work as linked to story. But, as a storyteller, I believe it is: you're telling the what, when, where, why, and how of the process or site you're measuring. The data a scientist collects are used to validate the story: the better the data, theoretically, the more sound the story. The worse the data, the more speculative the story becomes.

At Hilda Glacier, Dave took a picture of me sitting in the sun next to a huge block of stagnant ice up against the far west cliff of the proglacial zone. I am writing in my notebook—but am I making scientific notations or telling a story? Or am I doing a bit of both?

✷ My work at Hilda Glacier was part of a long tradition of research, exploration, and storytelling in the area, most recently by geologists Kathleen Hammer and Norman Smith who, in the 1980s, researched the ability of the proglacial stream to move rocks and gravel.[1]

Evidence of their presence appeared on site in the form of a battered old coffee pot from their camp and an orange-painted rock, both of which now sit on my bookshelf. They painted many rocks and placed them in the proglacial stream to measure how far they moved, using that information to figure out how much power the stream had to transport them. But long before Hammer and Smith poked around the proglacial zone, there had been two adventurous, science-minded women who explored the area in the late 1800s and early 1900s: Mary Schäffer and Mary Vaux.

At the age of twenty-nine, Mary Schäffer first visited the Selkirk Mountains in 1889 with her much older husband, Dr. Charles Schäffer. They travelled by train from Philadelphia to Glacier House, the first Canadian Pacific Railway hotel for wealthy travellers situated in the Rogers Pass region of British Columbia. Charles was not only a doctor but also a botanist, interested in the local flora. The couple travelled to Glacier House every summer to botanize and bring back stories and photos to their friends in Philadelphia society. Mary Schäffer was a skilled painter, and would press, dry, photograph, and paint the flowers that Charles collected, having learned the very specific type of painting required to show all the features of each flower. Ultimately, she used these skills to publish *Alpine Flora of the Canadian Rockies* in 1907.

Schäffer described herself as quite unadventurous during her early visits to the Rockies. In 1893, she and Charles went on their first camping trip, to Lake Louise. While she enjoyed the trip there and the views once they arrived, she didn't enjoy camping given the mosquitoes and the boggy landscape. She vowed never to do it again. She was destined to break that vow, however, as her interest in intriguing locations was piqued by stories from various explorers and climbers who had ventured into the wilds. These tales led her to stray farther from Glacier House on future visits, with a Philadelphian friend named Mary Vaux and her family.

Like Schäffer, Vaux was a talented painter of wildflowers and published a five-volume book entitled *North American Wildflowers* between 1925 and 1928. Schäffer joined the Vauxes on hiking trips, something she would never have attempted in her early years at Glacier House. But she didn't climb any mountains, being "scared stiff at rocks and precipices."[2] Vaux herself was not a dedicated mountaineer, though she was the first white woman to ascend Mount Stephen (3,199 metres) near Field, BC, in 1900. Vaux did attend the annual Alpine Club of Canada summer camps, traversing snowfields and glaciers as part of a larger group of adventurers, likely including ACC co-founder Elizabeth Parker.

Vaux first visited Glacier House in 1887, the year the hotel opened. She, her father, and brothers are credited with recording the first measurements of glacier change in the Selkirk Mountains. They photographed the nearby Illecillewaet Glacier before heading back to Philadelphia, then returned in 1894 to take new photos. Their images showed that the glacier had retreated significantly in the seven years since their last visit. This kicked off a family legacy of annual glaciology measurements at Illecillewaet, Asulkan, Yoho, Victoria, and Wenkchemna Glaciers, which started in 1896 and ended in 1922. The family selected landmarks around each glacier from which they took compass bearings of the ice and surrounding peaks, they made sketches of each glacier, and took repeat photos from set photographic points using heavy, large-format cameras with glass plates. They also set up metal plates on each glacier's snout, which they surveyed from a fixed point to measure annual glacier flow rates. These plates had to be moved regularly as the glaciers continued to retreat.

In 1903, Charles Schäffer passed away. Not to be robbed of her beloved trips to the mountains, Mary Schäffer travelled by horse pack train for five summers after that, from 1904 to 1908. In the first few years she collected botanical specimens for the book she and Charles had started to compile. In 1907 and 1908 she explored the valleys and passes that the current Icefields Parkway follows, and visited Maligne Lake in the newly established Jasper National Park. She was on the trail for several months at a time, mostly with her companion Mollie Adams and well-known mountain guides Billy Warren (Schäffer's future husband) and Sid Unwin. Maps of her travels show that she passed through the Hilda Glacier area on each of her summer visits. Schäffer's explorations took her to Wilcox Pass, Nigel Pass, and Mount Athabasca—all in the immediate vicinity of Hilda Glacier. She even set up a Camp Parker, near Parker Ridge where our unseen grizzly sow came from, the same ridge we had climbed during field school. Perhaps Schäffer saw a local grizzly or two when she was camped there.

Vaux took on her family's annual glacier measurements in 1911 and continued them on and off until 1922, after which her work was continued by surveyor Arthur O. Wheeler, president of the Alpine Club of Canada, who'd helped her with previous glacier surveys. Her scientific work was recognized when she was elected a member of the Academy of Natural Sciences of Philadelphia, one of few women to receive that honour, and she served as president of the Society of Woman Geographers.

In the early 1900s, society assumed that being outdoors "would have little appeal to the average woman whose time is divided between her dressmaker's, her clubs and the management of her maids."[3] But Schäffer scoffed at this description, saying, "We can starve as well as men; the [bogs] will be no softer for us than for them; the ground will be no harder to sleep upon; the water no deeper to swim, nor the bath colder if we fall in."[4] She was adamant that she enjoyed her outdoor adventures, and there was no reason those adventures should be limited to men. Vaux was equally enamoured with mountains over society, writing that "golf is a fine game, but can it compare with a day on the trail, or a scramble over the glacier, or even with a quiet day in camp[?]...Somehow when once this wild spirit enters the blood...I can hardly wait to be off again."[5]

Sometimes I thought I caught a glimpse of Schäffer's fringed buckskin jacket, just around the next bend in the Hilda Glacier trail;

it seemed if I walked a bit faster I might catch up with her. I imagined Vaux setting up her large-format camera in the proglacial zone, taking photos of the glacier, mapping its front, and surveying its extent with her early twentieth-century equipment.

In *Lands of the Lost Borders*, Kate Harris writes, "Explorers might be extinct, in the historic sense of the vocation, but exploring still exists, will always exist: in the basic longing to learn what in the universe we are doing here."[6] This is exactly how I think about Mary Schäffer and Mary Vaux, spending their summers exploring the mountains to discover their place in the world, to make sense of their lives through the work of wildflower collection and glacier measurements.

Working at Hilda Glacier, I felt a kinship with Schäffer, who was commissioned by the federal government to survey Maligne Lake in 1911, despite having no experience with surveying. She used a spool of measuring tape to determine the distance between survey points, but it fell into the lake and a new one was ordered from Toronto. She promptly dropped the replacement spool into the lake as well, but managed to have Arthur O. Wheeler, who had come with the replacement spool, retrieve it so she could continue her work. Then she experienced problems with a piece of metal in her wooden survey tripod, which affected her measurements for the worse, so she had to switch to using a piece of wood instead. Despite these setbacks—similar to some that I've had to deal with in the field—Schäffer persevered in surveying the lake and naming local peaks for friends and colleagues, including Mary Vaux. She submitted her survey data and place names to the National Geographical Board in Ottawa, where they were accepted and included on new maps of the area.

I also felt a kinship with Vaux, taking her measurements of Illecillewaet and other glaciers. I was immersed in the same kind of landscape that she explored: the rocky terrain of the proglacial zone, with the constant sound of rushing water and an ever-retreating glacier snout, but I was studying water flow instead of ice flow. I wondered if Vaux missed glacier surveying when she gave it up after 1922, or if she felt that she had come to the end of a family era.

Schäffer and Vaux were early examples of what women could be and do in rugged landscapes at a time when gender roles were highly circumscribed by society. They forged a path for future women and girls to become explorers, mountaineers, and scientists, through their pioneering trips in mountainous regions. Though they often had male guides or a husband with them, they were particularly independent and tough-minded: they knew what they wanted and set out to achieve it. They served as historical mentors for me: adventurous women in an era when women most often stayed at home; strong women who bucked social conventions and did so without apology.

✸ Following the downpour that second day, the weather improved and Dave and I enjoyed sunny, warm conditions for the rest of our stay at Hilda Glacier. But after five long days of climbing up and over the moraine and down into the rocky forefield with a heavy pack, and walking up and down the uneven terrain to the glacier and back, the knee I injured so long ago abruptly gave out.

Of course, this occurred when we were as far up-valley as possible. We were near the proglacial stream, just finishing up for the day, and now had to somehow find a way to get back to our vehicle. I couldn't put any weight on my injured leg, and didn't have any walking sticks to brace myself. Dave had to help me walk by acting as my crutch. He also had to carry both backpacks, so he wore mine on his front. I put my arm around his neck and held my bad leg up, stepping forward on my good leg while he absorbed the weight that my bad leg couldn't. Over the next few hours, we stumbled the two kilometres up the rocky ice-marginal moraine and down the trail past Hilda Creek, me leaning heavily on Dave as he struggled to maintain his balance. We finally reached the driveway to the hostel and the truck, a trek that took at least three times as long as usual. When we arrived at the bunkhouse, I hobbled up the front stairs using Dave's arm and the railing, then collapsed in a chair by the door while Dave got me an ice pack.

For the final five days of the field season, I was trapped in the bunkhouse with only an ice pack and my thoughts, while Dave took measurements and recorded observations without me. I was definitely not the best company when he returned each evening. "I hate having a bad knee!" I griped. "Why did this have to happen?" I was frustrated at being incapacitated, and felt like my fieldwork was cursed. Dave was helping, but it wasn't the same as seeing things with my own eyes.

Still, it wasn't all bad—staying at the bunkhouse and writing in my journal allowed me to think carefully about the project and the data we'd collected, and to consider how it all fit together. I was piecing together the story of Hilda Glacier, and Dave's continued data collection helped flesh out that story. I reminded myself that spending this time in the Rockies was immensely preferable to spending it in the clean lab at the university. This brief field season was a necessary break that helped me push through the last six weeks of my summer job.

* After ten days of fieldwork, some of my questions about Hilda Glacier had been answered. The glacier was reacting as most glaciers do: daily streamflow peaked a few hours after maximum sunlight, then declined as the sun set. Meltwater travelled out of the glacier and down through the proglacial stream, picking up dirt as it flowed and carving stunning ice caves into the banks of stagnant ice. At the end of the stream channel, that meltwater disappeared into the ground through at least two holes. These holes bubbled a bit like groundwater springs throughout the day, suggesting that either water was backing up in the groundwater system that they were feeding, or it was forcing air out of that system.

The silty flats provided evidence that the proglacial zone filled with water during high spring melt and other high-flow events, like heavy rainfalls. These high flows probably reached a threshold where they delivered too much water for the groundwater system to absorb. Although we only had one day of rain when we were there, I suspected that a lake sometimes formed on these flats, depositing silty clay before declining into a series of braided channels. To capture such an event, however, would have required a much longer field season—or even several seasons.

Despite all I had learned, some of my data didn't make sense, particularly the chemistry data. I ran my carefully collected and filtered water samples through the ion chromatograph back in the clean lab, but the results didn't match my electrical conductivity measurements. Experience has taught me that science doesn't always provide cut-and-dried answers to difficult questions, that sometimes there is no alternate hypothesis for your results, and that things often don't work out quite as expected. My conflicting results were just examples of these realities.

My project report was difficult to write up, given these limitations. I had to explain what went right and what went wrong, while also speculating on what might be happening between the end of the proglacial stream and Hilda Creek, since I couldn't physically measure it. This uncertainty solidified the importance of field observations to complement data collection, as much of what I knew about this complex system was based on what I had observed in tandem with what the data could tell me. Like the Vauxes and Mary Schäffer, I relied heavily on observation in my attempt to figure out Hilda Glacier's story.

It had been a challenging field season, but even an unsuccessful research project is a learning experience, never a waste of time. On the positive side, I had learned how to set up a research project on a shoestring budget, without a lot of high-tech equipment, and had made decisions on the fly in the field. I'd developed not only my field skills but also my critical thinking and data analysis skills.

I submitted my Hilda Glacier research report to a scientific journal but it was never published. It wasn't scientifically robust enough: too much story and not enough science. I presented my results at a national conference and was the youngest person there, standing in front of a room full of intimidating scientists in my one set of non-outdoor clothes. I talked nervously about numbers and pointed at graphs, but wished I had more solid evidence to show. I was stranded between science and story. I realized then that I preferred to observe and tell stories about landscapes, rather than analyze and quantify them—a revelation that should have set off alarm bells about my future career direction. I identified with what Canadian explorer Kate Harris wrote in *The Walrus*: "The end of all our exploring, then, is not knowledge but kinship—a deepened sense of connection to the planet and to each other."[7] Facing that room of scholars, I felt alienated from their society, yet strongly connected to the Hilda Glacier landscape, and to the people who had travelled through and studied the region in the past.

✳ In September 1998, I had one more term of coursework and another co-op work term to go. As my BSc came to an end, I had to choose between doing a two-year master of science degree starting in the autumn of 1999, or following my somewhat vague ambitions into writing. The problem was, I knew what an MSc would look like based on Dave's experience, but I had no idea what a writing career would look like. Who would I write for, and where would I begin? Alternatively, was I a good enough scientist to pursue an MSc? The goal of an MSc is to learn to be a scientist, not to start off as one, so perhaps it would help me expand my knowledge and improve my skills. Maybe I could become a writer *after* the MSc, and learn to craft the story behind the science.

3

PREPARING FOR TAKEOFF

WE STOOD OUTSIDE at two in the morning, in minus-forty-degree weather, running our truck so the engine block wouldn't freeze and the battery wouldn't die. All of the vehicles in the parking lot were idling while we owners chatted in the still night air, bundled up in down jackets and warm toques, our breath crystallizing in puffs of vapour.

It was Christmas of 1998, and I was spending the holidays in the Rockies with Dave. We were staying in an off-the-grid hostel that was so cold, the inside of the windows had iced over completely. We had returned to the mountains from Vancouver Island because we loved them so much, and couldn't imagine a year without spending time there. This time, however, we experienced the snow and frozen charm of a mountain winter, rather than the multicoloured hues of autumn or the unpredictable weather of summer.

The Icefields Parkway gets a lot of snow in winter, and we made the most of it. We went cross-country skiing on the Pipestone trails near Lake Louise, where Dave was convinced I was trying to kill him because of the cold and the fact that he'd never cross-country skied before. The trails were a bit hillier than I had expected; I went

(Top) The remains of a Rocky Mountain outfitter's cabin in the Canadian Rockies, December 1998. (Photo by D. Lewis, used with permission.) (Bottom) Dave snowshoeing up to the lookout over Peyto Lake, Canadian Rockies, December 1998. (Photo by the author.)

hurtling downhill several times, terrified of wiping out if my knees weren't strong enough to keep me in the tracks or allow me to make an abrupt turn at the bottom.

We also went snowshoeing, exploring the Mosquito Creek valley, happy not to have to worry about mosquitoes at that time of year. I enjoyed the rhythm of it: my leg muscles working hard, my butt pushing my leg up and out of the snow, my hip and thigh swinging my leg forward and then planting my foot, my snowshoe gripping the snow like a claw, then a slight tensing of my calf to roll forward into the next stride. Each step repeated until I had ten, twenty, thirty in a row, my walking sticks clicking and creaking softly in cadence with my stride. I was completely in sync, moving effortlessly through this white mass of crystals. This was the life, constantly in motion, feeling like a part of the natural system and not merely a blot on it. It was hard going in the deepest snow, though, and sometimes we accidentally slid into tree wells: depressions close to tree trunks where the lower branches prevent snow from collecting. Once you landed in a well, it was a challenge to struggle out of it.

We snowshoed up to the Peyto Lake lookout, first following the unplowed road and then turning onto a barely visible path to the lookout itself. The trees stood like sentinels cloaked in heavy snow and frost, their branches bent under the load. It was deathly quiet: no birdsong or sounds of other people, just our breath as we took in the view out over Peyto Lake—a pristine expanse of white, with milky green ice showing through where the snow cover was thin.

All too soon our trip was over, and we left the mountains to head back to the daily grind of university. But I carried the memory of that trip in my back pocket, ready to return to the Rocky Mountains in any season. That chance would come soon enough, as we moved to Edmonton in the autumn of 1999 so I could begin a master's program in glacier hydrology at the University of Alberta with Martin Sharp.

Before I finished my 1998 summer job with Martin, we had talked about potential thesis topics for an MSc and he suggested a lab-based project. After working in the clean lab all summer, however, I was definitely not keen on the boring repetitiveness of lab work, and hesitantly proposed a field-based project for his consideration. He was on board with that, so I was saved from measuring "carbon fluxes in recently deglaciated terrain," a topic that didn't interest me in the slightest. Instead, I'd study the flow of water on and through an Arctic glacier and collaborate with a British graduate student, Sean, to figure out how this affected glacier movement.

I was all for it—the more remote the fieldwork, the better, as far as I was concerned. My plan was to pursue writing in some way, shape, or form once I finished my MSc. The fieldwork and the master's degree would give me an environmental research background to write from, while also providing a fallback career in consulting or government work in case the writing didn't pan out. In the meantime, Dave would finish his MSc from the University of Victoria remotely, in Edmonton.

The move was a big change for us, from Victoria to a city almost ten times as populated, and from a small campus to one at least twice as big. But we were excited that our new home was only a four-hour drive from the Rocky Mountains instead of the two-day drive that we were used to.

* I had been fascinated by the Arctic since high school, after reading *Frozen in Time*, Owen Beattie and John Geiger's book about Sir John Franklin's doomed 1845 expedition to traverse the Northwest Passage. I was both drawn to the wide-open spaces and the unexplored territory that the authors described, with death just a knife's edge of poor judgment away, and horrified by the prospect of getting lost and stumbling across the barren tundra like an earthbound ghost.

Franklin left England in 1845, tasked with exploring the last unnavigated section of the Northwest Passage in the western Canadian Arctic. The expedition ran into trouble in September 1846, when Franklin's two ships became stuck in the sea ice in Victoria Strait near King William Island, rendering them captive as winter set in. The ice closed in around the wooden ships, crushing their hulls and causing them to list as it shifted around them. The crew stayed with the ships for nearly two years, finally abandoning them in April 1848, at which point Franklin had already died, likely of pneumonia. He and his crew were ill-prepared for Arctic survival, bringing their best silver cutlery, overkill for an Arctic expedition, and woollen clothing, which no longer insulated once it got wet. I felt for Lady Jane Franklin, as ship after ship—twenty-six in all—left England after 1847 to search for her husband, some lured by the British government's £20,000 reward. Each one returned without him. She was a widow before her husband had even had a chance to explore his Arctic surroundings.

When I was preparing to do fieldwork there, the Arctic was as hot a topic as it had been in the mid-nineteenth century. In the late 1990s, scientists worldwide were in the midst of determining whether or not the Arctic was responding to a changing climate. Were the environmental changes observed in the Arctic related to shifts in large-scale weather patterns, or were they caused by something else? Today we know that the Arctic is warming almost three times faster than the rest of the globe because of human-caused climate change, but at the time, my work was on the cutting edge of Arctic research. I would be examining how Arctic glacier hydrology developed, and would model what role environmental change played in that process.

✳ "Eight heads of broccoli!" Martin exclaimed, looking over our food list. "Who's going to eat eight heads of broccoli?!"

"Uh, *we* are?" I hesitantly responded. It was January 2000, and my fellow master's student Kathy and I were planning meals for four people in advance of our eight-week Arctic field season. We'd made lists of fresh food to be brought in by people joining us partway through the season: bread, vegetables, fruit, and cheese. Apparently, Martin wasn't accustomed to too many vegetables in the field. He did, however, give me a recipe for a dish he liked and asked that we make sure to get the ingredients. It was a stew of chickpeas, rice, and tomatoes, so it was easy to incorporate into our meal planning.

Our field season would begin in June, a month after the eight-month academic year ended. We'd be heading to the east coast of Ellesmere Island, Nunavut, to work on John Evans Glacier (JEG), a remote glacier about 1,200 kilometres south of the North Pole. Martin had started working on JEG in 1994, with an initial field crew that camped on the glacier from May until August. That must have been a serious adventure! The glacier encompasses an area of 160 square kilometres, about the size of Liechtenstein, Europe's fourth-smallest country. It stretches from Dobbin Bay in the north over barren rock to Allman Bay in the south. Poking out of the ice along its length are nunataks: islands of bedrock peaks that remained untouched by glacier ice as it flowed around them. High rock ridges outline the borders of ice watersheds, forcing ice flow downstream in viscous rivers. Meltwater from JEG flows into Nares Strait, which separates Canada from Greenland—not that far away.

The glacier was named by Vice Admiral Sir George Strong Nares, the strait's namesake. Nares explored the Arctic much later than Franklin as part of the British Arctic Expedition in 1875–1876, and he named John Evans Glacier for the head of the Geological Society of London at the time. His mission was to reach the North Pole, but he ran into thick sea ice and his crew suffered from scurvy so he turned back. Unlike Franklin, Nares survived and went on to explore the coasts of Ellesmere Island and Greenland. He collected scientific data such as weather observations, ocean temperature readings, descriptions of pack ice, and compass bearings of the landscape, and brought back to England samples of the so-called animal, vegetable, and mineral kingdoms, and photos of Inuit he encountered.

Doing remote Arctic fieldwork was almost as tricky at the turn of the millenium as it was during the nineteenth century. Our team would be deployed to our research site from the Polar Continental Shelf Program (PCSP) base and logistics hub in Resolute, on Cornwallis Island, also in Nunavut. The PCSP is a Canadian government department that coordinates travel from their base to remote field sites across the Arctic via planes and helicopters. They also provide camp supplies, including mess tents, individual tents, snowmobiles, two-way radios, satellite phones, camp stoves, generators, fuel, and more. There is a bunkhouse for researchers at the base: a blue-clad building with red trim that contains double-occupancy rooms and communal bathroom facilities, and a dining area that serves delicious cafeteria-style meals. The PCSP also has lab space that's used by researchers working out of the base.

The base is situated a few kilometres from the hamlet of Resolute, one of Canada's northernmost communities. Created in 1953, it was populated by Inuit from Inukjuak, in northern Quebec, and from Pond Inlet, Northwest Territories (now Nunavut), who were forcibly relocated there to demonstrate Canada's sovereignty in the Arctic. The people were hugely out of their element, particularly those from Inukjuak who weren't used to the twenty-four-hour daylight of summer and the twenty-four-hour darkness of winter. Both groups struggled with hunting and collecting local food because they didn't know the land, though they eventually learned to hunt beluga. In 1996, the Canadian government established a "reconciliation agreement," which created a $10 million trust fund for the families relocated in 1953. It wasn't until 2010, however, more than half a century after the original relocation, that the government offered an official apology to Inuit. Today there are approximately two hundred permanent residents in the hamlet.

✳ Since we'd be working in the remote Arctic, we had to get all of our gear up to the PCSP base, so it was ready to be flown into our field site once we arrived. We'd fly from Edmonton, Alberta, to Yellowknife, Northwest Territories, then catch a connecting flight to the base in Resolute, Nunavut. From there we would travel by plane and then helicopter to JEG. Our plane from Resolute would be a Twin Otter—an iconic bush plane developed by De Havilland Canada that can touch down on (and take off from) water, snow, or land, depending on what landing gear is installed.

Kathy and I had been thrown in the deep end of Arctic field preparation and told to swim. Having never experienced this type of remote fieldwork, we had to plan meals from scratch, or by asking other students in our research group who had been north before. Our daily breakfast, lunch, dinner, and snacks all had to be accounted for, so we had to estimate how much everyone would eat and drink. We had countless spreadsheets outlining menus, meals, and ingredients. It was cheaper to buy most of our food in Edmonton and ship it via plane, given the exorbitant prices of food in the North, where four litres of milk can cost more than eight dollars.

"How many chocolate bars do you think we'll eat?" I asked Kathy, going over our lists for the umpteenth time. "I don't know, let's say two a day per person?" she replied, thoroughly fed up with all this detailed planning. We would never eat that many chocolate bars normally, but given that we'd be walking on snow and ice up to fifteen kilometres a day, we figured we'd need the extra energy. It would be worse to have not enough food than to have too much.

We were all fairly easygoing about what we were willing to eat, and no one had any food allergies, so planning meals and shopping ended up being pretty straightforward. Based on our menus, we drew up shopping lists of canned goods, granola bars, oatmeal, pasta, bread, cheese, and more. Our trips to the local bulk grocery store invariably ended with us pushing two to three carts piled high through the checkout. "What are you going to do with all this food?" the cashier would always ask. "We're heading to the Arctic for eight weeks and need to bring everything with us," I'd reply, trying not to get into too detailed of a discussion. It was awkward to tell a stranger about our research plans; it was a privilege that so few people have, but also an experience that not many would understand.

In addition to these standard grocery items, we bought dehydrated food from a specialty supplier: sour cream, mushrooms, eggs, peppers, onions, and garlic. Dried eggs do *not* reconstitute well into scrambled eggs, but dried sour cream is great as a thickener for (again, dried) mushroom sauce for pasta. Once we got all the food back to campus, we stripped off as much packaging as possible, then sorted it into labelled Ziploc bags and packed it into large Rubbermaid tubs held shut with zip ties. We shipped the tubs to Resolute via Air Canada Cargo. Their office at the edge of the Edmonton International Airport had seen better days; it housed a well-scuffed countertop and rough-edged employees that were more than happy to take our money. We frequently showed up at the cargo office with something new to ship, resulting in a relatively large bill.

We weren't just sending food north, but also our research equipment. This meant designing our experiments and building and testing any equipment we needed well before we went into the field. It was difficult to come up with a research plan for a place I'd never seen. At least for my solo Hilda Glacier project, I knew the glacier well from having done a field school project there. But going to John Evans Glacier was a completely different kettle of fish: it was twenty times bigger, and infinitely more remote. We'd be spending a lot of time on the ice itself, whereas at Hilda Glacier I spent my time in the proglacial zone.

I found an aerial photo of JEG, printed it up at poster size to clearly show the surface, and identified locations where I would install my measuring equipment. The glacier looked unreal, like someone had squeezed a tube of toothpaste onto a crenulated piece of brown stone and let it flow into the valleys and around the ridges. Sitting in my cubicle in my shared grad-student office, I stared at that photo so intently that I felt I had been there already.

✶ Glacier hydrology is different from land-based hydrology, mostly in terms of the speed at which meltwater shapes glacier ice versus the same process on land. In land-based hydrology, water shapes rock on a long timescale. One of the best places to see evidence of this is in the flash flood–prone sandstone slot canyons of the US Southwest. There, water erodes the soft sandstone at a geologic pace, resulting in cathedral-like canyons with polished, sculpted walls, which can be explored during the dry season when they're not in danger of flooding.

Glacier streamflow creates similarly sculpted channels, but it also creates moulins (holes through which the water enters the ice) and waterfalls in varied shades of blue. The water melts and shapes the ice as it flows, carving out features much faster than it could in sandstone. Both land-based and glacial streamflow is driven by weather: warm, sunny days generate snowmelt in both systems. However, land-based streamflow is also driven by rainfall, which is often not the case in Arctic glacier systems. In the latter, rainfall often means cloudy days and cooler air temperatures, and snow at higher elevations, which can shut down melt and runoff altogether.

On JEG, my research goal was to figure out when the different components of the surface water system connected to one another, and when they drained into the moulins and initiated streamflow at the glacier snout. This would tell me how the glacier drainage system developed during the melt season, which would subsequently impact glacier flow and water chemistry.

To answer my research questions, I'd measure a range of variables in both the surface streams and proglacial river. By combining water level data with streamflow measurements, I could determine how much water was moving through the surface system over time. Like at Hilda Glacier, measuring the electrical conductivity of the water would tell me the concentration of ions in it. Low conductivity water comes directly from snow and ice melt, so it has fewer ions; higher conductivity water has been in prolonged contact with rock and sediment, so it has more. Some of the sources for higher EC water at JEG would likely include a lake at the base of a large mid-glacier nunatak, in which previous researchers had seen rocks and silt. The water coming out of the front of the glacier would probably have high EC values because it had filtered through the sediment underneath the glacier.

A key part of my research was to measure glacier melt across the melting zone, which in most years encompassed the entire glacier surface area below the nunatak. This would tell me how much surface melt was being produced and flowing into surface streams, crevasses, and moulins. An array of PVC ablation stakes had already been installed on the glacier by a previous field team—one for each elevation band, and on different aspects (north, south, east, and west). I'd be responsible for regularly measuring the height of each stake: as the glacier surface melted and more of each stake was exposed, my numbers would increase, providing a record of glacier melt over the summer season. One of my research partners, Sean, would use these same stakes to measure ice movement: as the glacier flowed downhill, the stakes would move with it. There were also three weather stations installed on the glacier, again by a previous field team, which I'd tap into to collect data on the variables that drive snow and ice melt: air temperature, wind speed, relative humidity, and incoming solar radiation. I would use this information to numerically model snowmelt, and match the output from that model to my ablation stake measurements. Near the lower weather station, three previously installed geophones would record icequakes (seismic events similar to earthquakes, but caused by moving ice).

Last but not least, I built a time-lapse camera setup that I'd use to observe the proglacial zone from on top of the glacier snout. Nicknamed "Leroy," the camera was housed in a Pelican case with a plexiglass hole for the lens, and would be mounted on a tripod and set to take repeat photos at specific intervals. Those photos would capture when the proglacial river appeared, and how it changed over the melt season. This would be inherently different from my experience at Hilda Glacier, where we worked in a narrow proglacial creek with gentle flows. I was expecting the proglacial flow from JEG to create a wide channel, more like a river than a creek.

Since I wouldn't be able to find a hardware store on the glacier, I crossed my fingers that the equipment I was bringing would do the job without malfunctioning. Where possible, I packed duplicate equipment to substitute for damaged equipment as necessary. Because, no matter how much you hope it won't, something always goes wrong in the field.

✱ I pestered Martin endlessly about what I'd observed on my poster-sized aerial photo of JEG. I specifically wanted to know how the drainage system was structured; I'm sure I must have become somewhat annoying.

"So there are five main surface channels?" I asked, again.

"Yes," he said. "Two of them come from lakes at the base of the ridge and the nunatak. The other three form directly on the glacier surface."

"And all five flow into the glacier in a moulin field partway down the lower section of the glacier?"

"Yes," he repeated.

"Can I gauge surface streamflow with a current meter?"

"Probably not," Martin said. "You don't want to risk losing your footing and sliding into a moulin. You might want to find a different way to measure it. Maybe salt slugs?"

Salt slugs? What were those? Off I went to figure out how to measure streamflow with salt. Turns out I'd have to dissolve an awful lot of salt in a bucket of water and measure its volume and EC. I'd then toss that salt "slug" into the stream and measure EC downstream to see how long it took for it to increase, peak, and then come back down to baseline values. I would graph the EC over time, and use that information plus the original volume and EC of the slug to calculate the streamflow. I made a note to put bulk salt on my shopping list and brush up on my math skills.

I had other questions. The water that entered the moulins on JEG eventually emerged at the front of the glacier—in the form of the proglacial river—but there was a delay between when it entered and exited the glacier. "Can I gauge proglacial river flow with a current meter?" I asked, wondering if the meter would be easier to use while standing in a stream that flowed over land, rather than on the glacier surface. "Maybe early in the season when the flow is low," Martin said. "But not later when it gets a lot higher."

How would I measure the amount of water coming into the system and the amount coming out if I couldn't use a current meter? I couldn't use a salt slug in the proglacial river; the EC would already be so high that I wouldn't be able to detect a conductivity spike that way. It would be kind of like adding an extra spoonful of sugar to a cup of hot chocolate—you wouldn't taste the sugar the way you would if you added it to a cup of coffee. I'd have to find some other method to measure proglacial streamflow at high flows, and nothing helpful was coming to mind. I might have to figure it out when I got there, which wasn't ideal.

Most of my data (water level and EC; weather) would be collected using sensors attached to data loggers: instruments that had to be programmed in advance to record the information I needed. I went to a training course to learn how to use them, which was an overwhelming immersion into becoming an electrician and a computer programmer all at once. As a field scientist, you have to wear a lot of hats.

Data loggers are basically circuit boards with a supposedly user-friendly interface attached to the top. I programmed them to read each sensor based on the channels they were wired into, using an archaic coding language that was specific to that particular model of logger. I was glad I'd taken a programming course during my BSc, even if it was pretty elementary.

I also learned to calibrate sensors to get the best measurements while out in the field. For example, I wired in a water level sensor, programmed the logger to read it, then put the sensor in a bucket of water and compared the output from the logger with the measured water level in the bucket. If there was a discrepancy, I added an extra line to the logger's program code to add or subtract a set value from what the sensor read to ensure that it provided the correct measurement.

These loggers are powered by an electrical connection to a deep-cycle battery (always connect the red "power" cable first so you don't accidentally create a spark!), which is attached to a solar panel that keeps the battery charged—and running the logger—for the entire field season. With such complicated circuitry, data loggers and batteries have to be sheltered from the elements; they will short out if they get wet. My challenge was to come up with a way to house them on the ice to keep them safe. I settled on small plastic toolboxes. I figured the toolboxes would sit on the ice surface: the bottom of the toolbox would protect the logger from snow and ice melt, while the lid would support the solar panel and protect the logger from rain and snowfall. This setup sounded practical when I designed it in my office, but I had no way of knowing how effective it would be in the field.

* For Arctic fieldwork, I needed completely different personal gear than I did in the Rockies. I had to invest in plastic mountaineering boots for glacier travel, a warmer sleeping bag for cold nights camped on the windy rock next to the glacier, a down jacket to wear in camp when the temperatures dropped, winter boots to wear in camp once I was out of my plastic boots, and windproof fleece to wear on the ice while working. Plastic boots are just as they are described—a plastic outer shoe with a felt liner bootie. You snug up the laces on the bootie first, then slide your foot into the plastic shell and tie up those laces, and you're ready to go. Plastic boots are designed to fit rigid crampons, metal claws used for traction on the slippery ice surface. Martin supplied the glacier safety equipment, including crampons, climbing harnesses, ropes, and ice axes.

My most important purchase was a pair of prescription wraparound sunglasses. I'd be out on the reflective glacier ice daily and needed to guard against snow blindness, just as Inuit did using goggles carved from wood or bone with tiny horizontal slits in the front. I also invested in a high SPF sunscreen and a broad-brimmed hat. For down days in camp, I brought books and playing cards; CDs of Ani DiFranco, the Tragically Hip, Soundgarden, and others to play on my Discman (yes, it was that long ago); and a good, peaty scotch. It all had to fit inside my duffle bag, which also carried my sleeping bag and mattress, field clothes and gear (walking sticks, etc.), and personal hygiene items.

Getting to the Arctic is not cheap, given the cost of food, scientific and personal gear, cargo shipments, and airfare. While Martin had funding to support our research, we had to offset some of the costs by applying for grants from various earth science–related organizations. This was something I'd done only once, for my small research grant to work at Hilda Glacier. For my work on JEG, I applied to the Circumpolar/Boreal Alberta Research grant, the Northern Scientific Training Program, the Geological Society of America, and the American Alpine Club. I was successful with each one, which helped pay for my personal gear and some of our shared field costs like helicopter and Twin Otter flights.

✳ Not only did we have to send all of our food and gear north, we also had to prepare for being in polar bear country. Each of us had to get our firearms licence and practise shooting a shotgun, as that was what we'd have in the field.

Kathy and I spent a series of Wednesday evenings taking a firearms course in a local hunter's home. He was an average guy, short, balding, and slightly overweight, who lived in a nondescript neighbourhood in north Edmonton. The house looked average, too. But upon entering his small, wood-panelled basement we were immediately confronted with guns of all types hanging on the walls, with trigger locks on them for safety. This was someone who was *really* into guns, so we hoped to learn a lot from him. He went through the course manual with us, teaching us the theoretical aspects of firearms use and safety: the difference between rifles and shotguns, the uses of each, how to load and unload them, how to store them safely, and how to carry them when out hunting. That was all the course covered; we didn't even have to touch a gun to get our firearms licence.

We told our instructor we needed some shooting experience, so he arranged for us to use one of his many shotguns to test our skills. One evening we went to a nearby field and he set up clay pigeons on fence posts for target practice. My hands shook a bit as I handled the shotgun—the thought of what terrible things might happen if I didn't do this right scared the crap out of me. I made sure the safety was on and loaded the shotgun with two shells. I used the pump action to chamber one shell, then held the gun up to my shoulder, took off the safety, and slowly squeezed the trigger. The gun bucked in my hands and slammed into my shoulder as it recoiled, its shell shattering the clay pigeon into small bits. I chambered another shell and repeated the process. Though I hit several targets, I was still uncomfortable around guns and would have benefitted from more hands-on experience. Once in the field we would practise with the camp shotgun, but this seemed like minimal training for something so serious.

I also needed a wilderness first aid certificate. Since so many students in the earth sciences department were going out on fieldwork, we all attended the same certification course and went through endless scenarios of potential field incidents. Our training covered things like splinting broken legs, diagnosing hypothermia, and recognizing the signs of heart attack and stroke. While it was fun to play the bandaged-up victim or be put in the recovery position, it was sobering to think of being isolated in the field and having to respond to a medical emergency. I paid close attention to the instructor, read the manual, and took copious notes, but ultimately my response to an emergency would depend on the information ingrained in my mind. I wouldn't have time to check my notes or consult the handbook. I'd have to act automatically, based on my memory of the scenarios we participated in during training.

We all knew there were many hazards associated with Arctic fieldwork, from potential aircraft crashes, to falling into a crevasse, to being attacked by a polar bear—not to mention countless other, less-dire sources of danger. Staff responsible for occupational health and safety at the university helpfully suggested placing a traffic cone at each hazard, which had us laughing for days as we imagined a forest of cones at each crevasse and moulin.

✻ The first eight months of my MSc wasn't all about fieldwork preparation, although it sure took up a lot of my time. I also took two courses: one on the environmental history of the Arctic, and another on Arctic glacier processes. The former was an upper-level undergraduate class; our irreverent professor, Dr. John England, was wiry and energetic, with a grey beard and a pointed, elfin face. He shared stories about his many years of Arctic fieldwork and bits of obscure Arctic history in between describing the area's geological history, and how geologists and geomorphologists studied it. He talked about the historical artifacts he'd found on his travels and the rich exploration history of the Arctic region itself.

Our course on Arctic glacier processes was entirely different from John's class. It was a directed reading course with Martin, for which Kathy and I read scientific papers that we discussed once a week. It was meant to help us better understand John Evans Glacier, and how it differed from the glaciers I'd seen and explored in the Rockies.

Glaciers in the Rockies are temperate, which means that the ice is at zero degrees Celsius, it flows downhill at all depths from the surface to the bed, and it can push up moraines as it moves. Water flows on and in these glaciers easily, and can speed up glacier flow at the beginning of the melt season by collecting at the bed of the glacier and creating a lubricated surface for the ice to slide on.

Glaciers in the Arctic, however, are either cold or polythermal. Cold glaciers are below zero degrees throughout their entire mass and are frozen to the ground; they don't build moraines because only the upper layers slowly flow while the lower layers remain static. Cold glaciers also mostly have surface streamflow, though water can enter the glacier through moulins and force a connection with the glacier bed. Once the water gets to the bed, however, it has nowhere to go: the glacier remains frozen in place.

John Evans Glacier is a polythermal glacier. These are a cross between temperate and cold glaciers. Like temperate glaciers, they have a zero-degree core, but it's surrounded by below-zero ice (also known as cold ice) that is frozen to the glacier bed at the margins—similar to a chocolate candy with a hard shell and a creamy filling. This means that water can get into the glacier and collect at its base, but it has to force its way out past the cold zone around the edges. Water that collects at the base can either jack the glacier up, or build up enough pressure to create a crack in the surrounding cold ice and spray out as an artesian fountain or a proglacial river. Polythermal glaciers are exciting beasts for glaciologists: the mix of cold and temperate ice results in major variations in water and ice flow relative to fully temperate or fully cold glaciers.

Martin's class was tough. I struggled to read the papers and extract the essence of what the authors were getting at, as I had no previous knowledge of the physics of different glacier types. Martin knew everything there was to know about those physics, and I scrambled to keep up with his advanced knowledge. I think sometimes he forgot that we were just learning, that it was all new to us. There were a lot of awkward silences in our weekly meetings, which took place in Martin's office. I tried, and often failed, to explain what I'd learned from the assigned readings while putting it in context of what we'd read the week before—much of which I'd already forgotten by then.

I spent hours in the university library, scanning the stacks for glaciology books and photocopying old journal articles about glacier hydrology. There had been a flurry of glacier hydrology research in the 1970s and 1980s, but relatively little new work since then. What did this mean? Was the research field quiet because there was nothing new to learn? Or were scientists on the brink of new discoveries, particularly on glaciers like JEG that hadn't been studied as much as temperate glaciers? And what about the mystery of climate change? The impact it might have on Arctic glacier hydrology was still an unknown. It seemed I was either at the cusp of some exciting new research, or digging into a musty old field that no one thought was important. I was hoping it was the former.

When I wasn't preparing for the field, in class, or in the library, I spent my time cycling the five kilometres to and from the university, and kept active by going to the gym and the pool. Unfortunately, my activities were curtailed as I re-injured my knee in January 2000, a year and a half after I'd injured it at Hilda Glacier. The orthopedic surgeon diagnosed a tear in the cartilage, which caused my knee to collapse suddenly when I was walking. He recommended surgery to nip off the offending piece of cartilage, which would keep me in hospital for only a day. This seemed like a smart thing to do before leaving for the Arctic, so I agreed.

I signed in for the procedure early one January morning, and had to mark the proper knee myself with a felt pen—apparently, surgeons sometimes make mistakes! I woke up with a couple of small incisions on my knee from where they inserted the scope and tools, and a knee brace to keep me from bending it for a week. Turns out the surgeon had not only sewed the cartilage down instead of nipping it off, but he'd removed a "floating body" and sanded the back of my kneecap—where that body had come from—to make it smoother and theoretically cause less pain. I left the hospital on crutches, not entirely sure when I'd be back to 100 per cent, but hoping that my knee problems were over. However, when I was later given an obnoxiously large knee brace with a hinge set to only thirty degrees of bend, which I had to wear for four weeks, I knew my recovery would be slow.

My knee didn't heal properly and instead formed a mass of scar tissue. It was impossible to bend it past a certain angle, and I wasn't able to exercise it for months. It felt weak and unstable, not strong and capable like I needed it to be for my Arctic fieldwork. I was distraught and frequently in tears, worried that I'd have to abdicate another field season to knee issues, just like I did at Hilda Glacier. The thought of losing yet another field opportunity was almost unbearable. Still, there was hope: the first field crew Martin put on the glacier in 1994 had one team member who'd injured his knee skiing right before going in the field. He couldn't walk at all, but managed by getting towed via sled to his sampling sites and then towed back to camp each evening. I figured there must be a way for me to do fieldwork while being similarly incapacitated, though I wasn't sure what that would look like. My research—unlike his—would involve a lot of long days walking across the glacier in deep snow.

* By late April, it was too late to ship any more cargo north, so we had to assume we'd already sent everything we needed. Anything

else would go with us as checked baggage. Our team was ready. Sean had arrived from the United Kingdom, a lanky blond with blue eyes and a ready laugh; someone I was sure I'd get along with in the field.

It had been a gruelling eight months of coursework, grant applications, field preparation, physical therapy, and adjusting to a new city and a new rhythm of life. As I pushed through every day of new challenges and new ideas, I journalled as much as I was able, and even made time for an on-campus writing workshop before I left for the Arctic. It was an immersive week of turning images into words, the scientist side of my brain packed away for a short while. My writing covered the outdoors, the adventures I hadn't taken and the ones I hoped to take, from climbing mountains to owning dogs. My experiences with shooting and wilderness first aid made their way into nuggets of stories, as I focused on the way the sentences flowed out of my pen and onto the page. I belonged in that room full of people discussing writing, more so than I did in a classroom reading glaciology papers. It was obvious that I was destined for a writing life after my MSc.

I wanted to be like Rachel Carson. She started college with the intention of becoming a writer, but switched to biology from English and got her bachelor's degree in 1929. She then moved on to Johns Hopkins University, finishing an MSc in marine biology in 1932 based on her studies at the Woods Hole Marine Biological Laboratory. She worked towards a PhD while also teaching at Johns Hopkins and the University of Maryland, but had to drop out during the Great Depression because she had become the sole financial support for her family.

Rachel's writing background came in handy: she was hired temporarily by the US Bureau of Fisheries to write short radio scripts about marine life. She was then brought on full-time as a junior aquatic biologist, becoming only the second woman at the bureau to hold a full-time professional position. She did freelance writing on the side, transforming scientific facts into lyrical prose that enchanted her readers and supplemented her professional income. Eventually she was promoted to staff aquatic biologist at the newly formed US Fish and Wildlife Service (USFWS), a position she held while writing *Under the Sea Wind*, the first of three books about the ocean, which was published in 1941. In 1946 she wrote several pamphlets for the USFWS, translating science about the new National Refuge System into plain language for the public, and started on her second book. In early 1951, she published *The Sea Around Us*, which was a *New York Times* bestseller and won the National Book Award for Nonfiction. The success of the book prompted a reprinting of *Under the Sea Wind*, which then became a bestseller as well.

As her writing career took off, Rachel resigned from the USFWS to write full-time and look after her family. She earned enough that she was able to build a house on the Maine seashore, where she spent her summers beachcombing and examining the life in tidal pools, enjoying the fresh air and the sounds of the ocean. She published her third book about the ocean, *The Edge of the Sea*, in 1955, fed in no small part by her endless beach walking and exploring. Given her former position at the USFWS, she had access to scientists across the country doing cutting-edge research, and used that research to inform her writing. She wrote with a holistic, ecological bent, emphasizing how the ocean's systems and organisms were interlinked and interdependent, rather than focusing on individual components of an ecosystem.

Rachel's last book was her most popular and prescient: *Silent Spring*, published in 1962. Written to be accessible to the average reader, it warned of the dangers of unchecked chemical pesticide use on human and ecosystem health—particularly DDT. The book led to congressional hearings on federal regulation of pesticide use, at which she testified in 1963. Some argue that the book also led to the creation of the US Environmental Protection Agency. Rachel came under fire from chemical companies and government officials who supported pesticide use; she was disdained as an alarmist "woman writer" who didn't understand the science she was communicating. The readability of Rachel's book led to it being considered too simple to tell the real story of pesticides; credible books about science were written in impenetrable prose not suited for public consumption. Though Rachel died of cancer only two years after the book came out, her legacy remains strong, and *Silent Spring* is still widely read and discussed. It remains relevant today, more than sixty years later.

Rachel Carson is one of my true heroes. I admire how she combined writing and science to forge a successful career path. She persevered with *Silent Spring* while fighting cancer, knowing that it was an important book on a subject that the public needed to be aware of. She shared her knowledge about the ocean in three popular books, all complemented by her thesis work and her professional work at the USFWS. Her writing life was just as much an ecosystem as the marine environments she described, with her work life informing her freelance work and vice versa. As an editorialist for the *New York Times* wrote, "Once or twice in a generation does the world get a physical scientist with literary genius."[1] This is what I aspired to—perhaps not to literary genius, but to writing clearly and engagingly, not only about science but also about outdoor adventures in remote places.

However, for now I just had to get through my field season—I could think about my future later. I had my head down, focused on getting ready for fieldwork and understanding as much as possible about Arctic glaciers, while trying not to worry that my delayed recovery from knee surgery would hamper my field abilities.

4

TWENTY-FOUR-HOUR DAYLIGHT

KATHY, SEAN, MARTIN, AND I ARRIVED IN RESOLUTE in early June 2000, and found everything we'd shipped waiting for us at the Polar Continental Shelf Program base. We piled it up along with our camp gear and some extra equipment that had been stored at the facility, then put it all on a scale. We had to make sure our load wasn't too heavy for the Twin Otter to carry, and to find out whether we could add a barrel of Jet B fuel for the aircraft that would be flying in to John Evans Glacier. Then we waited, like one does in the Arctic, for good weather so that we could fly out to our field site.

While waiting, I savoured the delectable food in the cafeteria. Breakfasts were a smorgasbord of eggs, bacon, pancakes, and cereal, while dinners were rich lasagnas, stews, or curries. Lunches were often a sandwich, or maybe another hot meal. Jars on the counter contained some of the best cookies I'd ever tasted. "I'm going to gain ten pounds before we even leave the base," I joked; the food was that good.

I also met other researchers, and learned about their projects across the Arctic. Some people studied seabirds, others looked at vegetation, and still others studied wood from a fossil forest buried

(Top) A helicopter sent to pick up supplies at the rock camp, John Evans Glacier, Nunavut, June 2000. (Photo by the author.) (Bottom) At the Polar Continental Shelf Project base in Resolute, Nunavut, June 2000. (Photo by K. Heppenstall, author's personal collection.)

by glaciers millennia ago. Everyone milled around in their field clothes, sometimes watching TV, reading, or lining up to use the computers to check email. Each field team was on tenterhooks, ready to go the minute the weather was clear and the Twin Otter was fuelled up.

Because there was still snow on the glacier and on the airstrip in front of it, the JEG team would be moved to our field site in stages. First, we'd fly by Twin Otter to the closest point the aircraft could land with wheels and offload all our gear. Next, the base would send a helicopter to move our gear in sling-loads from the interim landing spot to the glacier.

After a couple of days, the call came over the intercom: "John Evans Glacier, please come to the warehouse." We excitedly grabbed our personal gear from our dorm rooms and rushed off, not sure what to expect. We stood by as the crew loaded the Twin Otter, a white dual-propeller plane with a yellow-orange stripe around the middle. Once they were finished, we crammed ourselves in, twisting around the tubs of food and equipment, duffle bags of personal gear, a two-hundred-litre drum of Jet B fuel, and our tents and other camp supplies. As we took off, my stomach dropped and my heart raced. I looked down at the base below—we wouldn't be back for eight weeks. What had I gotten myself into?

The noise from the propellers made conversation impossible, and fuel fumes permeated the cabin. The landscape beneath us was completely treeless; its rounded, flat mountaintops like layer cakes of sediment dusted with icing-sugar snow. There were also jagged mountains rising directly out of the water in deep ocean fiords, piedmont glaciers flowing like icing down their slopes. Everything seemed huge: the mountains, the glaciers, the ocean. Despite the stunning scenery I dozed on and off, feeling the aftereffects of several restless nights in the dorm. After a three-hour flight we arrived at our first stop.

✶ Kathy, Sean, and I were dropped off in the most remote setting I've ever experienced. Martin had gone back with the Twin Otter to supervise the transfer, but would return in the chopper that would ferry us and our gear to the glacier. There was nothing but tundra beneath our feet and as far as we could see, the sky wide open above us. We were just tiny specks on the landscape, dwarfed by its immensity. I remembered Sir John Franklin's men, isolated and lost on the Arctic barrens after leaving their ship stranded in the sea ice. We heard no sound but the wind, and saw no life except scrubby willow shrubs that barely covered the rocky ground. The air smelled fresh and cool; a breeze blowing in from the north brought with it the unmistakable tang of distant ice and snow.

We were surrounded by a planeload of gear, including a shotgun in case of a polar bear, and a two-way radio in case we needed to contact the base. Now things were real: the threat of bears, the vast, empty terrain. The deafening silence after the plane departed. Kathy and I were quiet, overwhelmed by the sheer scale of the landscape. Sean roamed restlessly among the piles of gear, itching for us to be on our way. We were all paranoid about bears, having been told scary polar bear stories by other Arctic researchers, but had no real sense of what kind of dangers we might face. According to one account, a bear came into a two-person camp and got between the people and the tent that housed their gun. Luckily, one person managed to slide around the side of the tent and get the weapon, which he fired into the air to scare the bear away. I hoped we wouldn't find ourselves in similar circumstances.

Rationally, I'd known that working in the High Arctic was different from working in the Rockies, but it took being there to realize just how different it really was. Not only is the Arctic much more remote (no traffic on the nearby Icefields Parkway, for example), but the twenty-four-hour summer daylight takes some getting used to. There are no trees, and minimal wildlife: it's a world of rock, ice, water, and the few plants that can grow in inhospitable gravel. The remoteness was a stark reminder that the people I was sharing camp with were the only people I'd see for the next two months. It meant we had to get along to some extent and let small annoyances slide, or we wouldn't enjoy our time in the field. While we had common interests,

I was the only Canadian in camp: Kathy, Martin, Sean, and Sean's PhD supervisor, Paul (who would arrive in early July to replace Martin), were all British.

Our sole lifeline to other people was the two-way radio, which we used to check in twice a day, at 7:00 a.m. and 7:00 p.m. We'd listen as Eureka Station, one of the two northernmost research stations in Canada, called all the camps across the northern Arctic: "John Evans Glacier, John Evans Glacier, this is Eureka," the radio would sputter.

"Eureka, this is John Evans Glacier, how do you copy?" we would reply.

"Good morning John Evans Glacier, we copy you four by five. How are things?"

"All is well, Eureka."

"Roger that, Eureka out. Murray Ice Cap, Murray Ice Cap, this is Eureka…"

It was as though the camps were all gathered together for coffee instead of scattered across northern Canada. As we listened, we imagined what each camp was like based on the voices and locations that came over the radio: Tanquary Fiord, Lake Hazen, Expedition Fiord, Eureka Shore, Carl Ritter, Blue Mountain, Fossil Forest. Sometimes Eureka couldn't hear a camp's transmission, and they asked other camps to check in with them. But solar flares and ionospheric disturbances often dampened the radio signal to a meaningless buzz, and around the North camps were isolated. Silent. Cut off from the outside world and living in their own bubble.

When the radio was working, Eureka would sometimes pass along phone messages they had received. One evening they relayed a message to a member of another camp, saying "Your wife called and said 'I love you. I got the letter and everything's going to be all right.'" Speculation in our camp was rife as to what that was all about! After the nightly check-ins, camps sometimes switched to a secondary, informal channel to chat, and of course the rest of the Arctic switched over to listen in—a throwback to eavesdropping on telephone party lines.

✳ Eventually the silence of our stopover was broken by the distant sound of an incoming helicopter, bringing back Martin, along with a mesh sling to transport our gear to camp. We spread the sling on the ground and loaded it up, then gathered the corners together in one clip. The chopper hovered above us as we hooked the clip to the bottom; we then had to run to the side, crouch, and cover our heads as the pilot lifted the gear into the air and headed off to camp. After multiple sling-loads had been moved, it was finally our turn to board the helicopter. In the Arctic you learn to wait: for your turn to be sent out from the base, for the weather to be good enough for aircraft to fly, for the chopper to move your loads of gear—the list goes on.

The views from the chopper were phenomenal, from cerulean blue circles of water on bright white sea ice, to massive icebergs, to extensive ice sheets covered in snow and fresh meltwater channels. We were flying in an area so remote that if anything bad happened we were on our own; it would be a terrible place to have something go wrong. There have been several high-profile accidents in the Arctic, including helicopters crashing with well-known researchers on board. Every time it's a shock, and a reminder that the remoteness and ruggedness of the landscape makes Arctic research more dangerous than we sometimes care to admit.

✳ Once in camp there was a lot of setting up to do, but I was distracted by the unfamiliar scenery and the scale of the glacier. It loomed over our camp, as tall as a five-storey building, cooling the air around it like a giant ice cube. Behind us was a rocky ridge, flat brown in colour, made up of loose shale and sandstone. But the ice filled my vision, an ever-present mass that defied description. It was beautiful in a stark kind of way. And daunting to think of how we would get onto it, as the huge, white wall in front of us was a sheer cliff. Since it was early in the season, the glacier itself was quiet and still; the only sound was the wind coming off the ice, whistling down through camp.

Camp was a scree-covered slope with level spots for wooden pallets and tents, and well-beaten paths from previous years' setups. We started by clearing a circle in the snow for the mess tent, called "the igloo" because of its dirty grey-white exterior and rounded top. Inside the igloo went the camp stoves, which were hooked up to propane bottles placed outside, two folding tables, four chairs, and the radio. Once that was done, we brushed the snow off the pallets left behind from last year. We each set up our personal tent on a pallet, and threw our gear inside to deal with later. We lined up the food tubs along the path leading into the igloo, sorting their contents: chocolate bars and granola bars, canned meat and fish, chips, rice and pasta, bread and crackers, oatmeal, and so on. We put the cooler full of fresh food into a snowbank behind the igloo, where it would stay cold until the snow disappeared.

We melted snow for water at first, until a stream along the west margin of the glacier started flowing. Once it did, we would walk-slide down a steep shale- and boulder-covered slope with water jugs that we filled by plunging them into the flow of the stream. We'd then have to haul them back up the hill, the weight dragging on our arms and making walking difficult.

✴ After we set up camp, Martin took us to the edge of the glacier for a lesson in safe glacier travel. Traversing a glacier in spring is not for the faint of heart: snowmelt is just beginning and the crevasses are still covered in snow that is starting to rot. We'd need to travel in harnesses, roped to one another. The leader of our roped-up team would probe the snow for hidden crevasses and direct the rest of us around or over them. We'd also have our crampons on and our ice axes in hand, ready to self-arrest if we slipped and fell. Knowing how to self-arrest is critical if you're sliding down a slope that's covered in ice or snow; it requires that you flip abruptly onto your stomach and drive the head of your axe into the ice to stop your slide. I'll admit, glacier travel sounded pretty straightforward until I actually experienced it.

We dumped the glacier travel gear on the ground: harnesses, belay devices, carabiners, ice screws, slings, prusik loops, pulleys, and climbing rope. "Put on the harness like this," Martin demonstrated, stepping through the waist belt and placing each leg into a leg loop. "Then tighten up the leg loops and do up the waist buckle with an extra loop backwards for good measure." The three of us complied, clumsy with the unfamiliar equipment. "Tie a figure-eight knot in the rope and clip it to the loop on the front of your harness with the locking carabiner," Martin said. "Now wrap the prusik around the rope and attach it to your harness with another carabiner," he continued. "It will act as a brake on the rope if someone falls into a crevasse."

"What about the rest of the stuff?" Sean asked, pointing to the remaining gear. Martin said we'd attach it to the gear loop on our harnesses, so we each clipped on ice screws, a belay device, extra carabiners, slings, and a pulley to our waist belts. We'd travel as a four-person team connected to one rope, with the first and last person carrying extra climbing rope in a loop across their chest.

Martin explained that, if someone fell into a crevasse, there would be a massive pull on the rope and we'd all have to self-arrest. We'd have to anchor the rope into the ice with ice screws and a sling so that the person didn't fall any farther into the crevasse, and so that we could unclip from the rope to run a rescue operation. We would disconnect our figure-eight knot, untie it, and reattach the rope to our harness with the belay device, a U-shaped wire attached to a hollow square of metal. We also had to put something under the rope at the edge of the crevasse to prevent it from cutting into the ice and making it harder to get the person out. We'd then increase our pulling power by attaching a pulley to the rope so we could hoist the person up and out of the crevasse. It was complicated, and without a lot of practice I worried that, if we got into a tough situation on the ice, I wouldn't know what to do.

Crevasses scared me. When we finally ventured onto the ice, I feared the snow would give way beneath me at any moment, dropping me into a hidden chasm, and only Martin would be experienced enough to save me. Even worse, what if Martin fell into a crevasse? Could *we* save *him*? Suddenly I wasn't sure I was cut out for this outdoor adventure thing. Maybe it was just a lack of confidence, but I started to think I should have stayed home with my books and my journal.

✷ It took just a few days to acclimatize to our new daily routine. Get up at 6:30 a.m. to be ready for the radio check-in at 7:00 a.m. Eat breakfast and discuss what to do for the day. Pack lunch (bagel and cheese, or pita with peanut butter), snacks (granola and chocolate bars), and water, and assemble safety gear. Walk uphill on the scree slope behind camp, strap on crampons and hook into the rope, then climb onto the ice. Spend the day walking, observing and/or measuring, and installing instrumentation. Walk back to the edge of the ice at the end of the day, take off crampons and rope. Stumble into camp, switch to down-filled booties and fleece pants, followed by dinner before evening check-in at 7:00 p.m. Make sure solar panels are attached to batteries outside, to run computers and equipment the next day. Go to sleep with the sun shining high in the sky. Rinse and repeat.

Every day I wore my quick-dry nylon hiking pants, a T-shirt over a long-sleeved shirt, and a windproof fleece jacket. I laced up my plastic boots and put on gaiters to keep snow from getting into them. For sun protection, I had a wide-brimmed hat, 50 SPF sunscreen, and my wrap-around sunglasses. I also packed a rain jacket, a Thinsulate jacket, and an extra down vest for when we stopped for breaks on the ice.

We spent the first few days exploring the glacier, assessing the landscape, and getting accustomed to being in camp. On the ice, the snow was knee-deep with a thin crust that broke open beneath our feet and plunged us into the weak layers below, a mass of sugary crystals with no cohesion. The surface streams I was there to monitor were silent early on, covered in ice and bubbling mysteriously through cracks in their beds, and there was no sign of meltwater emerging from the glacier front.

Earlier field crews had installed three weather stations on the ice, and these needed to be adjusted for the summer season. We added instrumentation and uploaded new programs to the lower and middle weather stations, as these were accessible from camp; the upper weather station would have to be reached by helicopter later in the season. We also checked the PVC stakes that had been drilled into the glacier—across the expanse from the nunatak down to the glacier snout—to make sure none of them were melting out or falling over. Finally, we checked the geophones, to make sure they were ready to capture icequakes.

During that first week I installed four automated hydrologic stations that measured water level, water temperature, and electrical conductivity. Water level would tell me when the glacier's lakes and streams started filling and draining; water temperature would tell me the source of the water (snow and ice melt are near zero degrees Celsius; subglacial water is just below zero); and EC would tell me whether the water had been in contact with any sediment. I put one station in each of two lakes: the Nunatak Lake and the Ridge Lake. Each lake was situated on the ice at the base of a piece of bedrock poking out of it, and was therefore described as ice-marginal. The Nunatak Lake was at the base of the nunatak, and filled with water from surrounding ice melt. The Ridge Lake was at the base of a long bedrock ridge, and filled with water from melting ice around the ridge and from a glacier on the ridge itself. Previous field teams had observed that each lake drained suddenly in the middle of the melt season, sending water into the "stream" system that flowed down-glacier from it.

These weren't streams in the classic sense of the word, but ponds of water connected by channels through the ice, like strings of pearls. As the glacier ice flowed around the nunatak and the ridge, it created a seam downstream from each lake, where the ice stitched itself together again. These seams were weak spots, where water could collect and flow through. Given the low slope of the ice surface, the water flowed in tight meanders, which eventually got cut off from one another. These cut-off meanders became the pearls in the stream system. Each string of pearls ended in a crevasse field, where moulins formed. The moulins froze over winter, though, and needed a lot of summer meltwater to open them up again.

Several other streams could be found in the same area, but these were "real" streams, not pearl-like streams. They started halfway down-glacier from the Ridge and Nunatak Lakes, and formed where a small depression in the ice allowed water to collect and begin to cut into the ice as it flowed downhill. There was one such stream between the Nunatak and Ridge Streams, and two to the west of the Ridge Stream. These also ended in moulins, so they were an important component of the glacier drainage system, too. However, as with all field projects, I had to choose precisely what to measure and what to just observe, given time and available equipment; these streams I chose to just observe.

In that first week we also explored the front of the glacier, where it terminated in a rounded-off ice cliff that bulged forward at the top then tucked in a bit just below. Crampons were critical to carefully pick a trail down the glacier front, though I took them off once I reached the ground. Beneath my feet were stream-rounded cobbles and fine sediments left by ice-marginal streams and previous years' proglacial rivers. We discovered a waterfall on the west side of the glacier front: it had sculpted the ice into fantastically elegant formations as it crashed over the edge, some with fluted sides and impossibly high spires in the middle of the flow. Also at the west side of the glacier was the ice-marginal stream from which we collected water—when melt began, that stream would roar along beside the ice to emerge in the proglacial flats. At the east end of the glacier front, the ice had calved into another ice-marginal stream: cubes of white damming flow for a few days until they were melted through and the water could move again. There was no water coming out of the glacier snout yet—that would only happen once the surface water system had developed enough to send meltwater into the glacier via the moulins. This was what I was there to learn about.

I gradually got comfortable travelling on the glacier roped up, and my fears about falling into a crevasse diminished somewhat.

Within a week and a half, however, we were no longer using the rope, though we would wear crampons and carry ice axes for the rest of the field season. The snow had melted from the ice surface, and most of the areas we travelled had only a few small and highly visible crevasses. Such a relief to not have to worry about crevasse rescue anymore! The melt season had started, with surface (supraglacial) ponds beginning to fill and water collecting above the moulins and into the depths below. By the end of snowmelt, the pearls we had observed downstream of the Ridge and Nunatak Lakes were connected to one another and flowed as two streams.

This meant I was able to test the salt slug method for measuring streamflow at the Ridge and Nunatak Streams. To make the slug, I dissolved several cups of salt in a bucket of stream water. I measured its EC, then handed the bucket to Sean. I paced out a distance of twenty-five metres between the point upstream where Sean stood and the point downstream at which I would measure the stream's EC. Sean then threw the slug into the flowing water while I measured conductivity at the downstream location, recording the value every minute until the peak EC value had passed and EC had dropped back to background levels. Although the cold water in the bucket didn't dissolve the initial slug as much as I'd hoped, and I had to check my notes on how to do the gauging in the first place, it worked well as a way to measure the flow rate. It sure used a lot of salt though!

✳ Even though I grew up camping and was a hiking and backpacking fiend in high school, remote fieldwork was different in many ways. I liked being outdoors, observing, and leisurely walking. But I wasn't as enamoured with measuring and quantifying, something I had realized at Hilda Glacier as well. As interesting as it was to study environmental systems, it took some of the magic away from the beauty of the scenery. Though famous physicist Richard Feynman would disagree, saying that, for example, understanding the science behind a flower adds to its beauty, rather than subtracting from it.

At JEG, I was comfortable reading books and writing in my journal. Every evening I sat in my tent, writing about what had happened that day, how I was feeling, and what I wanted to do with my life. Writing was what I wanted to do, what I had wanted since I was a kid pounding away on my dad's old typewriter, when I was always reading and watching. Watching was part of the art of writing: observing life for details that formed a sentence, an image, or a character. A scrap of a phrase would come to me from somewhere and I would add words around it, creating an image inside my mind. The words didn't describe the image, they just put breath into it, stirring the hairs at the back of my neck with recognition:

> Outside everything was rock. Greyish-brown, slatey rock. It was easy to be fooled into thinking it was barren until you noticed the tiny clusters of pink and yellow saxifrage clinging to the sides of fine-grained frost hummock, or the moss patches nestled between boulders, waiting for a rainfall to hydrate them. The Arctic poppies sent their slender stalks to the sun, that twenty-four-hour candle.
>
> A faint line of flattened stones marked the path from my tent to the igloo, an island of white canvas and multicoloured plastic tubs among the mix of blue sky, grey-white ice, and beige rocks. Kitchen cloths flapped from the guy lines—all was domestic and serene.
>
> In the evenings my tent fly shook in the strong, cold, katabatic wind that blew down-glacier daily, pulling at the nylon fabric with stubby fingers, urging it to come and play. The wind was matched by the roar of the west-marginal stream as it spilled itself turbidly along the steep edge of the glacier, heading for the proglacial zone and the open ocean beyond. It churned itself up in anticipation of that freedom, grumbling downhill into the night.

✳ Two weeks after we arrived, Martin returned to camp from a solo outing more animated than I'd ever seen him. "The proglacial river is flowing, and there are several artesian fountains on the glacier surface near the snout!" he told us. This was exciting news.

It suggested that the water from the surface streams, which was all snow and ice melt, had now made its way down to the glacier bed. It was either coming directly out the front of the glacier, or had pushed water stored underneath the glacier out of the drainage system like a piston.

The geophones had recorded an icequake around the time that proglacial flow started, showing that the influx of water from the surface was jacking up the ice and making it slide downhill. I set up a hydrologic station in the small, sediment-laden river coming out the front of the glacier, using the same types of sensors as the supraglacial stations, plus a turbidity sensor that measured how much sediment was in the water. I also gauged streamflow using a current meter, the same as I'd done at Hilda Glacier, as the river was small enough for me to stand in to take measurements.

On the ice the next day, we saw that the Ridge and Nunatak Lakes had finally drained into their respective stream systems; the water in the Ridge system had turned from blue to green because of sediment refraction. We hypothesized that when the moulins opened and the streamflow entered them, it created a hydraulic gradient that caused the lakes to drain. The newly exposed lake beds were strewn with bunches of candle ice: crystals over thirty centimetres long in the shape of tapered candles, that tinkled faintly as they fell apart when tapped. The phenomenon was beautiful but eerie at the same time, a larger version of the needle ice we'd seen in the Rockies, and a remnant of the water that had been there just days previously.

My data logger setup had nicely captured the drainage of the Nunatak Lake. As is always the case in field research, however, something malfunctioned elsewhere: the water level sensor at the Ridge Lake had a spliced cable that had likely been compromised by water, so it didn't accurately record that drainage event. Martin added a new water level sensor to compare the readings between the two, but I worried that I hadn't obtained the data I needed for my thesis, and couldn't help feeling discouraged that I had missed something so important. Although I knew we'd need to adjust equipment regularly to keep up with the dynamic nature of the glacier's hydrologic system, not having a record of the Ridge Lake draining was a blow to my project.

✳ Travelling on the glacier in crampons limited the natural mobility of my knees, forcing me to walk with my feet pointed forward instead of duck-footed, the way I naturally walk. Once we made it off the glacier at the end of the day, we had to traverse an unstable slope to get back to camp. Only ten days into the field season, my bad knee started to hurt—the one I'd had surgery on just six months earlier. I knew I wouldn't last an entire season in this shape. Disheartened and angry, I cursed my knees for dictating what I could and couldn't do. It was like my Hilda Glacier project all over again, except this time I didn't have someone to do my work for me. Sean and Kathy had their own projects to look after, and I felt guilty that they had to carry my equipment to install on the glacier because I couldn't. Eventually, I screwed up my courage and talked to Martin. I warned him that I might need to leave the field in early July when the Twin Otter came to bring in Paul, Sean's PhD supervisor.

To my surprise, Martin appeared unfazed. He suggested dividing our single camp into two: a "proglacial camp" at the glacier terminus, and a "rock camp" where we'd originally set up. I'd stay in the proglacial camp and take on different duties so that I could remain in the field but not have to be on the ice as often.

"How about when Paul comes in, you and Kathy set up camp in the proglacial, out in front of the glacier?" Martin said. "Paul will stay in the rock camp with Sean. You can analyze Kathy and Sean's water samples and they can keep track of your on-ice sensors. You can go on the ice when your knee feels okay." It wasn't an ideal solution but it kept me in the field, in a fabulous location—though I was back to being a lab rat again. I agreed to Martin's proposal, and we told the rest of the team what was up.

Sean was fine with it, particularly since he wouldn't have to set up his water sampling equipment at the glacier snout and analyze his own samples. However, Kathy was a bit peeved to be away from the "action" in the rock camp and to have to travel the extra distance from the proglacial camp to the mid-glacier to meet the others for glacier travel. I also had second thoughts about the changes, as Kathy and I weren't exactly the best of friends to be sharing a camp. But perhaps I only envied her ability to walk on the glacier without crippling pain, to step lightly on the scree slope like a mountain goat, to climb effortlessly from the rock onto the ice.

✻ The Twin Otter arrived on July 5, landing on the airstrip that had been cleared on the proglacial flats several seasons ago. Paul emerged from the plane, tall and thin as a beanpole, wearing a wide-brimmed hat and an ever-present smile. He had a wicked sense of humour, which was largely predicated on poking fun at other people—usually Sean, his graduate student, who took the ribbing gracefully. After a round of introductions, we hauled equipment between the proglacial and rock camps. Martin moved his sleeping tent and personal gear down to the front of the glacier to join me, while the rest of the team stayed in the rock camp. Martin and Paul would overlap for a week so that the transition between them would be smoother. Kathy would move down to the proglacial camp with me after Martin left.

We had set up the proglacial camp on a flat section of gravel in front of the glacier, making use of the extra supplies that Paul had brought with him, including another igloo and a pair of camp stoves. Since the igloo would be our mess tent, Martin and I placed it five hundred metres from our sleeping tents, given the potential of a polar bear visit. Our camp also took the shotgun for the same reason. A series of braided streams crisscrossed the proglacial zone, and while the igloo seemed relatively safe from migrating water-ways, my sleeping tent was another story.

I set up my tent and paced the distance to the nearest stream bank. Eleven paces. Things were looking good. But as glacier melt increased, that stream began to rise. I paced the distance again the next morning: nine paces. Two hours later: eight paces. Before bed: three paces. Should I move my tent, or risk it and wait until morning? As I stood undecided, a huge chunk of stream bank hit the water with a resounding splash. That did it. I wrenched my tent pegs out of the gravel and hastily dragged my home several metres from the stream. The constant daylight was my friend as I sat, close to midnight, repositioning tent pegs and banging them in with a large rock. By the next morning, half of my old tent location had washed away.

For Sean's project, Martin and I set up an automated water sampler (pump sampler) that connected to the proglacial river through a hose held underwater by a rock. Sean would put harmless dye into moulins up on the glacier; both the ones at the termination of the Ridge and Nunatak Streams, and others farther up-glacier past the nunatak. I programmed the automated sampler to start collecting water an hour after the dye went in, and every hour afterwards. I analyzed the samples by running them through a fluorometer, which automatically measured the dye concentration. Then I measured the EC and temperature of the samples by hand. The concentration data would tell Sean how long it took the dye to get from the moulins to the front of the glacier and what volume of water was flowing through the drainage system, while the EC data would tell him where that water was coming from: the surface water system or the subglacial system.

I ran a different set of tests for Kathy's project. She collected small samples by hand from the glacier surface snow, from each of the surface streams, and from the proglacial river. She also had twenty-litre samples collected at the same locations. I measured the EC and pH of each hand sample, then ran the larger twenty-litre samples through resin tubes in a field-rigged ion chromatograph, similar to the one in the clean lab back at the university. Our hope was to capture sulphate-35 ions, but we weren't sure our makeshift chromatograph would work. These ions would be minimal in "young" water melting off the glacier (surface samples) and more prevalent in "old" water that usually came out the front of the glacier (proglacial samples). By sampling the proglacial stream, we'd find out if the water had been stored under the glacier for a while before making its way into the stream system, or if it was water from the surface that was immediately being flushed out the front of the glacier. That would tell us about the structure of the glacier's plumbing system, which was important for my research, but also affected water chemistry and would impact downstream aquatic systems.

As much as I disliked working in the clean lab at the university, I didn't mind doing lab work in the field. At least I was outside, in a spectacular setting that fewer than a dozen people had ever visited, and had time to myself in camp while the others were up on the ice. The lab work was finicky sometimes, but I adapted to it and developed a routine to get everything done. In between tasks I wrote in my journal: about the landscape, the work, and the incredible experience I was having.

✲ During the five days that Martin and I shared a camp, we talked about glaciology and Arctic research. It's not often you get your supervisor's undivided attention; they usually have other students plus various bureaucratic headaches to deal with. "Wouldn't it be great to have an ROV so we could see under the glacier?" I said, during one of our chats.

"They're already using those in Greenland," Martin replied. He explained that researchers there were using remotely operated vehicles (ROVs) to test their theory that marine-terminating glaciers were melting not only from the top—because of warming air temperatures—but from the bottom, where they touched warming seawater.

By far our most interesting conversation was when Martin suggested I turn my MSc into a PhD. "You could study how the weather influences the development of the stream system on JEG," he said. This seemed especially relevant, given that we were in the midst of a period of rain and fog that had significantly slowed down surface melt and proglacial river flow on JEG.

Only a few weeks earlier I had decided I enjoyed being outdoors and observing much more than I enjoyed the measurement aspect of field research, and now here I was, thinking of doing two more field seasons for a PhD. Part of me was excited by the idea, but I worried about the workload and the candidacy exam. And would I have to become a professor, filling my days with meetings and paperwork while somehow fitting in fieldwork? There was also the fact that Dave was going to Simon Fraser University for his PhD, so we'd be separated for three years. Perhaps I could pursue other interests while I worked towards a PhD. What I really wanted to do was write and publish essays. To turn the world around in my mind and see it differently, the way the sun on the rock walls around us exposed different features at different times of day.

One night my British camp-mates were talking about someone who completed a high-quality PhD then retired to the Scottish Highlands to install kitchens and write detective novels. They mentioned another PhD holder who moved to Whitehorse to make instrumentation for glaciology work. To me these were sensible people, but to my colleagues they were wasting their degree. That evening, wrapped in my orange down sleeping bag and propped up in my L-shaped camp chair, I wrote in my journal that I wasn't sure about the professorial route. Instead, I looked forward to a job where my evenings and weekends were mine and I could have a life doing outdoorsy things and writing about them. The question was, if I didn't want to be a prof, did I really want to be a field scientist? I wasn't sure I had the drive to build a career in field science, either. My journalling that night left me with more questions than answers.

When Martin left on July 10 I was still up in the air about whether I would switch to a PhD, and hadn't managed to sort it out in my mind or through my daily writing. The weather mirrored my indecision. Ten centimetres of snow had fallen and the glacier was covered in dense fog, dampening down the hydrologic system. It was safe enough to gauge the proglacial river manually without being swept away—but impossible to do much else. When we weren't gauging the stream, we hunkered down in our tents, reading and listening to music, coming out for meals and radio check-ins, and sometimes playing cards while sipping scotch in the igloo. It was a much-needed five-day rest from the everyday hustle of fieldwork, as we often worked long days to make the most of our relatively brief field season and the twenty-four-hour daylight. Of course, I used some of this downtime to capture our surroundings in words:

> *Down in the proglacial camp the rock walls rose up around us, steep and debris-covered, striped in various shades of red, orange, and black. Across Nares Strait was Greenland, a dark smudge on the horizon that disappeared when the fog rolled in, while directly behind us loomed the glacier, a solid mass of ice that breathed cold katabatic winds onto our camp, heaving and creaking as it prepared to greet the summer. Rivers gushed from its belly and there was a constant noise of rushing water, rolling boulders, and the whistle of the wind across the rocks. Now that I was accustomed to the scenery, it changed daily. Rockfalls marked the valley walls, waterfalls cascaded over the glacier front to carve new channels into the ice, and table-sized icebergs emerged regularly from the east-marginal stream.*

A week after the weather cleared, I decided it was time to get back on the ice. For the first time in three weeks, I pulled on my knee brace and hiked up on the glacier to survey the Nunatak Stream and check my hydrologic stations. It was glorious to be on the ice again after so long in camp, and to spend some time with the rest of the team. I took many photos and sketched the Nunatak Stream system and its pearls in my field notebook. My drawings helped me understand how it was structured, and observe the surprising amount of sediment that had been transported downstream by the drainage of the Nunatak Lake. The whites and blues of the glacier surface provided a welcome contrast to the grey-and-brown dreariness of the proglacial zone. Weatherwise, it was a balmy five degrees with blue skies and sunshine reflecting off the ice surface; I was grateful for my wrap-around shades. Our team walked for seven hours that day, and my knees didn't hurt until we had to clamber off the steep ice front.

I went up on the ice again a few days after that, this time to survey and map the Ridge Stream. I couldn't believe it had been almost four weeks since I'd last observed that system. Kathy and Sean had described for me how the system was developing but, as I'd learned from my undergraduate field school and my work at Hilda Glacier, it just wasn't the same as seeing it in person.

Two days later Kathy and I went up on the ice, joining Sean along the way. We chattered about our work as we walked, glad for an opportunity to discuss our thesis challenges without our supervisors around to hear us. We talked about what we'd do once we got home. Sean was focused on what he would eat, while Kathy and I were more interested in having a hot shower. Sean told us about the Scottish mountains he'd climbed to achieve his Duke of Edinburgh Award, and Kathy shared her passion for orienteering in the Lake District of northwest England. I told stories about the Rockies and all the fantastic experiences I'd had there in all seasons.

We did salt slug measurements in each of the Nunatak and Ridge Streams, in the stream between the Nunatak and Ridge, and in the two streams to the west of the Ridge Stream. It was another bluebird day, with clear skies and only a light breeze. One of the streams to the west formed a scene that was absolutely idyllic, almost like a tropical island, with deep blue water flowing from two directions around an icy white outcrop before disappearing down a moulin, all contained within a bowl-shaped depression on the glacier surface.

When the three of us returned to the proglacial camp at nine that evening, the proglacial river was in full flood. It was welling up from the front of the glacier and pushing large rocks around, overflowing its banks, encroaching on the igloo, and generally causing havoc. We stood as close to it as we dared, awed by its sheer, roaring power. A torrent of chocolate milk, it produced a standing wave at least a metre high just after it emerged from the ice. Boulders rumbled loudly as they rolled around the stream bed, shaking the ground next to the channel. Rocks shot out of the opening at the glacier's edge. As we stood there, the pump sampler tipped over on its side next to the raging river, ready to fall in. The glacier had woken from its winter slumber, and was coming alive in front of us.

We dropped our packs and raced to rescue our scientific equipment from the mayhem. I waded into the knee-deep water at the edge of the river, boulders hitting my shins as I shouted to the others over the thunder of rocks crashing underfoot. Together we detached the pump sampler from its intake hose and carried it to safety. My legs now cold and soaked, I went back for the rest of the equipment. Standing in the strong current, I felt the rocks beneath my feet being tugged at by the water. I became mesmerized by the waves that invited me in, but dragged my focus away to the equipment instead. "I can't get the sensor wires out of the logger," I yelled, fighting to keep my balance. Eventually the wires cooperated and I managed to save the data logger and solar panel. The sensors themselves—now compressed by the weight of boulders the size of basketballs—I left for dead.

Shortly after I scrambled out of the water, Paul appeared on the horizon—hurrah, another set of hands to help us move the igloo! We spent the next two hours ferrying equipment, food, and pretty much the entire proglacial camp away from the raging torrent and onto the relative calm of a gravel flat, six hundred metres away. Our eleven-hour day stretched to fifteen hours, and while the rush of adrenaline carried me far, it didn't carry me that far. I faded fast, slipping into a kind of rolling hobble to protect my painful knees. We quickly made some dinner and I shoved the food unceremoniously into my mouth: Kraft Dinner, soup, and apple crumble. By 1:30 a.m. I was in my sleeping bag, snug, comfy, and dead tired. Out like a light.

✲ As I limped my way to the newly situated igloo for morning check-in, the sun brightened the ridge ahead of me with an impossible light, making it stand out sharply against the blue sky behind it. Stark and rocky and leaning ever so slightly over the proglacial floodplain, it seemed closer and more touchable than it ever had before. I took advantage of the fact that Kathy was still in her tent and brought out my journal. I wrote a bit about the sights and sounds of the landscape and the details of fieldwork. Then a scene took shape on the page, a short story about an aging couple I had dreamed up, who were disturbed by a long-held family secret. I didn't know where they came from or what to do about them, but the writing poured out of me faster than I could think, until I had to put my journal away and get ready for the day.

After breakfast, I found some new sensors in our gear and redeployed the proglacial hydrologic station. But three days later the proglacial river flooded again, thanks to a massive melt event on the glacier.

Kathy and I had gone up-glacier to survey the stream systems to the west of the Ridge Stream and noticed that the ice surface looked darker; it had been stripped down to the previous summer's dirty bare ice. This meant more surface melt because the darker ice was absorbing more sunlight. That day it was ten degrees with a warm wind blowing from the northeast, and the surface streams were full and flowing fast. Spray rose from the moulins as water tumbled down them with a roar, like a subway train entering a station.

I headed for camp once I'd finished my surveys, leaving Kathy to finish her work. It was nice to travel the glacier by myself, to allow the white-grey expanse of ice to feed my rambling thoughts. Back at camp, a flotilla of icebergs had calved from the east side of the ice, blocking the flow of the east-marginal stream. I was distracted by the constant sound of rushing water and tumbling boulders as the marginal and proglacial rivers flowed towards the ocean several kilometres away. But I reined in my attention to focus on my lab work, enjoying the sun and warm weather.

A day later the proglacial river was still thundering out of the front of the glacier, and had cut into the sediment to form a channel so deep that the water was too far down for our hydrologic station and our pump sampler intake to reach. I rescued the sensors that were now dangling in midair as a result, and spent the day fiddling with the pump sampler. I'd gotten the program wrong a few times, and the hose kept rising out of the flow so it couldn't take a sample. Kathy and I tried to gauge the proglacial river but could walk only partway out because of high flows, and ended up gauging just one-quarter of the river's width.

That evening we were gifted a partial solar eclipse, the strange dimming of constant daylight made all the more eerie by the clouds that drifted across the partially obscured sun.

I went back up on the ice a few days later and met up with Paul partway to the moulin field. It was coming to the end of the field season, so it was time to pack up our gear and get ready to fly out. Paul asked about my writing; I was pleased that someone took an interest in it. "How much of what you write is 'what happened' versus 'thoughts and musings?'" he asked. I had to think about that for a minute. In the end I replied that it was a combination of the two. He then said, out of the blue, "Nothing we're studying on this glacier is really important in a larger context. It's only contributing to our understanding of general glacier dynamics, not environmental change or anything." I was taken aback by that statement. All of my grant applications talked about the importance of the research for Arctic environmental change. There had to be a larger purpose to this research—why would we be spending all this time and money doing it if it was futile? I didn't agree with him, but didn't have the depth or breadth of scientific knowledge to debate him.

When Paul and I reached the Ridge Stream we calibrated the sensors, downloaded the data, and dismantled the hydrologic station. We did the same at the Nunatak Stream, then walked all the way up behind the nunatak, somewhere I'd never been before. We adjusted the sensors on the middle weather station with help from Sean and Kathy, who were already there. The station had melted so far out of the ice that Sean had to sit on Paul's shoulders to slide the crossbar of the station down to a reachable level.

We then came down around the east side of the nunatak, and I saw the Nunatak Lake from above for the first time. I appreciated this different perspective on a feature I'd only seen from the shore, the one time I'd been there early in the season. My knees were killing me from the climb to the weather station, though, and I suffered during the subsequent downslope walk to get to my station at the Nunatak Lake—there was a reason I'd been there only once before. We downloaded and dismantled the last hydrologic station at the Ridge Lake, then piled all of the sensors and loggers on the ice by the moulins, ready to go when the chopper arrived in a few days. I was glad to participate in my own fieldwork again, even if the season was almost over.

That evening as I wrote in my journal, I replayed my conversation with Paul. His words really made me reconsider the idea of a PhD. Was my research that irrelevant to the wider field of Arctic environmental change? Would doing a PhD just put life on hold, even if it was only for an additional two to three years? There was such a world of possibility out there, and academia was so narrow in contrast. I kept coming back to the same thought: that being a professor, being an academic, would take up too much of my life, keeping me from writing and participating in outdoor activities I enjoyed. Maybe this field season of being stuck in camp highlighted what I was best at: writing and observing rather than doing academic research. Maybe I was better suited to a writing life and all that it entailed.

I was more of a bookish introvert than a hardcore outdoors person or a keen scientist. I liked to move at walking speed through a landscape, taking in everything around me and verbally polishing it up in my mind like a precious jewel. I liked being in the outdoors, but I didn't feel I had to challenge my limits or constantly analyze things I saw while out there. I was happy to come home to a warm house or sleeping bag, and to my journal or a book, after being out for the day.

✴ Because I'm not a hardcore outdoors person who had to push the physical and logistical limits of my science, I wanted to understand the life of someone who revels in extreme fieldwork. So I sought out Dr. Alison Criscitiello, the head of the Canadian Ice Core Lab (CICL) at the University of Alberta, who is maybe a decade younger than I am.

A National Geographic Explorer, Alison is an accomplished researcher and mountaineer, having guided clients up Aconcagua in the Andes and Denali in the Alaska Range, and undertaken expeditions in the Himalayas. She originally trained to be a climbing ranger for the National Park Service in the United States, but went back to school after several years to do graduate work in glaciology. "I fell in love with the frozen parts of our planet as a mountaineer and climber, which ultimately led me back to graduate school to study these places," she told me. She struggled with her master's program, however, noting that she probably would have quit if not for the mentorship of a female postdoctoral student in her research group.

She went on to earn a PhD at the Massachusetts Institute of Technology with a female supervisor. Being surrounded by sexism throughout her career definitely shaped her life choices, including the decision to go on several all-female expeditions. She suggested that women in science who want to pursue remote fieldwork should ask lots of questions, and get a feel for their potential field team members. "If the team is the right fit for you, go for it," she said.

Alison undertook several expeditions to collect ice core samples, to add to the ones already archived at the CICL. She climbed Mount Logan (twice!) to collect a two-hundred-metre core from a non-polar glacier. She also collected cores from Devon Island, Axel Heiberg Island, and the Agassiz Ice Cap in the Canadian High Arctic; from the Columbia Icefield, where we did our field school hydrology project; and from Mount Brown in Antarctica, where she extracted a core that spans the last ten thousand years.

Well aware of the limitations and barriers faced by women in the sciences, Alison co-created a Canadian offshoot of the Girls on Ice program. Founded in the United States, this program was designed to get high school girls interested in mountaineering and glaciology. Though it took five years to obtain enough money to run it, Girls on Ice Canada is now funded by the Natural Sciences and Engineering Research Council of Canada. Alison and her colleagues run three expeditions annually: Girls on Ice Illecillewaet, Girls on Ice Kootenays, and Girls on Ice Yukon.

Alison's adventures are the stuff of mountain legend—a far cry from my stay in the proglacial camp at JEG, scribbling in my journal and running lab tests on my colleagues' water samples. But we share the same love for the outdoors, and the mountains in particular. While I will never summit Mount Logan, I'll always love the frozen landscapes of our world and the peaks that surround them.

✳ It was early August and the 2000 field season at John Evans Glacier was coming to an end, the Arctic sun sinking lower in the sky. Nights were getting chillier although the days remained blue and sunny. Imagining what twenty-four-hour darkness must be like, after our experience with the partial solar eclipse, I was glad I wouldn't be around to witness it. Only two more sets of water chemistry samples to analyze—yes!

I puttered around in camp, inventorying equipment and food, wiring up data loggers for the winter season, gauging streams, and getting ready for our scheduled departure date. I'd enjoyed my time in the field, but was also excited and eager to go home and see Dave again.

As always happens in the Arctic, our plans changed at the last minute. Two days before we were to fly out, we got a message from the base that the helicopter and Twin Otter were coming a day earlier than expected. Paul and Sean were up all night collecting equipment from the glacier and packing up the rock camp. When the chopper arrived in the morning, the pilot took Paul to the upper glacier to service the weather station there, then ferried sling-loads of gear from the rock and proglacial camps to the airstrip. At long last we were ready, standing next to a pile of stuff, waiting (always waiting) for the Twin Otter to arrive so we could load up and go. It wasn't until we landed at the base that we realized we'd forgotten to pick up the sensors and data loggers we'd cached on the ice, near the moulin field. Guess the 2001 field team would have to rescue those.

The flight back in to Resolute was eye-opening—the landscape beneath us had changed significantly during our eight weeks on the ice. Unlike when we'd first flown out, all of the snow was gone, much of the sea ice had melted, and the glaciers now had well-developed stream channels and dirty white surfaces. Back at the base, we joined other research teams who had come out of the field at the same time; everyone was getting ready to head back to civilization and their desk jobs. We were delighted to put faces to camp names: "Oh, you're Lake Hazen! And we're John Evans Glacier!"

It was a culture shock, being around people again, adjusting to conversation about something other than what we were going to do in the field the next day. We took advantage of the base's good food, TV and internet, flush toilets and showers—all the conveniences we hadn't had for two months. We appreciated these luxuries after so long without them, particularly the meals. When we weren't eating, we sorted through our field gear and leftover camp food, leaving some behind at the base, and packed up our personal gear and other equipment that would be coming south to Edmonton with us.

✳ Seeing Dave again after two months apart was fabulous, though reintegrating into life in Edmonton was a challenge. I had to adjust to the now-unfamiliar darkness of nighttime and the slightly forbidding shapes of so many trees. Going to the grocery store was an exercise in overwhelm: way too much choice when I was used to picking from whatever was left in a Rubbermaid tub outside the igloo. Then there was the noise and the number of people. Dave and I went to an international heritage fair at one of our local parks and I was inundated by the smells of freshly cooked food and the sounds of music and overall hubbub. But it was fun to be back in the land of hot summer days and outdoor festivals.

Before this reintroduction to city life, however, I had a lot to think about on the plane journey from Resolute to Edmonton. I spent much of that time thinking about my research. I was excited to get to work on my field data, even though I knew some of it had been compromised by a logger flooding or sensors not working. Martin had suggested a three-step process to analyzing my data. First, I'd use weather station and ablation stake data to model snowmelt. Second, I'd use the results to figure out how much meltwater was getting into the surface channels and helping them develop. Third, I'd compare our observations of drainage development in 2000 with those from 1999. I'd have to track down the previous year's field team to get their timeline data.

I also thought about how my time in the Arctic had changed me. I certainly had more confidence in my abilities as a scientist than I did at the beginning of the season, despite having to rely on the rest of the field crew to collect most of my data. Looking back, it was the best field season I could have asked for—lots of time to think and write in an awe-inspiring setting that changed daily, punctuated by the occasional outing on the glacier. Realizing that I wasn't a hard-core field scientist but just a regular outdoors person came as a relief, in a way, in that it wasn't worth pretending to be one. The question of whether to pursue a PhD still lingered, but I was certain about one thing: I liked to get outside, then come home and write about it.

5

STAYING THE ARCTIC COURSE

IN AUGUST 2000, Dave and I made our usual late-summer pilgrimage to Vancouver Island. Walking along the beach, we talked about our future. Dave asked if I'd given any more thought to switching to a PhD. Before I could answer, he told me that if I wanted to do a PhD with Martin, he would stay in Edmonton with me.

"Martin said he could take me on as a PhD student, too. That way we can avoid a long-distance relationship," he said. The two of them had apparently had a chat in the Edmonton airport while they waited for my flight from Resolute to arrive.

I didn't know what to say. I hadn't even entertained the idea of Dave doing his PhD with Martin. And I was still wondering if it might be better for me to finish off the MSc and go on to write instead, especially after my conversation with Paul in the field.

"Do *you* think I should do a PhD?" I asked.

"That's up to you," he said.

I decided then and there that I'd commit to a PhD for the next three years, until I was well and truly done, and only then strike out away from academia. Dave would forgo his PhD at Simon Fraser University and work with Martin instead. I'd be going back to the

(Top) Proglacial camp at John Evans Glacier, Nunavut, June 2001. (Photo by the author.)
(Bottom) On top of the mid-glacier nunatak, John Evans Glacier, July 2001.
(Photo by D. Lewis, used with permission.)

Arctic for another two summer seasons! And Dave and I wouldn't have to live apart.

In September I returned to the University of Alberta for my second year, having completed all the paperwork to switch from my MSc to a PhD program. I'd take three more courses that year, all on hydrology, and expand my research topic to better understand not just the mechanics of glacier hydrology, but how it was linked to the weather and large-scale climate systems. Even though part of me wanted to avoid doing a PhD, a bigger part of me was glad I had made this choice. I was ready to take on the busy eight months ahead, full of coursework, grant applications, and analysis of the data I'd collected that summer.

After having spent a year on campus, I already knew several people and it was nice to run into them, or have someone stop by my office to say hi and chat. The university seemed smaller and more accessible, not as impersonal and impenetrable as it did during my first year. There were also new faces in our department: my former professor John England had a new graduate student, Mary, who became a good friend. Martin also had a few new students, including Jack, who was easy to get along with—which was good, since he'd be joining me, Sean, and Dave in the field that summer. He'd been to JEG when he was an undergraduate, as part of the first team to visit the glacier in 1994.

Though I was keen to take new courses, the two that I took during the fall term were more challenging than I had expected. One was a group seminar with Martin on ice dynamics and glacier hydrology, which involved difficult assignments and a lot of reading. It took me almost a full day just to read two papers, and most of the content sailed right over my head. The other was a civil engineering course in hydrology, where my professor and classmates spoke in equations instead of words. By the end of each class, the chalkboard was covered in symbols and numbers that I couldn't follow. What's worse, I always fell asleep: the course was at the inopportune time of 4:30 to 6:00 p.m., and I'd been up since 6:00 a.m. It wasn't a good class to fall asleep in. There were only eight of us, so it was pretty obvious when I jerked awake and my pen fell out of my hand onto the floor. All of my notes from that class started off legibly, then drifted off the page as an indecipherable scribble.

Aside from coursework, I was also applying for research funding to the same agencies as I had the previous year. It was time-consuming to pull together these applications and meet all the deadlines. My energy began to falter halfway through the fall term, and I found it hard to muster enthusiasm for my coursework and research project. I kept telling myself that in two short months it would be the Christmas holidays. Only two more months and I would start a new term, with just a single course and field preparation to keep me busy. I sometimes worried that I'd made a mistake by taking on the PhD—my life was being subsumed by schoolwork. I tried to make time for writing in the evenings, after my hectic day was done. But I was often too mentally tired, opting to zone out in front of the TV instead of tapping into my creative side.

All these demands on my time made me wish I was back in the Arctic, where the silence wasn't really silence but a natural soundscape: the icebergs jostling in the stream, the rock slides off the cliffs above the proglacial camp, and the stream banks falling into the river. The wind. Boulders rumbling along the bed of the proglacial river. Water thundering down moulins and the ice cracking deep, deep below. It wouldn't be long until the next field season, but it couldn't come soon enough.

While it wasn't the Arctic, one thing I enjoyed about Edmonton was the deliciously cold winter. The minus-thirty weather and a fresh snowfall made for the best hour-long walk to campus. I was bundled up in my heavy down jacket, my breath clouding the air in front of me, the vapour freezing on my eyelashes and frosting up my scarf. The cold air shocked my lungs and froze my nostrils shut. My route took me down into the river valley, next to the hushed quiet of fog rising from the North Saskatchewan. When it got really cold, circles of pancake ice scraped against each other in the current with a faint, slushy, grinding sound.

Once, when the river froze fully and there were no thin spots from incoming streams, I walked across it, from bank to bank. It was easy to imagine myself an explorer and the expanse of the river as a cold desert: white in the glaring sun, with slabs of bubbly, blue-green ice shining through along pressure ridges. The wind sent fine grains of snow across the slippery surface, whispering like dry corn husks in late summer. Small drifts piled up behind dead grass stalks that poked through the ice; similar drifts gathered behind my boots if I stood still for too long.

That term, despite everything I had on my plate, I signed up for an evening writing course with Ed Struzik, a well-known author and journalist with a decades-long career. I wanted to focus on my writing practice, which I'd been trying to keep up through regular journal entries, snippets of short stories, and a few unfinished essays. Working with Ed was an enlightening experience, given his expertise and familiarity with environmental writing. He gave the class examples of published writing to read, and we discussed what worked, what didn't, and why. He also provided writing prompts from which we wrote brief paragraphs. At the same time, each of us worked on a longer piece that we submitted at the end of the course.

Ed encouraged me to write popular articles about my research. On the last day of class he said that the piece I'd written about our 2000 field season on John Evans Glacier was quite good, and that I should submit it to *Canadian Geographic* or *Above & Beyond* magazine for publication. That was an exciting moment. *I had the potential to be published.* I was a good writer, maybe even a "real" writer! I didn't submit the piece right away, though. The thought of a rejection letter was too much to bear.

✳ In my PhD program, however, I wasn't feeling the same positive vibes. I dreaded my presentations in Martin's class. I worried that I would miss key topics, or show that I'd completely misunderstood a concept and be branded the fool at the front of the room. It was hard to keep up: the readings were dense and complex, and the assignments pushed the limits of my abilities. I was also barely staying afloat in my engineering class. I had to visit the professor's office every week to get help with the assignments. Even then, I still had problems understanding which equations had to be applied to which questions. My brain just wasn't wired for it.

Meanwhile, my ego was being pummelled into submission by Martin's comments on my grant applications. He kept changing his mind about what should and shouldn't be included in my proposals, and I kept writing words that he deleted no matter what they said. If there's one universal truth about a graduate degree, it's that it will tear you down then build you back up again in the shape of an academic who questions everything—including yourself.

In my case, I started to question my intelligence: was I smart enough to do a PhD? And what would I do with that degree? As I'd written in my journal the previous summer, I didn't see myself becoming a professor once I finished. Much as academic science needed women to show that they're just as capable as men, and to serve as mentors for female students—representation that was sorely lacking in my department—I didn't think that was my path.

Finally, Christmas came and I was free from the grind of schoolwork for several weeks. Dave and I spent a relaxing time on the west coast, walking on the beach, listening to the ocean, and hiking the local trails. "That was a tough term," I said, watching my footprints in the sand fill with water. Dave agreed, having also struggled through the first year of his PhD. We made the most of the holiday break, enjoying our favourite Parksville restaurants and visiting Dave's mom, grateful for this much-needed opportunity to recuperate and ready ourselves for the next term.

Since I'd only be taking one course and preparing for the field season, I planned to attend a writing retreat at the Banff Centre, hosted by the Writers' Guild of Alberta. I'd also sign up for the same annual writing workshop that I'd done in 2000 just before I headed to the Arctic. The need to write was as strong as the need to breathe, and such events were a way to keep writing in my life when homework and grant applications threatened to take over. I remained torn between what I wanted to do, what I needed to do, and what I was actually doing.

The 2001 winter term started off well. I had more free time to work on my thesis, which would take shape as a series of research papers. I was particularly keen on the first paper, in which I would study the massive melt event we'd experienced on JEG in 2000, when the ice surface was so dirty. I was starting to understand how this melt event fit with my new thesis direction, and I enjoyed being able to work on my own timeline despite taking one course. The lack of weekly assignments also allowed me to spend time with my journal in the evenings, untangling my fears and frustrations, and writing to prompts from a Natalie Goldberg's *Wild Mind*.

The course I took was in surface water hydrology, which I really liked, and found much more applicable than glacier hydrology. Our professor raised a lot of philosophical questions around hydrology and earth system science, based on the writing of Vít Klemeš, a Canadian hydrologist of Czech origin. This type of discussion had been missing from my previous courses, where I learned more about *what* research had been done rather than *why* it had been done. It appealed to my contemplative side, making me think more about how scientists design experiments and what biases we introduce. How do we decide what the key scientific questions are in a particular research field? We might inadvertently miss some of the important questions by focusing more on what we want to do, rather than on what gaps we can fill in the discipline as a whole.

✴ In February I drove the four hours to Banff for my writing retreat. The mountains started off as blue-grey silhouettes in the distance, rising out of the golden-hazed foothills under the brilliant sun. They slowly became more distinct, the snow on their flanks outlining dips and folds in the geology and the delicate peeling of rock exfoliation. Spruce and pine stood along the lower slopes like bushy arrows, a vast bed of emerald green. When I checked in at the Banff

Centre the receptionist handed me an ID card with the word *Artist* next to my name. It was a small revelation to think that yes, I was an artist—what an amazing thing to be called. How nice to have the creative side of me validated.

The retreat was everything I had hoped for. My days were full of writing and thinking, with meals made for me. I had a quiet room and views of the mountains for inspiration. When I took a break from writing, I walked into town or on the trails surrounding the centre, savouring the crisp mountain air and the sensation of being free of obligations, if only for ten days.

I didn't fit in well with my retreat-mates, however. At twenty-four, I was the youngest person there by decades and didn't have the publishing record that many of the other participants had. The writer-in-residence was a vain man who revelled in the attention of this small group of primarily women. I spent a lot of time in the centre's library researching Rocky Mountain history, discovering many stories and pictures of Mary Schäffer and Mary Vaux, my historical mentors from my Hilda Glacier work.

One day I was browsing the shelves at the Banff public library when someone called my name. I hadn't expected anyone I knew to be in town, so imagine my surprise when I turned to face one of my field school friends, Chris. He gave me a big hug and asked what I was up to. Chris used to be a hardcore tree planter, but was now an instructor with Outward Bound and an outdoor photographer. He told me that once he'd decided to get serious about photography, he was amazed at how quickly things clicked into place. He even had a business card! I envied him turning his passion into a job. Why couldn't I take the same plunge with writing?

Talking with Chris helped me see that my priorities were all wrong. Doing a good job on the PhD was non-negotiable. But when I wasn't working on that, I needed to prioritize writing. When life got busy, writing was a luxury, something I did once all my other chores were finished. But if I waited until then before I sat down with my journal, not much writing would happen at all. Perhaps by going to workshops and classes again, reading books about the art of writing, and yes, even just writing, I'd change my perspective and this luxury would feel more legitimate.

Why had I gone into science, then? Why didn't I just follow my heart into the arts? Because, beneath it all, I was practical. It was how I was brought up. I had to have hard, marketable skills to fall back on. But at the root of it, I didn't have the courage to write. I didn't trust myself to set aside time, craft an article, and get it published—and repeat the process over and over again. So science it was.

✷ For my second summer field season in the Arctic, I would be the only woman in our four-person camp. It didn't bother me. I knew all the men who'd be with me in the field and we all got along. They thought well of me, and saw me as someone who could do whatever they could. But it didn't escape my attention that my thesis committee and professors were all male, and that Arctic exploration—both historical and present-day—was a pursuit dominated by men.

In search of female mentors, I found Dr. Bea Alt, one of the first women to do Arctic fieldwork in the 1960s. I first met her in person at a 1999 meeting for the Cryospheric System in Canada (CRYSYS) research team, a group of Canadian scientists studying snow, ice, and permafrost across the country. When I talked to her more recently over email, Bea revealed that in the late 1950s she had originally wanted to go into space. However, women weren't accepted into the required meteorologist training program—mainly because there were no women's bathrooms on the air base where the training was held. But in her first year at McGill University, Bea met members of the McGill Outing Club who explored the outdoors in the Montreal region during the school term, and did fieldwork at the McGill Arctic Research Station on Axel Heiberg Island in the summer. That's when she decided she wanted to go to the Arctic. "Of course they just laughed at me," she said.

For her MSc, Bea's meteorology professor arranged for her to take part in the Icefield Ranges Research Project at the Kluane Lake Research Station in southwest Yukon. She was supposed to remain at the base, taking weather observations and using records from nearby glacier weather stations in her research. However, one of the scientists working on the ice fell into a crevasse, so she replaced him and ended up unexpectedly gaining glaciology experience by working in two on-ice camps.

For her PhD work, Bea was the only female member of a team of five researchers who rotated between camps on the Meighen Ice Cap in the Canadian High Arctic. She did fieldwork there in the summers of 1968, 1969, and 1970—an opportunity also facilitated by her meteorology professor. She really enjoyed fieldwork: the isolation, the weather observations and travelling on glaciers, the expansive feeling of the Arctic tundra and the St. Elias Mountains. "I wanted to become a climber," she told me. "I liked the physical and mental challenges that were created by the land."

But being in the field wasn't always that enjoyable. She had to deal with sexism, discrimination, and harassment, all of which went with the job in those days—and even now. She emphasized that she chose to be there, fully expecting to be challenged, which might not have been a very helpful attitude in the context of equal rights, but she was prepared to fight her own battles. She wasn't fighting for women's rights in general, just for her own right to conduct research. While she didn't have the physical strength of the men on her team, she learned to get by using brains instead of brawn. She was careful and hard-working and found that, in most cases, her colleagues were kind even if they didn't agree with having a woman in the field.

Bea didn't have any female mentors, as there weren't any around at the time. Her main mentor was her professor from Norway; she noted that Scandinavians weren't as gender sensitive as North Americans.

Given her experience, Bea paved the way for other women in Arctic science, though she was humble about her contributions. She told me she was pleased to see that a lot had changed in recent decades, with far more women dedicated to fieldwork now. However, she recognized that there was still a long way to go before all people were treated as equals in the field. I definitely benefitted from her trailblazing work. Very few women were doing Arctic field research in the 2000s, when I was there. But there were more than during Bea's time, and having women in camp wasn't so unusual anymore.

✳ Preparing for the field in 2001 was a bit less chaotic than in 2000. This time I knew what was involved: making meal lists, shopping for food, shipping gear and food north, and brushing up on my first aid skills. Sean and Dave had gone to John Evans Glacier in May, four weeks before Jack and I were scheduled to leave, so I enjoyed some rare time alone before the field season started. I spent part of that time at the same week-long writing workshop I'd attended the year before. I couldn't wait to immerse myself in writing again after all the technical thinking I'd had to expend to get through my PhD courses.

The Banff Centre retreat in February had taught me to be more open to creativity, so I applied those lessons in this workshop's classes and activities. I wrote stories, essays, and poetry, the words and characters spilling out of some secret well that, until then, I didn't know existed. I wrote about the outdoors, my piano teacher, my family, swimming. Nothing was out of bounds. It was so rewarding to leave behind my science skin and slip into my writing skin, like a selkie slipping back into her sealskin after a night in society, returning to the watery depths.

Before long, it was time to head back to the Arctic: on June 13 the adventure began. Just like the previous year, Jack and I flew by commercial jet from Edmonton to Yellowknife, where the mosquitoes were as big as small birds. We switched planes and flew on to Resolute, where winter still gripped the landscape. Once all our gear had been weighed and stowed in the Twin Otter, we flew from Resolute to Eureka to refuel. From Eureka we flew to Franklin Pierce Bay, which was the closest the plane could get to JEG without having to land on skis. There we unloaded all of our gear, which was then choppered into our field site by sling.

The team was again split into two locations, with Jack and me at the proglacial camp up against the glacier snout, and Dave and

Sean at the rock camp adjacent to the west margin of the glacier. What was different this year was that we had a snowmobile—Dave and Sean had used one all spring at the upper camp, near the upper weather station. They had been analyzing snow pits and monitoring the weather stations all spring, while also exploring the upper part of the glacier. They brought the snowmobile down to the lower glacier when Jack and I arrived. It would come in handy, at least until the snow got too rotten to hold its weight.

It was both strange and familiar to be back in the proglacial camp. I had a different camp-mate, and was still getting to know him. I didn't have the same acute knee problems I'd had the year before, so I hoped I'd make it onto the ice more regularly. But I was accustomed to the landscape, the calving of the east side of the glacier snout, the rockfall from the surrounding cliffs, and the shadow of Greenland on the horizon. I was also resigned to the fact that we'd have to move our camp at least once during the melt season to keep it from being flooded.

Since we had no supervising professor in the field this year and no dedicated field assistants, we had to dole out tasks as best we could to cover off everyone's projects. Jack did most of his work on the lower glacier, Dave and I worked on the lower and mid-glacier, and Sean worked on the mid- and upper glacier. We all had the same objective: to make the most of the field season and get the data we needed to move on with our degrees.

Down at the glacier snout, I set up Leroy the time-lapse camera. I put him on the ice above the 2000 proglacial river outlet to capture the emergence of this year's river and record its changes over the melt season. Several days a week I went up to the mid-glacier to check on my hydrologic stations; this year I placed an additional station in what I called the Huge Moulin Stream, located between the Ridge and Nunatak Streams. During the 2000 field season, I'd observed that this stream drained into a very large moulin, which was a conduit for getting surface meltwater to the glacier bed. It was an important addition to my other measurement sites, and the only stream that wasn't fed by a lake at its head. As usual, I measured flow in each stream, and surveyed the stream systems and the Ridge and Nunatak Lakes. Once meltwater inputs from the surface caused the proglacial river to emerge, I collected water samples from it with the pump sampler to capture Sean's dye tracers and to measure electrical conductivity. I gauged the flow of the proglacial river when it was safe to do so.

I was also in charge of servicing the glacier's three weather stations. This included changing them from winter to summer use by uploading new programs and adjusting the height of the sensors above the ice surface. Ensuring that the programs and sensors behaved as they should was finicky work, and I spent a lot of time in camp looking over downloaded data to see if it made sense. In addition, I looked after the geophones, which involved jumping up and down on the ice above them to simulate an icequake and make sure they recorded it.

Dave and I often worked together. We measured the ablation stakes scattered around the lower and mid-glacier. We also dug several snow pits to see not only how the snowpack was structured but how it evolved over the spring season and how fast it melted in early summer. Digging a snow pit was a bit of an undertaking given the metre-deep snowpack. Dave would excavate a hole big enough to sit in and clear a flat face of the snowpack to analyze. Seated in the pit, he used a paintbrush to clean up the snow face and identify different layers within it, which he marked with popsicle sticks. He then slid in thermometers to measure the temperature profile of the snowpack: one measurement every ten centimetres. He took snow density samples from every layer, and checked for superimposed ice—refrozen meltwater—at the bottom, between the ice surface and the base of the snowpack.

I recorded notes of what Dave was measuring in the snow pits, and we collected snow samples from each pit for Jack, which he analyzed for their chemical composition. We also measured how air temperature changed with elevation on the glacier, using sensors Dave had installed on stakes along the glacier centreline. Every few days he and I downloaded the sensors' data to make sure we didn't lose any.

Jack mainly stayed in camp. He worked in the so-called chemistry tent, analyzing water samples to see how much organic content was in the surface and subsurface sources that were feeding the proglacial river. He analyzed the samples we collected from the snow pits, and went up on the glacier now and then to collect ice samples. He also collected ice samples from the glacier margin down in the proglacial zone, especially in places where ice from the glacier bed was visible.

Sean put dye in up-glacier moulins to find out if the surface water system had connected to the subglacial system before it emerged from the glacier snout. His dye-tracing adventures were evident from one look at his hands, which were permanently stained pink from the giant, leaking barrel of liquid dye that he used for his work. He also surveyed the ablation stakes from the top to the bottom of the glacier, measuring downhill and vertical glacier flow. This would show whether the drainage of surface meltwater into the subglacial system had jacked up the glacier and helped it flow downhill.

Needless to say, our days ran long—sometimes until ten at night, given the number of chores that had to be done. I was prepared for that, though I was haunted by the previous field season, when I sometimes felt like a liability simply because I was less physically able to contribute than the rest of the team. While I had come to terms with being stuck in the proglacial camp for much of the 2000 season, I now needed to be more involved in my own research instead of doing work for others. I didn't want to be perceived as the weak link among the four of us, not when we had so much to accomplish. I had to overcome the spectre of 2000 and remake my presence at JEG.

✳ Being in the Arctic with Dave was something new. We'd been to field school and Hilda Glacier together, but I had been to JEG without him the previous year. I was happy to share the field season again, having meals in each other's company and travelling on the ice as a team. "Check out these fascinating crystals," he'd say, handing me the loupe and a handful of snow from a layer in the snow pit. We also talked through scientific problems with each other. "How can I possibly figure out how much water is entering the glacier?" I said, more than once. "You can't," he'd reply. "You just have to measure what you can and model the rest."

We had quiet moments, simply enjoying the view and living the same astonishing experience. It helped to have someone there whom I trusted implicitly, someone I relied on to have my back as I had his. We goofed around when out on the ice—"Look at my feet," I said one day, laughing. Dave immediately took a picture of the snow that had balled up in my crampons so heavily it had turned my boots into platform shoes.

Sharing the field season had practical implications, too. When we travelled the glacier, Dave carried the heavier items in his pack, saving my knees from the strain of hauling around too much weight. This wasn't something I could ask of the other team members, as it just wouldn't be fair. Dave and I each had our own sleeping tent because we were in different camps, but sometimes we would decide to share a tent. We agreed it was good to maintain our own space and not be together twenty-four seven.

Dave was there for my scariest episode while walking on the glacier. We weren't roped up as the glacier was snow-free, and I was covered head to toe in wet rain gear. I stumbled on an unexpected lump on the ice surface, and my crampons gave way. I slipped and fell on my back, hard. Gravity send me sliding towards a pearl in the Nunatak Stream system, picking up speed as I went. I knew this stream drained into a moulin, one that I'd disappear into if I wasn't able to self-arrest, but I didn't have an ice axe as I'd been using walking sticks to help my knees. My rain gear was slick against the surface, and I cried out as I hit every bump on the way down. At the last minute, I flipped over and jammed my crampons into the ice. I came to a stop on a small ledge, mere centimetres from the water.

Dave's head appeared over the lip of the pond I was lying next to; he'd been drawn to my cry. He said he'd watched in amusement as I vanished, that I sounded like a cartoon character as I yelled and bounced my way down the slope. Then he'd realized where I was heading and it wasn't so funny anymore. I lay there for a moment, trying to control my breathing and stop my body from shaking, before slowly climbing back to the main glacier surface.

* When Jack and I arrived at JEG in mid-June, both the glacier and our camps were snow covered. Melt hadn't yet begun. The streams on the glacier surface were starting to collect a thin layer of slush, but their pearl-like ponds remained disconnected and there was no water coming out the front of the glacier. Travel by snowmobile was still possible on the lower glacier, and we took full advantage of that in our first week. We rescued the pile of sensors, data loggers, and solar panels that had been cached on the ice in 2000 but hadn't been picked up at the end of the season. Of course, water had gotten into the logger enclosures and some of the loggers had died—an expensive mistake.

By the third week of June, the lower glacier surface was a slushy mess. We had to park the snowmobile above the nunatak and rely on foot travel from thereon in. Parts of the lower glacier were covered in cryoconite: small circular depressions that form when sediment on the surface heats up in the sun and "drills" holes into the ice. These holes contain both mineral and biological material, making them little aquariums on the ice surface. It was easy to catch a crampon spike in the edge of one and trip, and they crunched as we walked over them.

One evening, the camp at nearby Alexandra Fiord reported during radio check-in that they were experiencing a warm, windy weather event. On JEG, perhaps the same warm weather caused slush flows that blew out the surface stream channels and fed waterfalls on the glacier snout. Such blowouts were spectacular events to witness, generating a thunderous roar and a cascade of slush that flowed down the front of the ice.

The next day, Dave, Jack, and I walked up-glacier to my hydrologic stations. The snow was wet and heavy, and I was content to let the two of them break trail. My knees were not happy with the half-day slog up to the stream stations, though, so we opted out of continuing on to the lakes. Walking back down-glacier near the

Huge Moulin Stream, we sensed movement—like a freight train running beneath our feet—and heard loud cracking and creaking within the ice. It was a bit unnerving to imagine the glacier as a living organism on whose back we were standing as it shook off the remnants of winter. This event was an early sign of the development of JEG's drainage system, though none of the surface streams were flowing into it yet. And to think that I would have missed it if I hadn't been on the ice at the time!

The weather continued to warm up, and by late June the lower glacier surface was turning that summer-grey colour. Lots of supraglacial melt was coming off the front of the glacier, and the east-marginal stream was full of calved icebergs. I helped Dave with his snow pits across the mid part of the glacier; it was cool to see parts of JEG that I'd never been to before. I was proud of myself for having done more on the ice this year than last, for having taken things such as the geophones in hand, and even for making it up to the streams on foot from the proglacial camp.

By the end of June, the slush flows we'd seen earlier had moved farther up-glacier, retreating along with the snowline. They blew out the channels between each pearl-like pond until finally the Ridge and Nunatak Streams were connected throughout their entire lengths. Being a "normal" (non-pearl) stream, the Huge Moulin Stream was already flowing. However, the data logger at its station had completely flooded. We'd had much more melt than expected and the meltwater had ponded two to three metres above it. At that point, the surface meltwater had nowhere to go; it was just collecting in large lakes.

One day, Dave and I hiked to the Nunatak Lake to check the hydrologic station there, and were so happy with our progress that we thought we'd visit the Ridge Lake as well. That proved to be a mistake. We struggled through deep, slushy snow but couldn't find a passable route to our destination. We started off with soaked feet and, as we tried new routes, soon became soaked to the knees, then to the thighs. The day wore on and on and we began to curse and swear more and more; the Ridge Lake station was in sight but we weren't able to get to it. We ultimately retreated in defeat, and didn't arrive at camp until 11.30 p.m.

✲ I was having second thoughts about Arctic field science. I was tired of shitty spring conditions, the thigh-deep snow and quicksand-like slush. I craved a summer down south: to experience the annual city festivals, to go cycling, to hike in local parks. But at the same time I knew I would miss the field. I liked camping, sleeping in a tent, being outside all the time, watching the landscape change by the day, and writing about it.

This field season I felt pressed to work, especially to make up for last year. I was anxious about collecting proper data and stressed about potentially missing key moments in the annual development of the glacier drainage system. I worried constantly that I would leave without the very things I came for, that I would be physically unable to make it through the season, that I wasn't working hard enough. I also had less writing time: I often worked late into the evening and was spending more time on the ice. While the latter was a good thing, in that I was recording observations that I wouldn't get otherwise, science was overtaking my writing. And I wasn't sure how happy I was about that.

The problem was that we were juggling four individual field seasons—everyone had a major project to do and there weren't any extra bodies to help spread the workload around. We each wore two hats: researcher and field assistant. It was hard to get my own work done when I was busy helping a colleague with theirs. Not that I begrudged them that help; it was just logistically challenging. So I collected the data I could, gave it my best, and tried not to second guess myself or my work. I couldn't afford to let my worries and doubts slow me down.

✲ After returning to camp Dave and I had a midnight dinner. We finally made it to bed by 1:00 a.m., but were awakened at 8:00 a.m.

"Hey guys!" Jack called from outside our tent. "Sean was just on the radio! He saw some water spurting out of the glacier surface below the rock camp. It could be an artesian fountain!"

We'd intended to spend the day in leisurely recovery following the punishing travels of the day before. But this development meant that the lakes we'd seen on the glacier surface above the moulins had likely drained into the glacier, pushing stored subglacial water towards the front of the glacier. So we decided to get up, have breakfast, and go investigate.

In the time it took for Sean came down to the proglacial camp, the fountain he'd seen on the ice surface wasn't the only news: water was also flowing from three places along the glacier snout, forcing its way out of the sub-zero ice that was frozen to the glacier bed. At noon the proglacial river burst forth—not in the same place as last year, but directly behind our camp! We raced to get the igloo and our personal tents out of harm's way, to salvage crampons scattered on the ground, and to move everything else, like the food tubs and the chemistry tent. Even with three of us working as a team (Jack was busy collecting water samples, as it was critical for his thesis), it took several hours of running and stream crossing to relocate everything.

When I finally sat down around five o'clock to actually eat something, I noticed that my new tent location was still uncomfortably close to a stream. But the adrenaline rush had worn off and the previous day's exhaustion had caught up with me. I was too tired to move it. I'd do it in the morning. I slept lightly and tensely that night, expecting the stream to shift or rise at any hour, aware that I might have to quickly pull up stakes again. The joys of camping at the front of a glacier!

The next day the weather changed, enveloping us in fog and rain. The wind came screaming off the glacier and down into the valley. The clouds closed tightly over our heads, leaving the sun a mere glow behind a hazy gauze curtain. The streams persevered despite the sky's reluctance to provide energy, working hard to pump out water from the now-developed drainage system, but the toll was beginning to show. Every morning for the next few days the proglacial riverbed was that much drier, the sound of running water softer and less defiant.

Given the poor weather and low flow, we were able to gauge the proglacial river. One morning the river was pink—proving that the moulins higher up-glacier that Sean had been putting dye into were now connected to the glacier's internal plumbing system. But water from that system wasn't diluting the dye as much as we'd expected. This told us that most of the water coming out the front of the glacier was from the surface rather than the glacier bed, and low electrical conductivity measurements confirmed that theory. The same thing happened later in the season, when Sean calculated that it took fifty hours for water from the moulin to reach the proglacial river. It was clear that the glacier drainage system was a tortuous, inefficient maze of within-glacier and subglacial channels that didn't move water directly to the proglacial outlet.

I felt like I should be working on the ice, even in the bad weather. But if I couldn't see the ablation stakes, would I stray off course and get lost? Going into the fog alone was dangerous. When the fog first descended, Dave and Sean had become disoriented by the low visibility as they came down to the proglacial camp. They compared it to being inside a ping pong ball: borderless white in all directions. I decided to go up-glacier anyway, and found the experience limiting but liberating. Sound was dampened, hushed. My focus narrowed to the view of my plastic boots on the ground and the rhythmic click of my walking sticks on the ice. Freed from the sight of the long distance I had to travel to reach the lower weather station, I seemed to get there in half the time and with half the effort. The fog restricted my vision, forcing me to concentrate on my immediate surroundings rather than on distant landmarks. It showed me how far I'd come, rather than how far I had yet to go.

∗ Eventually the weather improved, and we got a resupply flight on July 5. We sent back some empty jerry cans, propane tanks, and garbage, as well as some water samples that required lab analysis.

We received fresh fruit (apples and oranges); vegetables (broccoli, potatoes, and carrots); and bread, but not much mail from family, so the plane's arrival didn't boost my morale as much as I'd hoped it would.

A good morale-booster, however, was the bird bath I took the next day, as I was in camp by myself. I boiled water in the igloo and stripped off my clothes, mixing the boiling water with cold to achieve the perfect temperature for washing. I scrubbed my face to rid it of the many layers of sunscreen and grit, enjoying the warmth of the washcloth against my skin. I boiled more water to wash my hair, which was in a constant state of bedhead from wearing a hat or a toque all the time. Such moments of self-care were a luxury, small bits of heaven in an otherwise nonstop field season. I finished off by doing a bit of laundry—underwear, socks, a T-shirt or two—and hung it on the guy wires of my tent to dry in the breeze. It turned our camp into a scene of domestic life, with washing on the line and the sun shining on the igloo.

Despite the weather lifting, the glacier's surface drainage system remained shut down, and there was wind-packed snow around the stream stations. The water that had ponded above the moulin at the end of the Huge Moulin Stream was gone. The Ridge Lake had also emptied, while the Nunatak Lake water level had declined and the Nunatak Stream and Ridge Stream had very low flow. I was anxious about the recent poor weather and the slow recovery of the hydrologic system, but realized this was all part of my research: how weather impacts glacier hydrology. I was experiencing first-hand how the system responded when the weather wasn't conducive to melt, which was exactly what I was there to do.

This year should have been better than the previous one for data collection: the weather generated a lot of early-season melt and I had more streamflow data in all stream systems, both surface and proglacial, and more information on the proglacial river from Leroy the time-lapse camera. The downside was that flooding had destroyed three data loggers: the Ridge Lake, Nunatak Lake, and Huge Moulin Stream loggers had all been submerged.

Major setbacks aside, I felt much more capable this season. I was able to get on the ice regularly thanks to Dave carrying some of the heavier equipment, and I managed to write in my journal a few times a week, even though I didn't spend nearly as much time in camp as the year before. Writing took a back seat to science, as I had limited time to collect the data I needed. I noticed, however, that whenever something interesting happened, I immediately wondered if I should measure it, and the joy of just observing it would dissipate. There it was again: my interest in observation over measurement, which had been piqued back at that Rockies field school. Maybe that's one negative thing about fieldwork—you never get away from the science.

✷ In the second week of July, Dave and I hiked up to the midway point on the glacier. He had convinced me to climb the nunatak for the first time ever.

"I'm not sure I can do this," I said, uncertain about my footing.

"Sure you can," Dave said, offering his usual gentle encouragement. "Just step here and onto this ledge. There's only a bit farther to go."

Once we reached the summit, one hundred and fifty metres above the glacier surface, we looked out over the lower part of the glacier. It was awe-inspiring to see the glacier's features from above, like the giant aerial photo in my office, but in person. There, right beneath us, were the streams I'd traced with my finger on the photo, and the crevasse field into which the streams disappeared! To our right was the bedrock ridge below which the Ridge Lake formed. The view was made all the more spectacular by the fact that I had managed to get myself up there, with Dave's support. We took a quick selfie with my small film camera—smiling, tanned faces in the sunlight with blue sky behind us—then headed back down.

At the top of the nunatak that day (and on two subsequent climbs that season), I couldn't help but notice how many surface streams weren't being measured and how little area the ablation stakes covered. I was capturing only a tiny slice of what was happening in the glacier hydrologic system, and could never hope to fully comprehend how it worked. Like my Hilda Glacier project, there was so much to understand, and not enough time or resources. That's why field scientists sample a small, representative portion of the larger environmental system, gather as much data and as many observations as they can, then scale it up with numerical modelling or remote sensing technology.

We spent the rest of the day checking that the middle weather station was working, downloading stream station data, and gauging streams with salt slugs. The hike back to camp was interminable; my knees ached from being forced into an unnatural gait by my unforgiving crampons. Upon realizing we still had seven kilometres of ice-walking to go I was in tears, wanting to curl up in a ball on the ice and not walk anymore. I steeled myself for the trek back to camp, knowing I didn't have to hike the next day.

After a good dinner and a couple of anti-inflammatories, I woke up the next morning almost forgetting about the previous day's travails. Then I stepped the wrong way on a rock and was quickly reminded of the bone-on-bone sensation in my knees. I forgave myself a little, but resented my body for being this way. So sore and weak. Was I not physically cut out for fieldwork? Some days it sure seemed like it.

Melt on the glacier surface finally picked up again in mid-July as the temperatures increased and the snow disappeared, exposing the ice underneath. We heard and felt more creaking and cracking near the moulins at the end of the Ridge and Huge Moulin Streams, where water was now entering the glacier, followed by similar noises at the glacier snout. The geophones also detected the movement of the glacier as surface water flowed beneath it. The proglacial river, which had shut down during the poor weather, now emerged from the glacier snout at different locations than previously. That made it difficult to measure, as we suddenly had more than one location to deal with.

One afternoon, Sean, Dave, and I went up on the glacier to measure the time it took water to travel from the Ridge and Nunatak Lakes to their stream stations. Sean put dye into the Ridge Lake and it turned the whole stream system a deep, vibrant pink. From our observation point at the end of the Ridge Stream, the water stood out like cherry Kool-Aid against the white backdrop of the glacier surface. We cracked jokes while pretending to drink the obnoxiously pink water, and took silly pictures—I still have one on the shelf above my desk: Sean and I standing in front of a pink stream, me with a sample bottle raised to my lips. Those shared research days were some of the best times I had on the glacier. We all worked together, clicking as a team, not worried about who was getting what done and whether we were doing the "right" things. That day was partially about the science, but also about having fun and observing how the stream system worked, rather than measuring anything and everything.

As is often the way in the field, however, other days weren't as good. Two days later I had a huge temper tantrum while trying to get the power connections on the proglacial data logger to work. What was meant to be a fifteen-minute job just kept dragging on; the equipment wouldn't cooperate and I was losing data by the hour. And I wasn't the only one who needed the data—Sean needed it, too. I could feel the pressure mounting, as every new thing I tried failed. Finally, I said "Fuck it!" and stormed away. When Dave asked what was the matter I screamed, "I hate the field and I want to go home!" I had never in my life yelled like that, and Dave wondered if it spelled the end of the season for me. I kicked a few rocks and threw some in the proglacial river, attempting to clear my head and get the agitation out of my system. Determined, I went back to the data logger and eventually got it to work. If I had learned anything from this field season, it was that I was more resilient than I thought.

By the third week of July summer had officially arrived, with hot weather and significant surface melt. As a result, the proglacial river thundered out of the glacier, producing a two-metre standing wave twenty metres from the glacier terminus and rumbling huge rocks along its bed. No way were we going to gauge that! We'd have to stick with the measurements of electrical conductivity, temperature, and turbidity from the proglacial hydrologic station, and photos from Leroy.

Meanwhile, a massive banging and crashing in the proglacial camp signalled that something new was going on. It turned out to be a major calving event: huge chunks of ice had fallen off the glacier and were blocking flow in the east-marginal stream. The event was so big that it shifted east-marginal streamflow across the end of our airstrip, which was about seven hundred metres from the proglacial camp. We hoped the water didn't affect it too much; we needed the entire flat strip for the Twin Otter to get us out at the end of the season. The shifting flow also meant that we had to move our camp yet again. Camping in the proglacial zone was getting tiring—this was the third time we'd had to relocate the tents. From the igloo we could hear the incessant thump of icebergs temporarily grounded in a slurry of river water and ice. Baby icebergs floated ponderously past our camp, beaching themselves on gravel bars and at the shallow edges of stream channels like flocks of migrating seabirds.

That night I had a bad dream. I dreamed of the proglacial hydrologic station being destroyed by the river, of Leroy falling off his perch, and of the stream gauging going very, very wrong. Kind of like the classic student nightmare, where you have to write an exam but suddenly realize you haven't attended class all year. I woke with a start, my sleeping bag tangled around me, but was calmed by the midnight sun shining high above my yellow tent. The glow was reassuring, but made me worry that I'd be uneasy in the dark again when we returned south. There's something to be said for twenty-four-hour daylight.

* I was a bit lonely on the rare days when Jack was on the ice late and I was the only one in the proglacial camp. I would pull out my journal and, as the shadows shifted after 7:00 p.m. check-in, I'd make a cup of herbal tea and write about what it was like to be there by myself:

Sometimes I feel vulnerable. At least the rock camp, where Dave and Sean are, is surrounded by obstacles: ice and cliffs. In the proglacial camp, Jack and I have only the ice at our backs and the wide-open plain stretching before us down to the sea—could wildlife come that way? The area often seems devoid of life, but you can spot the occasional willow growing in the proglacial sediments, or the remnants of an eider duck's nest, lined with soft feathers. One day, a gull-like bird flew overhead, and a lone muskox that must have become separated from its herd wandered across the far side of the proglacial plain. Not long ago, a fox loped into camp, a slinking shadow of motion that veered abruptly away upon smelling my presence. The scarcity of wildlife reminds me that other, less-harmless mammals roam these Arctic barrens, namely the polar bears our shotgun is meant to protect us from.

It was a strange existence in the field. We were thrown together in camp as friends and confidants and became almost a family—prone to disagreements or harmony, depending on how everyone was feeling. Jack missed his wife, but his water chemistry work kept him from dwelling on that. He often spoke of the calm he experienced while mowing his lawn, creating stripes in the grass that paralleled the sidewalk. Sean was pretty laid back, not likely to complain about things as long as he was getting his work done. Dave and I spent the most time together because our projects were so complementary and we both had regular on-ice tasks.

By the end of July, however, members of this almost-family were starting to grate on one another's nerves. It had been a long six weeks together—even longer for Dave and Sean, who had been at JEG for a month before Jack and I arrived. But there was still a lot to do before we left the field. Adding to the time pressure were insinuations that some of us weren't pulling our weight, and difficulties in scheduling the use of tools like the ice drill. We struggled both personally and professionally to keep our cool.

Nothing I did ever seemed to work the first time, and maybe not the second time, either. Whenever I assumed a task would take me half an hour, it took three hours instead. The computer would refuse to connect to the data logger, or the data logger would say that there was no data in the storage module. I'd sit down to calibrate the water level sensors and would still be sitting there an hour later, trying to make them read the correct values. As aggravating as this was for me, it also meant I had less time to act as a field assistant for other team members. The stress was palpable: each of us had to build a thesis out of our work, and we had to present that work at both a candidacy exam and a thesis defence. Each of us had a set of field responsibilities, and the rest of the team would be affected if one of us messed up.

Amid all of this tension, I needed to step back and take stock of my situation. I was a twenty-four-year-old PhD student, in charge of my own field research at a glacier I'd visited only once—when I was in the company of more experienced supervisors who managed the day-to-day of my field activities. This time, there was no one to blame but myself if something didn't go as planned. It was a heavy burden, so no wonder I was stressed. But I had survived many frustrations and found it rewarding when things went well. I obtained a few good datasets to use for my thesis, despite my flooded data loggers. Now my job was to examine that data, in combination with the data from the weather stations, to figure out how the weather influenced the development of the glacier drainage system.

I recalled what Paul had said during our 2000 field season: that our research wouldn't contribute to the bigger picture of environmental change, only to the field of glacier dynamics in general. With another year of research behind me and more confidence in my work, I disagreed with that statement even more. In fact, I was sure that my work on the relationship between weather and glacier hydrology was highly applicable to the environmental change field. Weather is the main driver of glacier hydrology: it determines which stream systems and lakes evolve and when, and how the water from those systems moves on and through the glacier to the proglacial river and beyond. The proglacial river didn't just stop at the edge of the ice—it travelled downstream and affected stream ecology and the mixing of fresh and salt water on the coast. I might not be studying those systems, but for the people who were, the results of my research would be important.

∗ August was approaching, so it was time to start thinking about packing up for the season. This meant a flurry of activity at camp and on the glacier as we prepared for our departure.

I made my rounds of the lower and middle weather stations, the hydrologic stations, and the geophones with my laptop and a few small tools, leaving enough room in my pack to carry the hydrologic equipment back to camp. I downloaded each station's data, dismantled the hydrologic stations, and adjusted the weather stations for the coming winter, so that their sensors would stay above the rising snowpack. I loaded myself up with sensors and data loggers, placing the heavier loggers at the bottom of my pack and the lighter sensors on top. I made a second trip to retrieve Leroy, attaching his folded tripod to my pack, and carrying his Pelican case by the handle. My feelings were mixed—on the one hand, I would miss the field and the simplicity of camp life. But on the other hand, I was ready to head back to civilization and not think about my research every day.

Dave and I inventoried what equipment was coming back with us and what was to remain in a cache at camp, including food. We stacked the wooden pallets on which we had set up our tents, and put several Rubbermaid tubs on top containing food that could survive the winter. We then tied a tarp over the whole thing to keep it dry from winter snow. We were heartily sick of the same old meals by then, having been reduced to eating rice with Cheez Whiz for dinner.

While we were busy organizing things at camp, Jack was collecting and analyzing last-minute ice and water samples, frantically trying to fit them into the last days of the field season. Sean did one last survey of the ablation stakes then packed up his equipment, ready to head back south.

The helicopter arrived on the first day of August, despite rainy weather and heavy cloud cover. The pilot flew me to the upper weather station to prepare it for winter like I had the lower and middle stations. It was tricky manoeuvring, as he had to stay below the clouds and navigate by the valley walls that enclosed the glacier. The light was flat, and it was hard to tell whether the glacier was sloping up or down. The pilot had flown in similar conditions in Newfoundland, though, and assured me he was comfortable with the weather and the extreme landscape.

Once I finished my weather station work, the pilot used a mesh sling to move most of the gear from both of our camps to the airstrip out in front of the glacier, then headed back to Eureka. All four of us stayed at the proglacial camp that night, unaware that the chopper would return at five in the morning. This early wake-up call was the pilot's way of making sure we could pack up and sling the last of the proglacial camp gear to the airstrip before the Twin Otter came. When he left, the pilot suggested with a wink that we tell the base the weather was good for flying, even though the cloud ceiling was pretty low all the way out to Nares Strait.

Three hours later, the Twin Otter roared in from down-valley, coming in closer to the ground than it should. The plane circled low a few times before landing on the airstrip. The pilots were justifiably perturbed to fly in such marginal conditions, which they hadn't expected from our weather report. But if we'd given the weather report we should have, they likely wouldn't have come, and it might have been a week or more before we'd get out—the weather gets more unpredictable later in the summer. We didn't want to wait that long. They took us to Eureka base first as they had some cargo to drop off. We made awkward conversation with the base staff, watched TV (Clint Eastwood's *Dirty Harry*), and enjoyed a lunch that wasn't a variation on bagels, pitas, or chocolate bars. From Eureka we flew the six hundred kilometres back to the Resolute base.

Once in Resolute, I examined myself in a mirror for the first time in two months. In contrast to my nut-brown face and hands, my legs and arms were only lightly tanned, as we'd had just a week or so when it was warm enough (six degrees!) to wear T-shirts and shorts. I'd also lost some weight from all the walking we did.

I immediately noticed the scarcity of women at the base, and was glad to reconnect with fellow graduate student Mary, who had spent the summer on nearby Melville Island. The banter between our two research groups crystallized around a male attitude that women were less capable in the field. Mary's group claimed that it was much better to have a male field assistant because you could get more done. With a woman, they argued, you were always wasting time getting ATVs unstuck and dealing with other small inconveniences. The talk became somewhat macho, which really bothered me. Though I had spent eight weeks being treated as an equal by my male camp-mates, the men from the other group didn't see me that way. I remembered Bea Alt's words, and considered the work that still needed to be done for women in science—especially field science. It seemed that we would never be deemed equal to men, that there would always be someone pointing out our shortcomings and proclaiming that we were inferior. A disheartening thought, especially after what had been a challenging but enjoyable field season.

We spent the few days before our departure savouring the wonderful food at the base, and sorting all of our gear into items that were going south versus items that would remain there for the winter. We packed everything that needed to be shipped back to Edmonton, including Jack's samples and lots of scientific and personal gear. Another field season was in the books—time to head home and deal with all the data once we returned to campus.

6

GOODBYE TO THE ARCTIC

IT WAS THE SUMMER OF 2001 and Dave and I were on Rathtrevor Beach, another after-the-field-season visit to Vancouver Island to see his mom. The sand at low tide stretched almost to the horizon; in the distance the surf gently lapped at the land. We walked slowly, watching for hidden treasures: sand dollars, starfish, or maybe chitons, a rare mollusc with a plated shell. As we walked we talked about the field season, the upcoming school year, and life in general.

"Do you miss the field?" I asked, poking a stick at the clams squirting water up through the sand.

"Sometimes," Dave said. "When I feel like there are too many people around." I agreed wholeheartedly.

"What do you think we'll do when we finish our degrees?" I asked.

Dave didn't have an answer—for the time being, we were just taking it term by term. Then Dave said, "What do you think about getting married?" I was surprised and pleased at the same time, and after thinking about it for a moment said, "Yes, we should." And there it was—a low-key engagement ahead of a wedding that fit our lifestyle, planned for the fall of 2002, after the final field season of my PhD program. Instead of an engagement ring, we exchanged engagement

---

(Top) Standing next to an artesian fountain over two metres high on John Evans Glacier, Nunavut, July 2002. (Bottom) A colleague (left) and I climbing up the side of John Evans Glacier, July 2002. (Photos by D. Lewis, used with permission.)

pendants: a moon for Dave and a sun for me. I wore my pendant close to my heart, and looked forward to our wedding throughout the long slog of the 2001–2002 academic year.

✷ By September I was back at work at the University of Alberta. Dave and I were taking a directed studies class on snow processes and snow hydrology, a relaxed and easy seminar. I understood the journal articles we read, and had good chats with Dave and our professor about fieldwork: how best to measure snowpack, what variables to incorporate, and what questions to answer. I didn't have to work as hard to understand the material like I did in my engineering and physics-based classes—it was comfortable, like my surface water hydrology course from the previous term. Dave and I talked about it one evening and I said, "Maybe I'm better at straightforward studies of surface water and snow hydrology, not the complicated physics of ice dynamics and glacier hydrology." Not one to sugarcoat things, Dave agreed. He'd also found Martin's ice dynamics and glacier hydrology seminar the previous year difficult, but he had thrived on the challenge whereas I had just endured it.

That fall, I also wrote a scientific paper about the high melt event we experienced on John Evans Glacier in July 2000, putting my hard-earned field data to work. I used data from the lower weather station to model glacier surface melt. I verified the output from the model with my measurements of the ablation stakes. From those calculations, I found that this warm, windy event was unprecedented in the seven-year history of data from JEG, and that the glacier melted at almost four times the usual rate. And where did all that meltwater go? Into the glacier drainage system, feeding the surface streams and lakes, roaring into the moulins, and substantially increasing flow in the proglacial river that gushed out the front of the glacier and rolled boulders along its bed.

The event was similar to a chinook, a phenomenon that happens often in places like southern Alberta: air rises over a topographic obstacle like a mountain range, then flows quickly down the opposite side, warming and increasing in speed as it goes. It was caused by a rare configuration of weather systems over the Arctic that resulted in strong winds from the northeast over JEG. As the jet stream shifts with climate change, this configuration of weather systems might increase in frequency, causing more extreme melt events. But in 2000, I was lucky to be on site to capture my data and observations, which were what led me to write the paper in the first place.

I submitted my paper to the journal *Hydrological Processes*, and several months later received a positive revise-and-resubmit response. This meant that the editors and peer reviewers saw something of value in my research. Though the requested revisions were extensive, I was ready and willing to make them. I was excited at the prospect of finally getting my research out there, and grateful that I had collected a quality dataset to use. I had tried to publish my undergraduate Hilda Glacier work but was stymied by the lack of good, hard data and my reliance on storytelling and assumptions to pull that paper together. With the "chinook paper" I was still telling a story, but this time I had the data to back it up.

Scientific papers tell a story in a very circumscribed manner, with a set framework of sections and specific language that wouldn't be used in writing for the public. It's almost like a different dialect of English that scientists have to learn to speak and write. This alone was enough to make me really think hard about my PhD. Did I want to invest time in learning this new scientific language?

Other doubts about my PhD had started to creep in as well. Halfway through the fall term, I realized that I'd hit the wall, which many PhD students do in their third or fourth year. It became a struggle to reconcile my thesis with "real life." I had made commitments—to myself and to Martin—to finish this thesis. I also appreciated the predictable school routine. But I could hardly wait to go home each afternoon and weekend. I knew I had research to do, and I did it, but my heart wasn't in it. I was more interested in books, in writing, in going out cycling and hiking in summer, and cross-country skiing and skating in winter. I felt myself separating from the narrow reality of school, looking for a life outside of it, away from the people who populated it. I was exploring my options; the world was opening up around me.

Dave and I spent many fall weekends in the mountains that year. We explored a number of glaciers in the Columbia Icefield area, and I was in my element, comfortable and at home. The landscape of rocks, water, and ice spoke to me as it had at Hilda Glacier, pared down and beautiful. There is joy in traversing the mountain landscape, in sitting among the soaring splendour while you eat lunch and ponder the route to come. Just looking, not thinking about measuring or collecting data. We even enjoyed an impromptu Thanksgiving potluck with the Parks Canada crew at Tangle Creek, whom we'd first met back in 1997 during field school. We'd kept in touch over the years and were happy to be invited to stay for dinner after stopping in to say hi to a few people we knew from back then.

For the holidays, we decided to spend New Year's Eve under the stars, in a tent in the Rockies, in sub-zero weather that froze our hands as we tried to read in our sleeping bags. When we woke up on New Year's Day, 2002, the tent's interior was covered in a thick layer of ice crystals from our breath, and we guessed it was around minus thirty degrees. We stayed cocooned in our sleeping bags as long as we could, but eventually nature called and we had to struggle into the clothes we'd kept in our sleeping bags overnight, then shimmy out of the tent to put on our cold boots and get ready for the day. We kicked off the new year by snowshoeing and cross-country skiing at Emerald Lake in Kootenay National Park.

Back in Edmonton, when we weren't doing coursework or writing research papers, we spent our spare time cross-country skiing and outdoor skating in the river valley, enjoying keeping active and engaged through the long winter. It was such a relief to be away from the flickering computer screen and dry scientific papers for a few hours, just using my body and letting my brain rest. I started thinking about the writing career I wanted to build during my PhD so that, once I finished, it would be ready to stimulate and support me. I needed to stay active during my degree, and backcountry skiing and snowshoeing trips to the Rockies would give me fodder to write about. What better way to exercise the writing muscle?

✴ We headed back to the university the second week in January 2002. I'd finished my coursework for good, and felt refreshed by the winter break. I had survived "hitting the wall" and was ready to take on my candidacy exam, which would determine whether I was prepared enough to continue in my PhD program.

For the first part of my exam I would write a proposal for my research—just as I would for a grant application, but with more detail. I would then be subject to an oral exam, which would start with me giving a brief presentation about my research. Afterwards, my thesis committee would ask me questions about the proposal in particular and my research program in general.

On Martin's advice, I met with my committee members to find out what I should be prepared to discuss, and if they had suggestions of relevant articles I should read. Only one member suggested I read up on a specific process; Martin, meanwhile, suggested I read everything I could about glacier hydrology and climate change. I drew up a list of key papers, made a pile of them on my desk at least three large binders high, and slowly worked through them, making notes as I went. I came across ideas that were helpful for my research that I hadn't seen before, but worried I would never get through such a mountain of reading, much less remember what each paper concluded. I started to fret about whether I could pass the candidacy exam, and what I would do if I didn't.

While I was methodically reading papers, I was also working on my research proposal, going back and forth with Martin as he edited each draft a bit more than the previous one, a stream of red comments turning into a sea as time went on. A week prior to the oral exam, when I was still fine-tuning the proposal, Martin suggested I wasn't ready. "It's not clear from your proposal that you know what your thesis is about," he said. I was furious that he would leave his doubts to such a late date, particularly because he didn't have a backup plan. Should we call off the candidacy? Downgrade back to an MSc? Reschedule the exam for later in the year? Or what? I had no clue what he expected me to do so, instead of worrying, I decided to persevere. I would prove him wrong. I would blow my committee away by being a super-intelligent, insightful, and independent-thinking woman.

I submitted my proposal to the committee just after Martin's bombshell. In the days before the oral exam, I put together my research presentation, my stomach turning nervously in anticipation. On exam day, I put on my favourite T-shirt and burgundy fleece vest, saved my presentation on a memory stick, and walked into the conference room where the exam would be held.

My committee was already there: four middle-aged white men chatting and catching up on university gossip. The tables were arranged in a U shape, with the open end of the U at the front of the room. The men quieted when I came in, and Martin delivered a short introduction as I fiddled with the computer and brought up my presentation on the projector screen. Sweat beaded on my upper lip, and I was sure my face was as red as a tomato. I tried to ignore the unsteadiness in my hands. As soon as everyone was settled, I gave my presentation, watching the committee members' faces to make sure they understood what I was talking about. Then I sat and braced myself for the inquisition.

But the inquisition never came. To my surprise, the oral exam ended up being an interesting discussion among equals about my research program, rather than a grilling aimed at finding holes in my logic. I was relaxed and comfortable within ten minutes, and found that the remaining eighty minutes went by quickly.

I had no problem passing the candidacy exam, and partied hard with my research group and a lot of gin and tonics to celebrate my success. But the desire to prove my doubters wrong never left me; it only grew stronger. That attitude would lead me to make some major life decisions that perhaps weren't in my best interests, but fed into my just-watch-me ethos. It also made its way into my future reference letters from Martin, who noted that my strong will might cause me problems in my research career.

Regardless, I was proud of myself: for having upgraded from an MSc to a PhD, for having gone from basic Hilda Glacier fieldwork to cutting-edge Arctic research, for doing quality fieldwork despite my physical limitations, for being a woman in science, for passing my candidacy exam, for having my own ideas about how I wanted my research to go. I had a good quality of life, which wasn't as much about accomplishments as it was about living life to the fullest and doing what I enjoyed.

✳ As the winter term progressed, however, I was getting discouraged with Martin's lack of availability, especially when I was looking for some guidance in designing my last year of field data collection and revising my chinook paper for resubmission to the journal. It wasn't just me, though; my entire research group was struggling. We were all trying to do our work without the support of a supervisor, because he was overburdened with administrative tasks and short on time to invest in his eleven graduate students.

In the first year of my graduate program, Martin popped into my office regularly to talk about research, to suggest new articles to read, or just to check on how things were going. But that was a long time ago—I couldn't remember the last time he had stopped by of his own accord. He couldn't make time for all of his students, so he focused on the ones who were closest to his office, which was in another building. He mentioned at one point that, when he went for a coffee break, he avoided the hallway where most of us had our offices so that he wouldn't be sidetracked by a student request. This evasiveness taught us to be independent, I guess, in a strange and convoluted way.

Being part of such a large research group was also beginning to wear on me, mainly because of the office politics. *How many hours were you at work today? How long were you in the field? How much time did it take you to write that paper? Which other Arctic researchers do you associate with?* I had a threshold tolerance beyond which interactions with others became too much. I needed time alone. That's what made me a good field scientist: I wasn't bothered by being isolated in the field, where I was away from all the on-campus drama.

I wanted to be like author Chris Czajkowski. I'd read all of her books, mentally transporting myself to her cabins in the backcountry, with their hand-hewn logs and homemade furniture. Her accounts of adventure were the focus of many of my dreams (and they were just that—dreams) about living off the grid and away from society, especially her stories of hiking in the remote wilds of BC where few non-Indigenous people had travelled.

In the mid-1980s Czajkowski, a British-born Canadian, built a cabin on a small part of the wilderness property of Jack and Trudy Turner. The Turners homesteaded on their plot in the southeastern part of Tweedsmuir Provincial Park, in west-central British Columbia, for thirty-four years. They helped Czajkowski build her cabin using logs cut and milled on site. There she spent several years witnessing the wonders of nature, such as the tracks of wildlife in the winter snow, and enjoying the silence of the outdoors—though it wasn't that silent during winter storms. Czajkowski wrote about her experiences in *Cabin at Singing River*, sharing the trials and joys of the life she had chosen, noting how she'd always wanted to live this way despite having no backcountry knowledge. All of it was new to her: the isolation, the hand-building of cabins, the wilderness. She said if she could do it, anyone could, which further inspired my admiration of her lifestyle.

Ultimately, however, the Turners returned to the city and donated their land to Tweedsmuir Park, so Czajkowski had to leave as well. She moved to a new alpine location at 1,525 metres above sea level, sixteen kilometres south of the boundary of Tweedsmuir Park. She named her new home Nuk Tessli, which means "west wind" in the Dakelh language. She built two log cabins, this time on her own, again using lumber milled on site as well as some brought in from town. To document these exploits, she wrote *Diary of a Wilderness Dweller* and *Nuk Tessli: The Life of a Wilderness Dweller*, books I gobbled up like candy when they first came out.

But Czajkowski's situation wasn't all idyllic, as she had to make money to support her lifestyle. A garden wouldn't grow in those high alpine soils, and she had to pay for supplies and their transport by floatplane to her home. So she compromised: each year she'd close up her cabin and head to Nimpo Lake and beyond to sell her books and paintings, making enough money to return to her cabin and live the free life until it was time to leave again. One year a grizzly broke into her cabin while she was away, a discovery she handled with equanimity and practicality. These days Czajkowski no longer lives in the bush. She had to move closer to civilization because of health problems, though she is still off-grid on forty acres accessible only by a rough road.

Like her, I wanted to live in the wild away from the hustle and bustle of people, to explore the untracked outdoors and see the landscape in all seasons. To watch the forest change from bare to green in the spring, and from green to gold in the fall. To watch the snowline come down the mountains as winter arrived. To trek for a day and a half to and from the nearest town for supplies and mail. To watch moose and wolves, to bushwhack up surrounding peaks and take in the view from above. And to write about it all.

It wasn't actually that different from what I did in the Arctic—although I wasn't alone, we were much farther from civilization, and there was limited wildlife. I trekked across the glacier regularly, taking measurements and observations of the glacier surface landscape. I used solar panels to recharge the batteries that powered my laptop, and I took time to write as often as possible, filling field notebooks and journals with data and story ideas. In a sense, I lived Czajkowski's life for two months of each year, and maybe—if I was honest with myself—that was enough for me.

The place I called home was vastly different from Czajkowski's, however. I was living in the middle of a pulsing, electric city, with wild places limited to the river valley that bisects it. There were other wild places I could escape to, about an hour out of town—like Elk Island National Park, or the Cooking Lake–Blackfoot Provincial

Recreation Area, where the rolling aspen parkland dominates the landscape. But here in the big city I was deadened by the noise, the concrete, and the constant smell of exhaust. And the people—always the people. Even when I walked through the river valley, I was often pushed off the trail by groups of runners or pelotons of cyclists.

Now that I had passed my candidacy exam, I was no longer a provisional PhD candidate—I was an official one, able to go on with my research without the exam hanging over me. I had one more field season coming up and then a thesis to write, some of which I'd already started with my chinook paper. I was moving from the data collection phase of my research to the communication phase. I was exhilarated and exhausted all at once, as the thesis was taking over my writing time—a situation I had tried to avoid, despite the PhD being my full-time job. Could I really juggle academia and writing?

✴ In 2002 I headed back to the Arctic for my last and longest field season as a PhD student. Because I was going into the field in May, almost a month earlier than usual, I couldn't attend the writing workshop I'd been to in the previous two years. Dave had already gone up to JEG with a grad student named Alex four weeks before, so I would be flying north with Martin's new graduate student, Maria. Martin himself would be joining us on the glacier sometime in July. Before I left, I resubmitted my chinook paper, hoping my revisions would pass muster and the journal would agree to publish it.

Maria and I arrived at the Polar Continental Shelf Program base in Resolute on May 18. We wouldn't come back until the first week of August: a ten-week stint this time. I would get to see the glacier before it started melting, when it was still a quiescent, snow-covered mass of ice.

I was relieved to have finished all of my field preparation and gotten up to the Arctic with no major hassles. Once in Resolute, we had to wait several days for our flight to JEG. By now I felt like an old hand at Arctic fieldwork: I ran into some pilots who remembered me from previous years. I also met the warden from Tanquary Fiord, whom I'd only heard over the radio, and his new work partner for the season. I was keenly aware that, other than me and Maria, there were only men at the base.

After a few days we made it to the glacier, with 644 kilograms of gear plus two frozen tubs of food and two turgid personal duffel bags. We flew the scenic route across Ellesmere Island: the first two hours to Grise Fiord to refuel, then to the Prince of Wales Icefield, where we emptied the plane so that the pilot could fly two researchers to their ice-coring site. We then reloaded the plane and headed to Eureka to refuel, finally landing on JEG after seven hours of travel. We unloaded the plane and ferried our gear by snowmobile to the upper camp, near the upper weather station. We didn't get to sleep until well after midnight.

This was my first time on the glacier in winter, a season that would last until our spring camp change in mid-June, when we would move off the ice and onto the adjacent rock. Sean and Dave had started the season at the upper camp in 2001, so Dave was used to the logistics and temperatures. I wasn't. It was minus twenty and windy overnight and I was bitterly cold despite wearing several layers and snuggling into my down sleeping bag, which was enclosed in a synthetic overbag. While it wasn't as cold as our New Year's camping trip, the wind found all the tiny openings in my tent and cooled things down considerably. Camping on the ice also meant having to regularly shovel snow away from our tents so they wouldn't collapse during snowstorms, and having to melt snow constantly to have enough water for drinking and cooking.

Once again I was in charge of the geophones, hydrologic stations, and weather stations, except for two new weather stations that Dave had set up at intermediate elevations: one between the lower weather station and the middle one, and another between the middle weather station and the upper one. I would take the same hydrology measurements as in previous years, crossing my fingers that none of the data loggers flooded again. I had two time-lapse cameras this year: Leroy would again be placed at the glacier terminus to monitor the proglacial river, while a camera named Elmer would be installed on top of the nunatak to capture changes in the surface hydrology. As usual, I planned to collect streamflow data in the proglacial river, and to measure the evolution of the surface glacier drainage system over the complete melt season and its relation to the weather. It was going to be an exciting season for glacier hydrology—and for me.

Dave would dig snow pits again to measure snowpack processes and superimposed ice formation. His new weather stations, in combination with the temperature sensors he'd installed along the glacier centreline last season, would give him a sense of how air temperature varied with elevation on the glacier, and how that might relate to superimposed ice formation. As in 2001, he'd measure ablation stakes to document surface melt—data that was also useful for my research.

Maria was there to study the microbiology of glacier environments. While Jack had focused mainly on organic matter from under and on the glacier in 2001, Maria was interested in the genetics of that matter. She would sample surface, subglacial, and proglacial snow, ice, and water using extreme clean sampling protocols to prevent contamination by any external bacteria or microbes. She would also measure water chemistry as Jack had done, to connect it with her microbiological data.

Alex was—well, I wasn't sure what Alex was there for. It had something to do with mercury transport and contamination in Arctic environments. He would collect snow and ice samples for analysis back at the university.

This year we had handheld radios for regular safety check-ins when we were on the ice, which was a huge improvement. Before we headed north we'd also taken an official crevasse rescue course taught by a certified mountain guide. He took us out to the flats of the Sunwapta River, near the Columbia Icefield, where we used huge snowdrifts as makeshift crevasses. We worked in pairs in the wind and cold, taking turns being the rescuer and the victim. We'd put on our harnesses and gear and rope up together. Then the victim would jump over the snowdrift and fall into the void below, pulling on the rope and making the rescuer move into emergency mode. The rescuer would quickly secure the rope with what's called a deadman (a metal plate with holes in it that gets buried in the snow), then unclip from the rope and initiate a crevasse rescue by using a belay device and a pulley to hoist the victim up over the lip of the snowbank. This was crucial training that increased my confidence immensely; I came away knowing how to save someone from a crevasse if necessary. That type of hands-on experience is invaluable when learning safety procedures.

✳ I started the field season inauspiciously, by injuring my back. I had wanted to go to the lower weather station to check that it was recording data properly, but no one was available to come with me so I took the snowmobile and went by myself. It seemed fine to go alone. There was a packed snowmobile trail down the glacier that I could follow; Dave and Alex had made it earlier in the season. Still, I was terrified of driving into a crevasse, so when I accidentally veered off the trail and got the snowmobile stuck in deep snow, I panicked. Now I had to get off the machine, which meant I might *step* into a crevasse. It wasn't logical: I knew from previous seasons on JEG that there weren't any crevasses on the lower glacier. But the fear was real. I wanted to spend as little time as possible off the snowmobile, so I wrenched it out of the snow as though I was He-Man, tweaking my back in the process.

The pain wasn't helped by shovelling out from a spring snowstorm in camp the next day. I was so disappointed in myself. What was wrong with my body that it kept failing on me? Was I trying to make it do things it didn't want to do? If it wasn't my knees it was some other part that was injured. For the next five days I lay flat in my tent, waiting to heal and looking over weather data while I recovered. I also wrote in my journal, mostly rants about not being able to do what I wanted and needed to do, rather than notes about essays or stories.

Finally, it began to warm up. I was no longer freezing in my sleeping bag at night, but the sunny, warm weather (four degrees!) also meant that melt was starting early, relative to other years. It wasn't unusual to have a puddle of water around my tent, and the floor of the igloo was sometimes wet. By the end of May melt had started on the lower glacier; a few days later, it started in the proglacial area and water was flowing in the Huge Moulin Stream. The snow around the nunatak was getting slushy and the snow surface had dropped significantly on the lower glacier. I would soon need to install the time-lapse cameras and my hydrologic stations if I didn't want to miss out on any important data.

By the beginning of June I was mobile again, and snowmobiled down to the nunatak to install Elmer. The mountains around camp were turning brown as the snow disappeared, and the ponds in each surface stream system were starting to fill, as were the Nunatak and Ridge Lakes.

* That field season was marked by more exploration of the landscape around JEG than in previous years, which was great because I'd never spent any length of time on the upper glacier. Dave had spent four weeks there in both the previous and current field season, so he was happy to show the rest of us around. We walked up the ridge west of camp and looked out over JEG, then climbed what we'd nicknamed Mount John Evans to see Dobbin Bay, to the north of JEG. Through binoculars we spotted many polar bear tracks in the distance, but not the bears themselves. I found a fossil on one of our hikes—a curlicue of a shell impressed in sandstone—something to take home as a memento. We also skied from camp to another lookout over Dobbin Bay, testing our abilities on legs that hadn't skied in a while. One evening, at Maria's suggestion, we went tobogganing at a nearby slope, whooping and hollering as we sped down the hill on Rubbermaid tub lids, hoping we wouldn't injure ourselves. Another evening we skied out to a ridge overlooking a valley full of piedmont glaciers: the scene looked like cake icing had flowed downhill then pooled in a circle on the flat terrain of the valley floor. Only a handful of people had ever seen this fascinating landscape; it was a privilege to explore it.

Even though we'd seen the polar bear tracks near Dobbin Bay, we were surprised to find similar tracks next to the lower weather station the following week. They were maybe a week old, but a bear had definitely walked down-glacier, past the weather station, and out to the edge of the ice. It reminded us to watch out for white fur moving against a white glacier background, and to keep the shotgun handy. What would I have done, had I encountered the animal when I went down-glacier at the beginning of the season? Would I have been prepared? Maybe, but it probably would've helped if we'd practised firing the shotgun a few times—or even cleaned it recently.

As usual, I crammed as much as possible into each day to get my work done. One night I was working on the upper weather station at eleven o'clock, trying to get it to run by rewiring it and rewriting the program. Once I'd succeeded, I accidentally crossed the ground and the power wires when reconnecting to the twelve-volt battery. I was worried that I'd zapped the logger and killed all the data it had recorded, and was angry about my mistake. When I checked it the next morning, I was relieved to see I hadn't fried it after all, but it still took me all day to figure out why it wasn't working and to fix the problem. Rarely do things go smoothly in the field—especially when it comes to electronics. Maybe Dan Smith was on to something with the thirty-year-old analog equipment that we used at Hilda Glacier.

✷ After waiting a week for the weather to clear, first in Resolute and then on the glacier, a plane finally arrived in the first week of June to bring in our field assistant, Mary, who had been in the Arctic the previous year as one of John England's graduate students, and was also a good friend. The same plane would also be flying Alex out, as his field season had ended. I can't say I was disappointed to see him go. He occasionally did things like wander out on the glacier on skis without knowing how to ski. He wouldn't tell anyone where he was going or when he'd be back, and was oblivious to the dangers of crevasses and potential weather changes. It was difficult to get work done with him in the field, as he was always having to be "rescued" from tough situations.

Mary's arrival and Alex's departure brought about an interesting reversal in field team composition from the previous year: instead of three men and one woman, we were now three women (Maria, Mary, and me) and one man (Dave). Having Mary as a field assistant would be immensely helpful, as she was there solely to help team members with their research. We wouldn't have to repeat last year's complicated dance of figuring out how to help one another while still getting our own work done.

In the middle of June, a helicopter came to move us from our on-ice camp to our summer rock camp at the edge of the glacier, and to do a visual stream survey. Dave and I cached gear at the upper camp that would be needed the following year but not for the rest of the summer, and had the rest of the gear slung down to the rock camp. This would be the first season I stayed in the rock camp rather than the proglacial camp; it was nice to be around my field companions and not be split into two groups. I enjoyed my birds-eye view of the glacier during the stream survey flight, though I wished the flight had been later in the season so I could see more stream channel development. The upper glacier was still a vast expanse of white snow, hiding crevasses and stream channels.

When we went out on the ice after our camp move, I discovered that, during the previous field season, Dave and Sean had found a new way to get onto the glacier. In 2000 with Martin, we walked up the shale slope beside the glacier until we found a place where we could just step onto the ice surface. With Dave and Sean's method, however, we navigated the rocky slope from camp down to the west-marginal stream, crossed the stream, and climbed up the sheer side of the ice with only our crampons and ice axes to keep us safe. While this route got us on the ice more quickly, the climb was sometimes harrowing, and when viewed from camp we looked like tiny specks against a towering wall of ice.

At that time, the lower glacier was starting to get sloppy—bad conditions for the snowmobile and the usual terrible conditions for walking. Still, we managed to cache the hydrologic station equipment on the glacier so we could set it up later, and replaced the film in Elmer before we had to leave the snowmobile at the nunatak for use above that elevation.

As the melt season progressed, Dave and I set up my hydrologic stations in between digging snow pits, and observed the development of the stream channels. We also set up Leroy at the glacier terminus. The Huge Moulin Stream was flowing by mid-June, but wasn't entering the glacier; instead it created a huge lake above the moulin that had frozen shut over winter. There were bubbling crevasses in the area, and many cracking noises accompanied by subterranean thumping and rumbling. The glacier drainage system was slowly coming to life after the long winter, as small amounts of water began to trickle into the ice.

After a period of bad weather in the third week of June, during which I caught up on some much-needed journal-writing and reading, I climbed the nunatak to reset Elmer. *Climbed the nunatak.* It sounds so innocuous, but that feat would have been inconceivable during my first year at JEG. Now it was easy, like walking on the glacier. I'd never been on the summit that early in the season, and from my perch I saw many surface lakes forming that I hadn't seen previously. All of the stream systems were filling but they weren't draining. As I made my way back to camp there was a tremendous cracking and creaking below my feet, almost as though a wave had propagated through the ice. Fresh crevasses on the ice surface showed that the glacier was beginning to move, but there was no sign of water coming out of the glacier front yet.

Two days later, the Huge Moulin Stream, which had ponded on the ice surface five metres above the moulin, drained catastrophically. Dave and I went up on the glacier where water from the stream was thundering down the now-open moulin; the lake was completely gone and in its place were an old shoreline and several new crevasses that stretched across the empty basin. We gawped at the newly revealed landscape. What would it have been like, to see and hear that volume of water disappearing down the moulin like bathwater going down the drain? Dave walked down into the lake bed near the crevasses to provide scale for my photos; he was tiny from the basin edge, given the size of the basin itself. The best part was that my data logger and sensors had captured the whole thing—I finally had the data I needed to figure out how water from the surface got to the glacier bed, and I hadn't flooded any data loggers. My data showed that the lake had drained in just an hour, sending a massive input of water to the glacier bed.

The moulins at the end of the Ridge and Nunatak Streams had also opened, as had the moulins at the end of the two large unmonitored streams to the west of the Ridge Stream. That same day, crystal-clear water with high electrical conductivity burst out of the glacier snout; it must have been stored under the glacier over winter and was pushed out by the water coming in from the moulins. The next morning there was an artesian fountain over two metres tall shooting out of the top of the glacier, close to the snout. We took photos of each other standing next to it, sure that no one would believe us otherwise. Water from the fountain also had high electrical conductivity values, which dropped the longer it flowed. The fountain increased in size for hours, until it shrank later in the day. Large crevasses extended longitudinally along the glacier surface behind it, and it created a waterfall off the front of the ice.

✻ While all was well on the science front, our field team's situation was not as rosy. Maria's inexperience with remote camp life put a strain on our group. She had problems navigating on the glacier, and often stayed in her chemistry tent to avoid having to contribute to camp duties. As an MSc student on her first trip to JEG, she understandably had a lot of questions about her research that Dave and I tried to answer. These were mostly logistical in nature: How should she sample the proglacial river once it started flowing? Where should she collect her samples on the glacier surface? But after we'd answered her questions, she'd call Martin on the satellite phone to confirm that we'd answered correctly. Fieldwork requires that you trust your camp-mates. It also requires letting small things slide, if you hope to make it through the season without irritating one another. Unfortunately, that didn't happen this year.

In the second week of July we waited for a helicopter to come and take Dave and Maria out and bring Martin in. As usual there were delays due to weather, but eventually the day came. I said goodbye to Dave before he boarded the chopper; with a tight hug and quick kiss he was gone and I was left on the ice with Mary and Martin, snow just starting to fall.

The tenor in camp changed when Martin arrived. His behaviour was different from that of our first field season, back in 2000. This time, he didn't do things like figure out what equipment he needed for the next day or charge batteries for that equipment. He was reluctant to take on dinner duty, and would often disappear into his tent to "do some work" when it was time to cook. On nights when neither Mary nor I cooked, we had sandwiches for dinner.

After about a week, Martin got more comfortable and began talking to me as an equal. We discussed faculty and students being overworked, family issues and mental health, and the minimum standard for passing a thesis defence—to "keep the system from falling into disrepute," as Martin would say. But he didn't seem interested in my hydrology work or in Dave's superimposed ice work; he was more enamoured with the microbiology work, for which he was collecting additional samples for Maria.

While Martin had seemed preoccupied on campus that year, I had assumed that would change once he was in the field. But his behaviour was mystifying. During my first season on JEG, Martin had contributed to all camp duties, from cooking to looking after equipment. This year he avoided all of that. Mary and I speculated endlessly as to what was causing this apparent shift in attitude. "Do you think he has too much work waiting for him at the university?" I said. "I don't know," Mary said. "Maybe he's not that interested in the research?" Perhaps he hadn't worked out exactly what he was going to measure in the field, and was busy mulling that over. Regardless, I was somewhat disappointed. I'd switched to a PhD based on my first season's impression of Martin as an interested and engaged supervisor, but that impression was substantially changed by what I witnessed in the 2002 field season.

✳ One good thing that happened with Martin in camp was that he initiated a trip to the east side of JEG, where a small part of it flowed into a tight valley—an intriguing place I'd never visited before. He had brought a ground penetrating radar machine to "see" what might be under the ice. The surface was a maze of lakes and streams, with turbid water emerging from crevasses at several locations. Frazil ice also formed there: water that ponded in a thin layer then froze into a variety of crystal shapes. It was a different world—even the air was still and quiet, the only sound the bubbling of water as it made its way over the glacier surface. Our work was plagued with problems, however, beginning with me forgetting to bring a crucial bit of equipment, followed by the battery not being charged enough to run the radar unit. We finally got everything sorted out for one day of radar measurements, but I'm not sure if Martin got the data he wanted.

My biggest day was in the third week of July, when the helicopter came to drop me off on the side of the nunatak and take Martin and Mary to the upper camp. My job was to set up a GPS base station—complete with its large, heavy battery—on the nunatak. When I was done, Martin and Mary would walk down from the upper weather station with a roving GPS unit that constantly connected to the base station, which was the unit's static reference point. They would survey each ablation stake along the way. The results of the survey would tell us how much the glacier had moved, both downstream and vertically, relative to the last time the survey was done.

I had the base station working in camp that morning, and had written down exactly what buttons I had to press to set it up. But of course, once I'd scrambled to the top of the nunatak from where the chopper pilot had deposited me, lugging the base station and the giant battery and wearing a top-heavy backpack, the station wouldn't work. "I fucking hate electronics!" I swore, loudly, to nobody but myself, ready to pitch the whole apparatus off the summit. Fortunately, I got it working just as Martin and Mary radioed that they had started their survey.

Since it was late in the season, there was a lot of extra work to be done. I clambered back down the nunatak, collecting Elmer as I went. I cached him next to the middle weather station, where I downloaded weather data and installed the winter program. I spent the rest of the day downloading all of my stream and lake hydrologic stations, then dismantling them and caching them in a pile on the ice. I started at the Nunatak Lake station, packed it in my backpack, then headed to the Ridge Lake and added that station to my already full pack. I walked slowly down to the moulins, weighed down by the equipment from the lakes. I left my pack and its unloaded contents near the moulins, then walked between the Ridge Stream, Huge Moulin Stream, and Nunatak Stream to collect my stations and add them to the equipment pile. Once I'd tidied up the pile into data loggers, solar panels, and instruments, I put my pack back on and walked down to the lower weather station, which I downloaded and switched to the winter program. I also downloaded the geophones, which would stay in the ice for the winter. Along the way I downloaded and measured the height of four of Dave's temperature sensors. It was an amazingly productive day, all powered by Soundgarden's *Badmotorfinger* on my Discman. I was thrilled that I had accomplished so much, but it was bittersweet knowing I'd soon be leaving JEG for good.

The next day a Twin Otter did a double flyover to say hello, adding a little bit of fun to what had been an exciting season, hydrology-wise. We'd had a few days of nice weather; Martin returned from an outing and reported that the proglacial river was raging, with a standing wave just beyond the snout. The good weather meant that lots of melt was entering the drainage system to produce significant proglacial flow.

Those nice days were quickly forgotten when a snowstorm confined us to camp for the next four days—we ended up getting half a metre of snow! This presented the perfect opportunity to write in my journal and read books, and play cards and drink scotch with my camp-mates in the igloo. After the storm the weather was beautifully sunny, so I got back to work. Because of the shift in weather since the last time I'd been there, I downloaded the lower weather station again but had technical problems; it took three hours to do what should have taken fifteen minutes. I uninstalled Leroy, as the proglacial river had been reduced to a trickle after the recent poor weather. Given the amount of snow we received at the rock camp, I suspected much more had fallen on the upper glacier, shutting down melt and subsequent water inputs to the glacier. It was a good time to wrap up a successful field season.

On our last day in the field, the chopper came and the pilot took me to the upper weather station to get it ready for winter. The amount of snow up top confirmed my suspicion about snowfall shutting down melt. The pilot then took me to my on-ice caches at the middle weather station and near the moulins, and we brought all of the cached equipment to the airstrip in the proglacial zone. We had packed up our camp in the days before, so the pilot slung all of our gear to the airstrip and then flew us down there. The two-way radio had stopped working so we had to rely on the satellite phone to talk to the Resolute base and coordinate our flights.

We hung out by the pile of gear, waiting (as always) for the plane to come. I was giddy with excitement about leaving the field. I ran down the airstrip with a towel on my shoulders, pretending it was a cape. Even Martin got in on the action by waving around a net radiometer as though it was a magic wand. We were being silly, goofing off to release some steam, relieved that we'd managed another field season without mishaps and had obtained some good data.

This would be my last season at John Evans Glacier. I wouldn't be returning to fuss with data loggers and hydrologic sensors; I was done worrying about getting equipment set up on time or about floods taking out our camp. This year's data was the best I'd ever collected. It would go a long way towards telling the story of how the development of the glacier drainage system was linked to the weather. I would miss the quiet of the field—the lack of human-made sounds. I'd miss the camaraderie I had with my camp-mates, as strange as it was at times. I'd miss my little tent, my home in the vast Arctic landscape. But there were two things I wouldn't miss: the slushy season, when it was difficult to travel anywhere on the ice; and living my work, which made it difficult to disengage when I was in camp. I was ready to head back to Edmonton and enjoy the rest of the summer. Plus, I had a wedding to plan!

✶ After I returned from the field in the summer of 2002, Dave and I bought a used thirteen-foot fibreglass trailer. It would be the perfect home on wheels for our trips to the Rockies: small and compact, with just enough room for cooking and sleeping. In late September, Dave and I and our immediate families travelled to Jasper National Park for our wedding. We set up our trailer at a Jasper campsite, then headed to the cabins where our families would be staying. My parents and sister were sharing one cabin, Dave's best friend and his partner were in another, and Dave's mom was in her own.

The next day we headed to Hilda Glacier for the ceremony. Hilda was our favourite Rockies location and the place we'd met so many years ago at field school. We had custom wedding rings made that showed our love of the mountains. We wrote our own vows and, instead of bringing in a stranger, made one of our friends a justice of the peace for a day so he had the authority to marry us. We wore Gore-Tex, fleece, and hiking boots—not exactly a traditional wedding, but exactly how we wanted it.

When we arrived at the trailhead, it was spitting rain and threatening to snow. "It's too cold," my mom complained, cuddling my one-year-old nephew, Stephen. "Maybe I'll stay in the car with Stephen. You go ahead without me." That wasn't happening. I managed to coax her out of the car and everyone headed to the glacier. We walked up the trail, me toting Stephen in a child carrier on my back as my dad and future mother-in-law darted on and off the trail, taking pictures and enjoying the scenery. The clouds became heavier—would we marry in a snowstorm? By the time we reached the top of the outer moraine, next to the stone cairn that marked the trail down to the proglacial zone, the sky had lightened up. We started the ceremony and, as it came to an end, the sun came out. It was a beautiful day, and my heart thumped hard a few times as I absorbed the immensity of the commitment we had just made to each other. My dad was particularly pleased about the venue. "If this was a regular wedding we'd be getting into expensive cars and driving to a restaurant for dinner," he said. Instead, we hiked off the glacier moraine and went back to the guest cabins in Jasper for a wedding dinner that we'd prepared.

We stayed in Jasper for a few more days, visiting Mount Edith Cavell with our guests the day after the wedding, and then travelling up the Whistlers Mountain tram after everyone left. We hiked to a local vantage point to catch the view down-valley, fall colours lighting up the evergreen forest like tongues of flame, yellows and oranges and pale lime greens, brilliant in the sun against a dark-green backdrop of pine. And we were treated to a fabulous display of the northern lights, green and spectacular against the crisp darkness of a late-fall mountain sky. It was just the two of us—newly married and enjoying fall in the Rockies.

✶ Upon returning to my desk after three and a half months away, I learned that my chinook paper had been accepted for publication. I was elated. Having my first scientific paper published in a respected journal validated both my ability to communicate my research, and the field program I'd designed to collect the required data. What's more, I could confidently include this study in my thesis.

Despite having my paper published, I didn't excel at being a scientist—I was still learning how to fill that role. I was at a disadvantage because I'd skipped my MSc. A master's degree would have eased me into the scientific world with a well-defined and relatively small research project that could be completed and written up in two years. I might even have published a paper or two from it. It would have given me more experience with delivering presentations, writing papers, and defending a thesis, which would have been helpful preparation for my PhD candidacy exam. Not having had that experience, I was playing catch-up all the time, thrown headlong and unprepared into a science career. If I had to do it again, I'd have stuck with completing an MSc first, then decided whether or not to tackle a PhD.

Instead of worrying about experience I didn't have, I started thinking about what I'd do after my PhD. If I wanted to make a living as a freelance writer, I'd have to start building a portfolio. That November, I pitched an article to Edmonton's weekly entertainment magazine about one of my favourite topics: books. I visited all the second-hand bookstores in a popular Edmonton shopping district, then wrote a blurb about each one to create a guide for locals and visitors alike.

They printed it. It was my first published article in a popular magazine! I was a "real" writer now! Of course, I spent way too much time on it for the amount I was paid, especially given all the reporting that didn't end up in the article and the endless hemming and hawing about what to include and what to leave out. But the experience was so satisfying that I pitched them another article—this time a book review—that was accepted and published in January 2003. Writing those articles showed me that it *could* be done, that writing could be a job—a career, even. It would take some time to get established, but it was possible. Nevertheless, I still had a thesis to finish. I needed to spend less time thinking and planning for life after it, and start getting the data analysis and writing done to finish it.

Rather than shelve my writing ambitions, however, I signed on to write for the University of Alberta's Public Affairs office: they published news articles about events around campus and focus articles on different research groups. When they gave me my initial assignment in the spring of 2003, I had no clue what I was doing. I had to write about a new math centre at the university, and wasn't sure how I was supposed to cover it. Who should I talk to? What should I ask? What was important and what could I leave out? My position with Public Affairs was like an internship, so they coached me a bit about what to expect, then sent me out to do my thing. I was apprehensive and hesitant in the beginning, but once I'd made it through my first article, it got a bit easier. I wrote about a rooftop garden on campus, a research group that did cryopreservation, a scientist who studied the cumulative effects of industrial development—I even wrote about Martin's research and my own fieldwork. It was validating to be entrusted with reporting on news items that were relevant to the university community, and that were published regularly online and in the university newspaper, *Folio*.

During this time, I also attended evening and weekend writing workshops and editing courses to develop my skills. One night at dinner, Dave asked me why I stayed in academia when I was clearly getting more out of writing than I did out of my thesis. I finished chewing my mouthful of food before responding. The PhD afforded me the flexible time and steady scholarship income to pursue my writing interests, I explained. I wasn't ready—and indeed didn't know how—to subsist on an unpredictable freelance income and hustle for work every day.

The problem was that my public-focused writing was starting to butt heads with my scientific writing. They were too different: one was more open-minded and malleable, the other subject to strict structures and conventions. I kept writing for the university, but I was struggling on the science front. My papers were returned from Martin with blocks of red text where he'd rewritten or commented on what I had on the page. I could communicate with the public through my freelance work, but I had trouble communicating with other scientists through my research work. I was frustrated; I knew I could write, but I just couldn't seem to write *this*. My brain was wired for more creative forms of expression.

Despite my difficulties, I toyed with the idea of taking on a post-doctoral fellowship after I finished my PhD. It would be a research position at another university in a related field that would build on my existing work. I'd get a year or two to focus on a specific research topic, without coursework or a thesis to distract me. Ideally, I'd publish a few papers during that time. It seemed a natural career progression, and would give me the same financial security—and time to write on the side—that a PhD did. But I wasn't sure I was enamoured enough with science to spend more time doing it.

✳ In between weekend trips to the mountains with Dave, I spent the summer of 2003 writing and submitting my second scientific paper to my dream publication, *Geophysical Research Letters*, a journal that only accepts brief articles with significant scientific impact. The experience was a whirlwind. I submitted the paper in June, got the peer reviews back within three weeks, and then had three weeks to address them and resubmit. I worked hard on the article and was proud to see it published; it remains one of my more-cited papers two decades later. Based on my data and observations from the Huge Moulin Stream, I provided new evidence of how water gets from the surface of an Arctic glacier to its bed through a process called hydrofracture.

Of all the water that ponded at the end of the Huge Moulin Stream, a small amount seeped into the moulin but refroze when it contacted the sub-zero ice. This refreezing released heat, which warmed up the ice and allowed a bit more water to penetrate deeper into the glacier. My water level record from the Huge Moulin Stream showed these small, early drainage events quite nicely. As the water delved deeper into the glacier, the weight of all the water in the lake above the moulin began to press down on the frozen tip of the moulin, far below the ice surface, causing the tip to widen. As it widened and more water flowed down it, the turbulence of the water helped erode a channel that eventually connected the surface lake to the glacier bed. The water at the glacier bed acted like a lubricant, allowing the ice to flow downstream and pulling open the moulin into which the water was flowing. As the moulin was pulled open, the surface lake drained catastrophically into the subglacial system. The fresh crevasses in the empty lake basin that I'd photographed Dave standing next to fit this hypothesis, showing that glacier flow sped up downstream and the ice fractured as it flowed. The geophones also recorded icequakes while this was happening.

The time and energy I put into the paper was well worth it. I met several scientists at a meeting not long after it was published who told me how groundbreaking my study was. They said it had changed the way they thought about water getting to the bed of a polythermal glacier. This was good for my scientific career, and though I was pleased I didn't really know what to say in response. I was learning to write the language of science, but I still had problems speaking that language unless it was in a well-rehearsed presentation. Off-the-cuff discussions of detailed science were difficult. I often felt out of my league and feared I would be found out as a sham—classic impostor syndrome. I was a very young woman with a lot to learn among a group of older, male glaciologists. I wished I had a female mentor to talk to about my graduate student experiences, someone who would champion me and help me understand the vagaries of the research world. Someone to help me conquer my impostor syndrome and feel at home in the world of science. But I knew few women in earth sciences, and even fewer in glaciology. There just wasn't a big pool of mentors to choose from.

7

NOT "PAYING ATTENTION"

AFTER A BUSY SUMMER WRITING my hydrofracture paper, I felt ready to tackle the rest of my thesis. But first Dave and I made a fall trip to the Rockies. In early September 2003, we met up with Dan Smith and his field school for a weekend. We stayed at the Wilcox Creek campground, just south of the Athabasca Glacier. Dave went hiking with Dan's group for two days, while I had my own private writing retreat in the trailer. That getaway was an ideal combination of mountains and writing—something I hoped we'd do again soon.

My health had other plans. The effort I'd put into the hydrofracture paper had finally caught up with me. I was starting to feel trapped in school, like I should hurry to finish so I could get out and feel like myself again. As the autumn days became shorter, I fell into a deep depression. There was only so much I could do before my energy ran out. I couldn't focus on my work. I had nightmares regularly, and couldn't get a decent night's sleep. I was alternately restless, anxious, irritable, and angry. I hardly left the house: my days were spent on the couch watching TV, and my nights were spent lying in bed, desperately awake.

(Top) The nunatak weather station at Andrei Glacier, northern Coast Mountains, British Columbia, July 2006. (Photo by D. Lewis, used with permission.) (Bottom) The helicopter that ferried us to and from weather station locations at Andrei Glacier, July 2006. (Photo by the author.)

I started going to counselling and taking Paxil, a relatively new antidepressant. Within a month I was experiencing terrible reactions to the drug, including an episode of severe suicidal ideation while just sitting in a classroom, learning about editing. Suicidal thoughts were a well-known side effect of Paxil, so my doctor started me on a schedule to wean off it while putting me on another antidepressant to tackle the unrelenting depression. I began to wonder if I would ever be "better," if my brain would heal or if it would go rogue on me indefinitely. Would I ever be able to be a writer, let alone an employable academic?

In the midst of these challenges, I was waiting to hear back from another journal. Earlier that year, Martin and I had submitted a co-authored paper about the seven-year weather data record from John Evans Glacier, describing it as an excellent resource for modelling glacier mass balance. I was hoping the journal would accept it for publication; it would be great to have another published research paper to include in my thesis.

Glaciers are dynamic masses of ice that advance and retreat depending on the weather. Mass balance is the difference between how much mass a glacier gains through winter snowfall and how much it loses to summer melt. Because of climate change, the majority of glaciers have a negative mass balance—they lose more mass than they gain, causing them to retreat and get thinner. Winter snowfall can no longer make up for increased summer melt, especially in regions where snowfall has declined. Long data records, like the one collected at JEG since 1994, are critical for calculating changes in mass balance due to climate change. The data can be used to calibrate a model that simulates mass balance, and then to run that model to project potential future climate change scenarios. But the paper was rejected for publication, which only heightened my impostor syndrome and was a huge blow to my depressed psyche.

Given that rejection, I pared my thesis back to three papers: the chinook and hydrofracture papers, plus one more that I hadn't yet written. The final paper would focus on using a numerical model to calculate glacier melt, runoff, and mass balance responses to climate change. I would use my weather data from JEG to run the model, first making sure it was working properly and simulating the melt I'd observed in the field. Then I would change the input data—by increasing air temperatures, for example—to simulate a warmer climate. The new output data would tell me how the glacier would respond to a warming climate.

Computer model output is only as good as its input data, and I knew I had collected quality data in the field. However, I was using a model written by one of Martin's previous students that had some baked-in problems that made my research difficult. Plus I had to learn the appropriate modelling protocols for examining the impacts of climate change. I ran the model. Again and again. It seemed as though all I did every day was plug in numbers and press the Run button, then look at the model output and wonder what the heck to do with it.

What did any of it matter, anyway? Who cared if I could model glacier melt? What was it worth in the grand scheme of things? I was an insignificant blot on the paper of the universe, a tiny stitch in the fabric of time, a luminescent zooplankton on the dark canvas of the ocean, a drop of oil in the gears of the world. The light of life had gone out and I couldn't find a spark to rekindle it. I just wanted to go to sleep for a long time and wake up to find everything new and bright again.

By November, Dave and I knew that something had to change. We decided to move back to Victoria after the holidays, where I would finish my thesis from afar. The coast had always had a healing effect on me, and living there again might help repair my brain. Dave had already given up his PhD with Martin as he hadn't passed his candidacy exam. He'd just been diagnosed with diabetes at that time, and was having difficulty balancing his blood sugars and stress levels. His blood sugar had spiked then crashed during the oral exam, and he wasn't able to answer the committee's questions.

I had to tell Martin about my plans, which reminded me of when I had to tell him I didn't think I could complete my first field season because of my knee. He had been surprisingly accommodating then, reconfiguring the field season so that I could stay. This time, I sat down in his office, took a deep breath, and told him that I was struggling with depression and couldn't work on my PhD. I explained that we were moving to Victoria in January and I would work on my thesis from there. He hemmed and hawed a bit, and I imagined he was trying to be sensitive and not ask too many questions while also grappling with where we would go from here. It was an awkward conversation, though I knew from our discussions in the field that he'd encountered similar situations with other students throughout his career. Perhaps he was worried I'd drop out altogether and end up being a stain on his supervisory record. I would finish, no matter what, because I had committed to it. And I was so close that I couldn't justify letting it go.

I managed to get through my conversation with Martin rationally, without breaking down, and we settled on a timeline for thesis completion. But I was uncomfortable admitting to what I considered to be a weakness. I didn't see any other students talking about depression or struggling with it. Why wasn't there more discussion around mental health in academia? Statistics show that graduate students have higher rates of depression and suicidal ideation than the general population, yet few graduate programs are set up to address these issues. Students are taught to work harder, not smarter, and many professors don't know how to support students in distress.

Dave and I spent November packing and purging, selling and giving away items we didn't need. Thanks to counselling, I was learning a new way of existing in the world, which was a far cry from my usual, regimented, must-get-things-done approach to life. I was trying to be gentler with myself, trying to do what worked for me instead of what I thought I "had" to do. Exploring my wants and needs instead of running roughshod over them just to keep being "productive." Living this way was an experiment, to see if it would help the depression. To complicate matters, however, the schedule for weaning off the antidepressants didn't work as well as I'd hoped. I suffered from dizziness, shivers, nausea, and extreme fatigue—like a flu that lasted for weeks. By the end of November all I was doing was sleeping, eating, watching movies, and going to the counsellor. My thesis wasn't even on my radar. I had no idea how long I would take to recover from this difficult and scary time.

In January 2004 we left Edmonton and moved back to Victoria. We found a rental house with an extra room that would serve as my office. The house was on a quiet quarter acre, within walking distance of the university, a regional mountain park, a library, and a grocery store. That spring, in between sleeping and working on my thesis, I planted my very first vegetable garden. It grew prolifically and provided a surprisingly big harvest. I also took up quilting to complement the gardening—simple pastimes that were easy on my mind and fed my creative side.

I wrote another article for the University of Alberta, focusing on the Bamfield Marine Sciences Centre on the west coast of central Vancouver Island. Dave and I drove a long, lonely, and potholed gravel road to reach this research and teaching facility, where students take field courses and learn first-hand about ocean and forest ecology. The main building is situated next to the beach, with a beautiful view of Barkley Sound. The University of Alberta is one of a handful of universities that support the centre, which is why they were interested in a story about it.

I also finally submitted the story about my 2000 field season that I'd written in Ed Struzik's environmental writing class. The story was published in *Above & Beyond: Canada's Arctic Journal*. I was gratified to have a feature article in print, complete with my own field photos, something I never imagined I'd accomplish. It increased my confidence in being a writer, even though I was still struggling with the depression.

I was slowly putting my world back together and learning what life outside academia was like for the first time in nine years. It wasn't about writing papers and competing with other graduate students for my supervisor's attention. It was about gardening, going for walks, reading, and sewing. It was more balanced and fulfilling, something I should have taken more notice of at the time.

In September 2004, I finished my thesis. Dave and I drove back to Edmonton so I could defend it before Martin left for fieldwork in Antarctica. I still wasn't well, and wasn't sure that I could pull off a good defence. I barely registered the trip across beautiful British Columbia, caught in a haze of depression that muted my emotions and disconnected me from any sense of time or space. Thank goodness I had already published two of my thesis chapters. They were accepted by the scientific community, so I knew there weren't any errors or problems my examination committee could home in on. By using numerical modelling in my third and final paper, I aimed to show that I wasn't just a field scientist, but was more well-rounded and could use my field data for other purposes.

My heart pounded as I waited in the hallway for the committee to call me into the room—the same room in which I'd had my candidacy exam. Once summoned, I gave my presentation, distilling my entire five years of fieldwork, grant applications, research publications, and coursework into a fifteen-minute talk. I stumbled through it with a quaver in my voice, then took a seat and waited for my hands to stop shaking as I readied myself for their questions. Except for one cranky committee member, the all-male panel asked questions that were straightforward and relatively painless to answer. My external examiner, a researcher from another university who was brought in to make the process more impartial, asked about my already-published papers. The other members focused more on my last, unpublished chapter. By the end of it I was buzzing with nerves, but held myself together long enough to respond to their questions.

I waited in the hallway again while the committee deliberated. After what felt like an eternity, I was called back in. I had passed with revisions! I was pleased to have overcome this hurdle despite the depression. All I had to do was revisit some sections of the thesis—notably within the last chapter—and revise them according to the committee's suggestions. Since Martin would be in Antarctica until late December, I had a lot of time to finish those revisions.

What I *didn't* have was a lot of time to get them approved by Martin and submit the final thesis before I'd have to pay tuition for the winter term in January.

I spent a month revising, going through every committee member's comments in the text and re-running the numerical model as required. I received Martin's approval via email, as soon as he returned from the field. I printed off my thesis according to the university's strict guidelines: must be printed on cotton paper, page numbers on the bottom right, and large tables rotated ninety degrees to fit on the page. Dave and I drove back to Edmonton again in January 2005 to submit my thesis as soon as the university opened after the holiday break. I walked into the office eager to hand in my printout, but the thesis administrator made me change a few nitpicky details before she'd accept it. I scrambled to find a computer and printer to make the required changes, and carefully substituted the updated pages for the incorrect ones in the printed copy.

It had been a dizzying few weeks, but I had officially completed my Doctor of Philosophy in Earth and Atmospheric Sciences! I was relieved but exhausted. I had used up all my energy on that final push to finish. Dave and I shared a bottle of bubbly in a hotel room on our drive back to Victoria, a low-key celebration during which I felt shell-shocked and not entirely present. I was ready to put it all behind me and get back to my gardening and sewing.

When I next spoke to Martin, he asked if I planned to go into science communication. It was a simple question, and one that made sense in light of all my side jobs in science writing, but I perceived it as a comment on my abilities as a scientist. His question seemed to imply that I wasn't cut out for an academic career. My just-watch-me attitude kicked in and I perversely wanted to prove him wrong, just like when he doubted my readiness for the candidacy exam. That's when I decided to switch focus, choosing to follow the academic path instead of paying attention to my desire to write, negating what I'd learned in counselling about being gentler on myself and taking my own needs and wants into account.

Martin also asked if I would be going to convocation that spring, and I think he was disappointed that I didn't plan to attend. Convocation for a doctoral degree is a different process than for a bachelor's degree: you cross the stage with your supervisor at your side, as a sign of your research partnership and that you have attained this achievement together. In hindsight, I should have attended to mark the completion of a significant milestone in my life, and to share with Martin the granting of my degree. We had worked together for seven years, since the summer of 1998 when I ran samples in his lab. It would have put closure to what had become a difficult chapter in my life, and might have helped me feel proud of what I had accomplished. Instead, I was just relieved to be done. I had a long road of healing ahead of me.

✳ The Victoria rental house turned out to be fantastic—not just because of the garden, but because the landlord allowed us to get a dog. Tsuga, a German shepherd cross, was my therapy dog. I took him hiking at the local "mountain," walked him through the neighbourhoods, and took him to a nearby schoolyard with Dave to practise recall. We snuggled with him and took photos of him and played in the yard with him, where he would sometimes run through the vegetable garden as it didn't have a fence around it. We looked forward to have him accompany us on our adventures for many years.

In the meantime, I started a postdoctoral fellowship at the University of Victoria with Dan Smith, my field school advisor. I hadn't planned to do a postdoc, but Dan offered me some funding and a project, so I accepted and dove into a new research field. He also brought Dave on as a PhD student. Dave was studying the history of glacier change in the Coast Mountains of British Columbia.

Dan and I were using tree rings to reconstruct historic snowpack levels across BC. Tree rings have been used successfully to describe past climates: the thickness of growth rings in spring and early summer, or in late summer and fall, correlates with rainfall and temperature. My project involved a new way to apply tree ring research. I knew it would be challenging to learn about this new field, but it was a terrific opportunity to work with my original mentor. I spent my time in Dan's lab, the University of Victoria Tree-Ring Laboratory, searching for snowpack datasets from across the province and familiarizing myself with the world of dendrochronology.

I also taught a course in January 2005 on snow and ice hydrology. It was my first experience being the professor at the front of the room. I couldn't believe I had finished my PhD at the age of twenty-seven and was now teaching undergraduates the ins and outs of my own research topic; I was more than a bit intimidated. On the first day, I paced around the room before class started, nervous about how the students would respond to me. Some mistook me for one of them, assuming I was too young to be a professor. The class was a success, though, with good evaluations from the students. Things were changing for the better.

At the same time that I was working with Dan, I was actively searching for my first academic position. Finding jobs that I wanted to apply for was difficult, as most universities are in big cities and I preferred to live in a smaller city. Dan recommended I apply for a job opening at the University of Northern British Columbia (UNBC). In the spring of 2005 I successfully landed an eighteen-month position in Prince George, BC, as an assistant professor in UNBC's geography department. I would be filling in for a professor who was on leave, and teaching first-year geography, third-year hydrology, and fourth-year fluvial geomorphology. I saw this temporary contract as a way to continue my recovery from my depression and ease myself back into the academic life. Dave would come along and finish his PhD from afar.

Dave and I drove up to Prince George in May 2005 to find a house, but the pickings were pretty slim. We were staying at a bed and breakfast a little ways out of town, adjacent to an extensive trail network. The owner of the bed and breakfast knew that her neighbour was thinking of moving, so contacted him and asked if he wanted to sell us his house. We liked it more than anything else we'd seen and ended up buying it on the spot. The location was perfect, and the bed and breakfast owners became not just neighbours but friends.

Soon after I arrived on campus, one of my colleagues handed me a stack of books on rivers and geomorphology. "These will help with your courses," he said, condescendingly. While the books were interesting, and I accepted them graciously, I bristled at the suggestion that I was unprepared to teach. It was a classic example of mansplaining, which I nimbly manoeuvred to avoid alienating a new colleague.

I was pleased that I was teaching courses on topics that I was familiar with, and had the opportunity to develop a field program for my students, just like the one I enjoyed when I was an undergraduate. I took them to the university's research station on the Quesnel River, where they did stream gauging, surveyed the river, and observed the make-up of the watershed that fed the river. It was fantastic to be out in the field, sharing my knowledge with my students like Dan had done so long ago.

I wasn't only teaching, however; in my contract I had negotiated funds to undertake a research project of my own. Of course, I wanted to continue studying glacier hydrology, but I didn't have enough funding for helicopter support. Luckily, Dan and a colleague at the Geological Survey of Canada (GSC) both happened to be working on a particular glacier, and offered to let me piggyback on their flight time if I chose to study the same one. This led me to do research at Andrei Glacier, located in the remote Boundary Ranges of the northern Coast Mountains of BC. The glacier flows from the massive Andrei Icefield, which is larger than the Columbia Icefield in the Rockies. Olav Mokievsky-Zubok, who did most of the glaciological work in the Coast Mountains in the 1960s and 1970s, named the icefield and glacier after his son.

Andrei Glacier was originally meant to be one of the GSC's benchmark monitoring glaciers in northwestern BC. Their plan was to install ablation stakes and a weather station on it and measure the changes in the glacier's thickness over time. They would then compare it to other glaciers along a north–south line from the southern Coast Mountains up to the Northwest Territories. Though they installed the ablation stakes, the GSC never got around to putting up the weather station. Within a few years, their research at Andrei Glacier was abandoned in favour of the Bologna Glacier in Nahanni National Park Reserve, a project that today is co-managed by the GSC and Parks Canada.

Dan's fieldwork involved visiting the northern Coast Mountains each summer in search of trees that had been pushed over by glacier advance and subsequently exposed by glacier retreat. Carbon dating and tree ring analysis of this wood helped him figure out the historical record of glacier extent in the region. Andrei Glacier was one of his field sites.

For my research project, I planned to install weather stations at three locations around Andrei Glacier. I'd use data from my stations and daily maps of regional weather systems documented by the US National Centers for Environmental Prediction (NCEP) to understand four things: how air temperature and other weather variables changed with elevation; how they were linked to large-scale weather systems; what that link meant for glacier melt; and how melt would be affected by climate change.

Andrei Glacier is only accessible by helicopter from Bell II, BC, a remote destination in the Skeena Mountains, almost eight hundred kilometres northwest of Prince George. Bell II is home to a lodge that serves as a heli-skiing base, and a landing site carved out of the coastal temperate rainforest. At the time, an ATCO trailer and a travel trailer had been set up to house Lakelse Air, the company flying out of the area. On one side of the company's airstrip was a stockpile of black fuel drums, used to refuel the choppers flying in and out of this end-of-the-world location.

In July 2006, I drove my rental truck from Prince George to Bell II in a day, bringing with me one of Dan's graduate students who would be in the field for the rest of the season. Lisa was an easygoing woman with long dreadlocks that she kept in a ponytail, a good sense of humour, and a calmness that was refreshing after the chaos of the school term. At Bell II we met up with Steve, an independent contractor from Lake Louise, Alberta, who did a number of glacier surveys for the GSC. One of the sites he serviced was Andrei Glacier, so we'd all be flying in together. Steve was a hardcore outdoors person and professional field assistant, with a well-equipped Toyota van that doubled as a camper and had all his gear stored inside.

As with Arctic fieldwork, we had to wait to fly out; the clouds were thick around the mountaintops, socking us in overnight. Lisa and I set up a small camp at the side of the airstrip, having a granola bar for dinner before settling into our shared tent, while Steve spent the night in his van. The next day we packed up the chopper with field equipment and personal gear and flew over the Boundary Ranges, headed for Andrei Glacier. Below us stretched an untouched landscape of brilliant green, black, and white—the verdant green forests thriving in the rainy, overcast summer climate; the black of exposed alpine rock; and the white of many glaciers sustained by heavy winter snowfalls. Andrei Glacier itself was crevassed and dirty, with V-shaped flowlines on its surface. We landed on a nunatak to the south of it, on the other side of which was Forrest Kerr Glacier. The chopper then went to fetch Dan and his team, including Dave, who were at a field site nearby.

After the chopper's final noisy departure, we were stunned by the silence and looked around shyly at our new field companions. Dave had been in the field since June, and I was obviously glad to see him again. But public displays of affection were a bit awkward with the field team gathered around, so we settled for a hug and a smile with the promise of a more appropriate welcome later. Dave and Dan were accompanied by a field assistant, Ben, and Nicole, another graduate student from Dan's lab. Lisa would be joining them for the rest of the summer.

Once introductions were out of the way, we began to sort out our gear and set up camp. Everyone had their own orange tent, and there was a main area for cooking away from the sleeping tents. Food was packed in large blue plastic drums, to keep it safe from water, rodents, and bears. Not being part of either Dan's or Steve's camp, I hovered at the edge of the group, feeling out of place as they followed their regular camp routines. Eventually I threw my personal gear into a tent I would share with Dave, leaving my field equipment piled on the ground outside. He and I sat together and had a snack as he told me stories about the fieldwork he'd been doing. It sounded tough: climbing steep moraines and chainsawing logs that had been mowed down by the glacier centuries ago. Carrying a chainsaw and slabs of wood over steep, gravelly terrain didn't seem like much fun to me.

∗ My research at Andrei was particularly relevant for policymakers. In 2003, the BC government had approved a run-of-the-river hydroelectric project on the Iskut River, which captures runoff from the Andrei Glacier and other glaciers in the area. This type of project is touted as being environmentally friendly because it uses turbines that are installed either directly in a river or in a side channel diverted from a river. The flowing water spins the turbines, which in turn creates electricity without fully blocking the flow like dams do. What hadn't been taken into account was that the Iskut River is fed by glacier melt, and as the glaciers retreat because of climate change there will be less river flow to generate power. My study would hopefully provide information on how much melt Andrei Glacier could produce, and how much water would be available for future power generation as glaciers in the area continued to shrink and retreat.

On the day we arrived at the glacier, we had enough time to set up a weather station on the nunatak where we were camped. Dave and I unfolded the metal tripod and secured it by placing rocks around each leg; we couldn't use stakes because it was on solid bedrock. We then attached the instruments and wired them into the data logger. I was using a different brand of equipment than I'd used in the Arctic, so I no longer faced the hassle of programming a data logger with computer code and wiring in each individual instrument. Instead, all of the instruments plugged into the data logger enclosure with telephone cable connectors, and the software made it easy to set up the data collection intervals. A piece of cake, compared to what I had come to expect.

Each weather station was about two metres tall and looked a bit like a robot from *Star Wars*. It had a central steel tripod that bristled with various instruments for measuring different aspects of the weather. Using the air temperature data at each station, I planned to calculate how it varied with elevation, and link it to regional weather systems documented daily by the NCEP program. With methods I described in the last chapter of my PhD thesis, I'd model the length and intensity of the glacier melt season. The temperature data I'd collect would allow me to calculate glacier melt, the wind data would tell me which direction the weather systems were coming from, and the rainfall data would show days when glacier melt was reduced by cloudy conditions. All of this information would give me a snapshot of weather at the glacier at a given time, and allow me to calculate how much meltwater was leaving the glacier.

I was glad to have a chance to test the nunatak weather station overnight. If it worked properly, I would know exactly how to set up the other stations so they would work as well. In the morning I discovered that it had rained while we slept, which was perfectly captured by the rain gauge and recorded by the data logger. All of the sensors were doing their jobs—and I didn't even have to swear at them.

That day, the chopper pilot flew Steve down to the glacier surface where he would measure the GSC's ablation stakes, just as our team had done with the stakes on John Evans Glacier. The pilot then flew me and Ben down-valley to set up the second weather station in the proglacial zone, two kilometres from the glacier snout. The glacier sat in the distance, a crevassed tongue of ice that fit neatly into the valley around it. Where Ben and I were, however, was perfect grizzly territory: alder thickets and scrubby evergreen forest, and lots of flat land for easy travel. I unpacked the tub of gear quickly and we set up the station in record time, barely testing it before getting in the chopper to fly back to camp and pick up the last station.

With the equipment for the third weather station on board, we flew to the mountain on the north side of the glacier to set it up. Conditions were snowy on the mountaintop, which corresponded with the dusting of snow we observed on all the surrounding peaks, the white contrasting with the black rock around it. As at the nunatak, we secured the station legs with rocks and tested the sensors. The local weather makes for some interesting flying; you can be stranded for a few hours or even a few days without much warning. Ben and I experienced this first-hand when a snow squall blew in that day, making it impossible for the pilot to come back for us when he was supposed to. After an anxiety-filled half hour, conditions cleared up and he was able to return.

I stayed in camp one more night, making the most of my time in the mountains and visiting with Dave. I wouldn't see him again until the field season was over. The chopper pilot returned the next morning and I flew out of the site just two days after my arrival, Andrei Glacier receding behind me as I left the weather stations to do their thing.

My research philosophy was based on Mary Oliver's advice: "To pay attention, this is our endless and proper work."[1] So it was strange to not spend the summer monitoring the weather stations and measuring glacier parameters like snow and ice melt, to not watch the glacier change over the melt season. I was doing field-work, so to speak, but I wasn't in the field. Unfortunately, I didn't have the budget to stay at Andrei Glacier all summer, nor did I have a field assistant to help me. I was immensely grateful that Dan and the GSC had shared their chopper time, to allow me to undertake this project.

✳ Dave returned to Prince George from the field in late July. In September it was time to collect my three weather stations, so we drove back up to Bell II and flew in to Andrei Glacier, again with flight support from the GSC.

From the chopper we watched in awed fascination as a large grizzly bear attacked the proglacial weather station. It had a good hold on the station with its front paws, and was gnawing on one of the instruments as we hovered above. Loose wires snaked all over the ground, and the rain gauge had been tossed a few metres away from the station. We circled overhead several times until the bear fled, then set down to rescue the equipment. The station lay on its side, the rain gauge was punctured and bent, and the shield for the air temperature sensor was covered in tooth marks. The data logger enclosure had been nibbled on but not breached, while the cables connecting the sensors to the data logger had been severed. I worked quickly to right the station and dismantle it, constantly looking over my shoulder. I was relieved when we finally lifted off again. We then collected the other stations and downloaded the data for analysis back on campus. We flew the equipment out in a metal cage attached to the exterior of the helicopter; one that was meant for storing skis on heli-skiing operations.

The sight of that bear reminded me that the region was wild and remote enough for grizzlies to roam wherever they liked and attack objects at will. Dave had told me stories about the grizzlies and wolverines they'd seen during their fieldwork in the area: this definitely wasn't the Arctic! I still have the rain gauge that was punctured by a tooth or claw—it sits on my bookshelf next to the coffee pot and painted rock I'd found at Hilda Glacier while doing my streamflow project.

* Some couples can't work together, but Dave and I had been working in the field with each other since my Hilda Glacier project back in 1998. We had a strong partnership that could weather the challenges of fieldwork, and each of us often knew what the other was thinking, or going to say, before they even said it. Our relationship brought to mind explorer Phyllis Munday who, along with her husband Don, climbed many peaks in the southern Coast Mountains and elsewhere across British Columbia from the 1910s to the 1940s.

Phyllis was an outdoors person from a young age, a tomboy who enjoyed daring exploits like crossing deep ravines by walking on logs that spanned their depths. After her family moved from

Nelson to Vancouver, Phyllis spent her spare time climbing Grouse Mountain on the city's North Shore. She would go alone or with a few friends, but always made it from the streetcar to the summit in three hours. She joined the BC Mountaineering Club as a teenager, and climbed her first "real" peak at the age of sixteen. From then on she was an active member of the group, signing up for many climbs around the province's Lower Mainland.

One thing she found difficult was that she hiked and climbed in her bloomers, but couldn't be seen in public without a skirt over them. So she would take her skirt off, hide it under a log, and make sure to retrieve it and put it back on before returning to civilized society. One day, she and her friends weren't able to come back the same way they'd set out, and were denied passage on the streetcar back to Vancouver because of their state of (un)dress.

Phyllis met Don when she was twenty-four, at a military hospital in Vancouver where she volunteered as a nurse. He was also a climber, though he had injured his left arm in the war and was somewhat limited by this disability. They climbed together regularly as members of the BC Mountaineering Club, and married in 1920. They spent their honeymoon in a cabin on Dam Mountain—there was no other place they wanted to be. In 1921 they had a daughter, Edith, and eventually moved to North Vancouver for her schooling. But they kept climbing the southern Coast Mountains in their backyard.

The Mundays also climbed on Vancouver Island. As the story goes, they were standing on Mount Arrowsmith near Port Alberni, looking across the Strait of Georgia, when they spotted a massive peak on the mainland. It rose well above the adjacent peaks in the southern Coast Mountains, and they only glimpsed it for a moment before it was once again wreathed in cloud. They got a quick compass bearing ahead of its disappearance, however, and named it Mystery Mountain; the couple would dedicate the next twelve years of their summer travels to finding and summiting it.

While they knew roughly where to search for the mountain, there were no roads leading into the area, so their first hurdle was to access the mountainous terrain from the coast. They had to make their way inland from sea level, battling alder and devil's club as well as streams and rivers. They tried several routes up various coastal fiords before settling on Knight Inlet as the best way to reach the glaciers of the southern Coast Mountains and Mystery Mountain itself.

They attempted to summit Mystery Mountain (named Mount Waddington in 1927), the highest peak in the Coast Mountains, sixteen times, and came close to succeeding once. Sometimes they were thwarted by weather, other times by food running out, and once by not having enough pitons and rope. The expeditions weren't all failures, however, as they made first summits of many nearby mountains on days they couldn't access Waddington. And when they returned from their Waddington trips, there was always the Alpine Club of Canada summer camp to attend, where they may have rubbed shoulders with Elizabeth Parker, the woman who co-founded the club and for whom Parker Ridge in the Rockies is named.

The Mundays weren't just mountaineers, they were also scientists. They took compass bearings, field notes, and panoramic photos of the areas in which they climbed, areas that were virtually unknown by white settlers. They used their data to make detailed photo-topographical maps of the new terrain they had explored, opening up the area to future adventurers. They wrote articles for the *Canadian Alpine Journal* (for which Phyllis served as editor from 1953 to 1969), outlining the peaks they'd seen and climbed, and providing elevations and names for others. More thorough records of their climbs can be found in Don's book *The Unknown Mountain*, in which he recounts their expeditions to reach Mount Waddington.

While Phyllis did much of the scientific work without recognition (common for women at the time), Don belonged to a number of scientific organizations, including the International Commission on Snow and Glaciers. It's unclear if Phyllis's contributions were shared with these organizations, or if they were assumed to be solely Don's work. Phyllis also assisted the Royal BC Museum, preserving insects for them that she and Don gathered on their travels. She found that "collecting and mapping made them [her and Don] see and observe a lot of things that they might have missed otherwise."[2] This was exactly what I had learned from Dan at field school: to do science in the mountains I had to look carefully at the landscape and observe the environment at work, seeing things that I might not notice otherwise.

Unlike many women of her era, Phyllis didn't let motherhood stop her from climbing. She took Edith with her—starting when the child was eleven weeks old—first in a cradleboard, then in a backpack fitted with a mosquito net and a hood to keep her safe from the incessant rain and ubiquitous insects. When Edith was more active but not yet old enough to keep up with Phyllis and Don, she stayed with family for the summer. Edith came back into the wilds with her parents when she was in her teens, around the same age Phyllis was when she started climbing with the BC Mountaineering Club.

Phyllis was a revolutionary woman who summited many peaks in many different locations. Her accomplishments and contributions to mountaineering were recognized with a wide variety of honours, including the Alpine Club of Canada's Silver Rope Award in 1948 for climbing leadership, and their badge for outstanding service in 1970. She was appointed to the Order of Canada in 1973, and received an honorary doctorate from the University of Victoria in 1983.

Phyllis and Don described themselves as "a climbing unit something more than the sum of [their] worth apart."[3] This was partly because of Don's injury; he sometimes needed assistance from Phyllis on tricky parts of climbs. Don wrote, "we relied on each other for rightness of action in emergencies, often without audible language between us," and "my wife and I bring to this...travel a glad confidence in each other that one not knowing us well might brand foolhardiness."[4] This was why their relationship made me think of mine with Dave: like the Mundays, we were a pair working together to travel and document mountain landscapes.

I understood Phyllis's enjoyment of the outdoors. She wrote, "on a mountain you are so very close to nature...I always feel a friendship with mountains, almost as if they were human."[5] I felt the same thing when I was in the field: a friendship with the peaks that surrounded me, even if I wasn't planning to summit them. While I didn't want to become a climber, I shared her passion for the mountains, her scientific observations of those landscapes, and her connection with her partner, all of which made fieldwork so important to me.

✶ After packing the truck with the weather stations retrieved from Andrei Glacier, Dave and I headed south from Bell II to Prince George. We hadn't driven far when Dave turned to me and said, "You've never been to Stewart!" That statement was certainly true, so we decided to take a detour and visit.

Stewart, BC, is located on the northwest coast at the head of the Portland Canal, close to the Alaska Panhandle. It's an old mining town that had its heyday in the years prior to World War I, when it boasted a population of over ten thousand people. It now has a year-round population of about five hundred, with summer tourists coming to visit what was once a thriving frontier town, and snowmobilers and skiers coming in winter to play in some of the deepest snowpack in the province—about six metres on average per year. We went there mainly because of the Bear Glacier: from the highway leading into Stewart, you can see its retreating and shrinking mass. We toured Stewart's quirky toaster museum, and crossed the border into Hyder, Alaska, which is only accessible by road via Stewart. We took pictures of the massive annual salmon run, keeping an eye out for grizzly bears feasting on the dying fish, and marvelled at the dripping and lichen-covered Tongass National Forest, a classic example of a coastal temperate rainforest.

Even though I hadn't spent my field season exploring a glacier, I got to explore somewhere I'd never have considered visiting if it hadn't been for fieldwork. Stewart was too far off the beaten path for me to travel to otherwise, but it was a fun side trip from my work at Andrei Glacier.

＊ That fall, to help with my research, a colleague at UNBC used aerial photos and satellite imagery to calculate Andrei Glacier change since 1988. The results showed significant retreat and major thinning almost halfway up the glacier, with the greatest thinning—caused by summer melt—happening on the lower parts of the glacier where the air temperatures were the highest. This is consistent with what researchers see on mountain glaciers worldwide: air temperatures increase with climate change and summer melt exceeds winter snow accumulation.

Back in my office, I examined my weather data more closely. The proglacial weather station had been in its own microclimate, caused by katabatic winds pushing cold, dense air down-valley from the glacier surface. All stations recorded similar temperatures during warm weather events associated with high-pressure systems, and during major low systems that brought a lot of rain. The proglacial station had the highest air temperatures and the nunatak station had the lowest, meaning that the glacier terminus was melting much faster than ice at higher elevations; the temperatures recorded at the mountain station were in between. This validated what my colleague's remote-sensing analysis had shown me.

Beyond these basic observations, I didn't know exactly what I was looking for in my datasets. I should have had a weather station on the glacier itself, to measure conditions directly above the ice surface and give a sense of how that changed relative to the other stations and with large-scale weather patterns. While the data from each station told me something about the conditions at each location, I struggled to figure out how to integrate the three datasets to determine what was happening with melt and weather at Andrei Glacier. It felt like my Hilda Glacier project all over again—too much story, not enough science.

I put together an abstract with preliminary results for the American Geophysical Union's annual meeting in December 2006, and was invited to give a poster presentation. At the conference I was treated as a young graduate student: researchers asked me whose lab I worked in (mine) and what year of study I was in. I had an unsettling run-in with a professor from the University of Lethbridge, who also assumed I was a graduate student and creepily asked if I would come party with him and a few other students. Needless to say, I declined.

In hindsight, I should have used the model I'd used during my PhD to calculate glacier melt using data from only one of my weather stations. Had I done that, I could have linked specific melt events to large-scale weather systems from the NCEP dataset. However, not only could I not decide which station to use to calculate glacier melt, I was overwhelmed with teaching responsibilities, and didn't have a lot of spare time to think about the data and how to analyze it. I either hadn't come up with a proper research hypothesis or hadn't set up the correct instrumentation for the hypothesis I did have, so now was stuck figuring out what to do after the fact. I was ill-prepared and out of my depth. Science began to feel like lonely, difficult work, and I wondered again if it was really for me.

8

INTO THE FOREST

WHEN DAVE AND I MOVED TO PRINCE GEORGE IN 2005, we were alarmed by the number of dead pine trees—not just in the city, but in the region as a whole. Large swathes of rusty red forest stood out like a cancer against the surrounding green trees. The trees were dying because of an outbreak of the mountain pine beetle, a rice-sized insect endemic to forest ecosystems in western North America. Climate change had allowed the beetle population to swell to epidemic proportions in the northern forest. The region's pine trees were stressed by summer heat and drought, which made them susceptible to insect infestation. On the other side of the coin, winter cold spells weren't long enough—or cold enough—to kill overwintering beetle larvae.

The mountain pine beetle, like all wood-boring insects, can be extremely destructive. The real culprit, though, is the blue-stain fungus that these beetles carry on their mouthparts. As they munch beneath the bark, the beetles transfer this fungus to the tree. Along with staining the wood blue, the fungus shuts down the tree's phloem, cutting off the flow of water and nutrients. As a result, the trees die, turning red at first, then grey as needles and fine branches fall off.

(Top) Checking the weather station in the clearcut at François Lake, central British Columbia, November 2006. (Bottom) Tsuga and puppy Jasper help me dig a snow pit in the dead forest stand at François Lake, January 2007. (Photos by D. Lewis, used with permission.)

By the time we arrived in Prince George, approximately 8.5 million hectares of pine across British Columbia had been killed. The infestation peaked in 2004 and, almost two decades later, the infested area had grown to over 18 million hectares: more than five times the area of Vancouver Island.

In the early stages of the infestation, the provincial government gave forest companies the go-ahead to cut down, or "salvage log," these dead forests for timber production. This assumed that the beetle-affected forests weren't good for anything else, which overlooked their role in local ecology and hydrology. Leaving dead trees standing supported biodiversity in plant and animal communities, and moderated the impacts of the reduced forest cover on hydrology and soils. Forest companies soon learned that the trees had to be harvested within a few years of infestation or they would become so dry they'd shatter on impact with a sawmill's blades. Thus, they hastily clearcut dead pine stands in a race to preserve the wood's commercial value. We regularly drove past a sawmill near Prince George that had an uncountable number of log piles, each several storeys high, waiting to be processed.

Even though they'd approved salvage logging with minimal scientific data to support the decision, the BC government still wanted to find out all they could about the impacts of pine beetle infestation on ecosystems and timber supply. They put out a call for research proposals on various pine beetle topics. One of the things they wanted to know was how snow would be affected in beetle-killed forests. The water supply in much of the province is dominated by snow hydrology: spring snowmelt is a key feature of the ecosystem. Forest disturbances like beetle infestation and salvage logging would change how winter snow was trapped in and around trees, affecting when and how much meltwater reached regional streams and rivers.

This type of research was right up my alley. While it wasn't about glacier melt, it was about cold regions hydrology, and I had a lot of experience studying snow and snowmelt. The physics of snow are pretty much the same wherever you go; you just have to take local factors into account. In this case, instead of studying snow on a glacier surface that didn't interact with either the ground or vegetation overhead, I'd study snow in a forest where it interacted with both the ground and the trees above it. I'd use some of the same methods that I used in the Arctic, both field and numerical modelling approaches. What was different this time, was that my research would be *applied* rather than *basic*—so my results would make their way out of academia's ivory tower. Policymakers, not just scientists, would be interested in my findings because they would be important to communities and ecosystems.

I poured a lot of energy into my first grant proposal as a university scientist. I explained that I would find out how snow accumulation and melt changed in beetle-killed forests, and laid out how I'd design an experiment to measure this using tools I'd used on glaciers in my previous research. I outlined the ways in which my study would be useful for the government, and put together a budget that took into account all of the items I'd have to purchase and the travel costs I'd incur to do the work. I looked up equipment needs and secured quotes for all of my field gear, from weather stations to snow pit kits. I didn't budget for a field assistant, though—which I should have done, as Dave would help me with weather station setup and data collection.

If they accepted my proposal, I'd have to get used to an entirely different type of fieldwork. While my Arctic work involved spending eight to ten weeks each summer in the field, my forest-snow work would take place in winter and wouldn't require the same level of attention. I'd visit my research site every two weeks to measure changes in snowpack, but the forest itself wouldn't change over that time. Since I was no longer a graduate student, I'd need to fit my research around my university responsibilities. The work would happen on weekends, when I didn't have to teach and could take the time to go in the field. It was a shift in perspective: I was going from being steeped in fieldwork to it being just another part of my job. It certainly wasn't like my Arctic fieldwork, where I was immersed in my research for months at a time.

To increase my chances of funding success, I also had to familiarize myself with the field of forest hydrology—quickly—so I pored over dozens of journal articles about forests and snow. This task was a lot easier than it had been during the early years of my PhD program, as most journals now had digital copies of papers online; I could search research databases from my office and not have to wander the library stacks. I learned on the fly, noting how the methodologies that others applied were similar to what I knew from glacier hydrology. I also made sure to figure out what work had already been done, so that I could build on it instead of reinventing the wheel. I went over my proposal many times before submitting it, certain that this was a key funding opportunity that could get my career off the ground. Then I sent it in and waited.

✻ In the meantime, I scoured the web for other academic positions I could take on after my eighteen months at the University of Northern British Columbia were up. In the fall of 2005, I applied for a job at the University of Otago in New Zealand and was invited down for an interview. Trouble was, my passport had expired and they were expecting me in a matter of weeks. Dave flew to the passport office in Victoria with my renewal form and returned with the new passport, probably the most expensive one I've ever owned! Thanks to him, a week later I was on a plane to the bottom of the world.

In all, I spent four days at the university. The interview went well, and the department administrative assistant thanked me for delivering an accessible research presentation that she actually understood. The department was so welcoming; everyone took a break together at 10:00 a.m. in the coffee room. Some faculty participated in a lunchtime game of badminton and invited me to join them. It was friendly but competitive, and left me sweating in my interview clothes; I hadn't considered bringing gym clothes with me! A fellow Canadian faculty member took me to see the South Island's beautiful sandy beaches and abundant coastal life, just minutes from downtown Dunedin. Sea lions barked out in the bay and waves lapped at the empty beach—a perfect place to take a dog for a romp.

The morning before I left, I was summoned to the dean's office. "We'd like to offer you the job," he said. "Think about it on the way home, and I hope to hear a positive response when you get there." I was floored. Here I was in a foreign country, one to which I had barely made it given my passport issues, and I was being offered a tenure-track job. I told him I'd think about it, emailed Dave to tell him the news, and then wrestled with my decision for the entire sixteen-hour flight back.

I had enjoyed the departmental atmosphere, which was collegial and inclusive. There was also a high level of openness: all candidates were interviewed in the same week, and we ran into one another several times on campus and in the department. This was markedly different from North American academic job searches, where you only find out by accident—usually after the fact—who else has been interviewed. I also loved the landscape, the proximity to the ocean, and the relatively small size of the city of Dunedin.

But by the time I landed in Prince George, I had made up my mind. I told Dave I wouldn't be taking the job. Even though he would have been game to go there with me, it was too far from home: at the edge of the world, two small islands floating in the Pacific, thousands of kilometres from anywhere else. Also, Tsuga would have to remain in quarantine for six months in a facility on the North Island, far from Dunedin, as New Zealand is very strict about bringing pets to the island nation. We couldn't leave him alone in a kennel for that long, not just because he was so young, but because he was an integral part of the family. Since then, the New Zealand government has reduced the quarantine period to ten days, but even that is difficult for a furry family member.

Nevertheless, the interview and the offer showed that I was well-prepared for the job market. If the University of Otago recognized my potential and wanted to hire me, then surely another university would.

✽ I returned from New Zealand to find that my pine beetle and snow research proposal had been funded for one year, so I immediately set about putting my experiment in action. My first trip into the field was in January 2006. I chartered a helicopter to fly over the area west of Prince George, hoping to identify places reasonably close by that would make good study sites.

I was looking for three forest stands within close proximity: healthy green pine, red or grey dead pine, and a clearcut. As we flew, I stared intently at my topographic map to find landmarks and then match them with the same ones on the ground below. Switching focus like this while flying was not a good combination, and the helicopter pilot had to set down quickly as I vomited into an airsickness bag. The fresh air helped, but I was embarrassed; I'd never gotten airsick in all my time flying in choppers and Twin Otters. When we lifted off again I put the map away, not wanting to make the same mistake twice—not that I had anything left to throw up. Ultimately, the flight helped me identify the stands that would work for my research. They were in a private woodlot, so I contacted the owner and got permission to work on their land.

As a naïve scientist who hadn't run a research project with a healthy budget before, I didn't know the ins and outs of managing my own grant funds. I had to buy a laptop to activate and download the data loggers in the field, so I phoned the program manager to make sure that was okay, as it wasn't in the original budget I'd submitted. He'd probably never had someone ask him a question like that; most people just use the money as they see fit. "Yes, that's fine," he said, impatiently. I had assumed the funding agency would compare my purchases to my budget and ding me for items that didn't match, but it turned out that they just wanted the work done. The budget was there to give a broad sense of the total cost.

My three pine stands represented different stages of forest cover: healthy green, which were few and far between; beetle-killed; and clearcut. The clearcut was the reference stand: it would provide a record of how much snow had fallen in total, and show when and how fast the snow would melt if there weren't any trees around. It also served as a proxy for a salvage-logged stand—what remained on the landscape after forest companies harvested the beetle-killed trees.

The healthy green stand would tell me how the snowpack behaved in the absence of pine beetle infestation. The beetle-killed stand would tell me how infestation affected snow processes relative to the live and clearcut stands. I would use all of this information to figure out the impacts on the timing of spring melt and how much melt there might be.

Though the project fell under the umbrella of cold regions hydrology and I had my Arctic snowpack experience, I still faced a daunting learning curve. I'd never worked in forests, so I needed to learn what to measure and how to measure it: tree height, tree size (determined by diameter at breast height, about 1.3 metres above the ground), canopy closure, and other data. All of these variables affect how much snow is caught by tree branches and needles, and how much sunlight reaches the snow surface.

Even though I'd be working fairly close to Prince George, it was still a remote site out in the bush. But I was used to that: the forest started across the street from our house, complete with bears, some of whom had climbed the crabapple trees in our front yard—the only fruit we'd forgotten to harvest. Prince George had always struck me as a city plunked down in the wilderness, one that would be completely overgrown in a year if it was ever abandoned.

✳ In late January 2006, Dave and I rented an SUV, piled all of my scientific gear and Tsuga the field dog in the back, and travelled an hour west of Prince George towards Vanderhoof, the geographical centre of British Columbia. My research site was located about forty-five kilometres southeast of Vanderhoof, near McKay Lake. It was an easy drive that took us from the hilly pine and spruce forests of the province's Northern Interior to the relatively flat landscape of the Nechako Plateau and the farmland that surrounds Vanderhoof.

There was a road into the woodlot, but the SUV wasn't a good choice for fresh winter snow and it bogged down fairly quickly. Dave and I had to walk most of the way in, carrying the equipment. We wore snowshoes to make the travelling easier, and I'd picked stands that were accessible from the road, but there was a lot of gear and our packs were heavy. Tsuga gambolled along with us, sometimes breaking trail and other times trying to ride on the backs of our snowshoes. To him it was a big adventure in the wilderness, a great opportunity to spend the day playing in the snow.

My three forest stands were about a fifteen-minute snowshoe trek from one another. This was intentional, not only for convenience but to ensure they all experienced the same weather conditions. Each one encompassed an area about the size of a tennis court and represented a specific set of forest characteristics that I measured to define the differences between stands. Because it was a coniferous forest with few deciduous trees, I was easily able to record which tree species were found in each stand (none in the clearcut, of course). I counted the number of trees in each species, measured the average age of the trees using tree rings, and calculated the canopy density. I also installed a weather station in each stand—the same stations I used at Andrei Glacier. We spent the day setting them up, then headed back to Prince George until it was time to collect the first set of snow measurements.

Dave and I visited the research site every two weeks that winter and spring; our final visit took place in the middle of April to confirm that the snowpack had melted in all three stands. Each visit was an all-day affair, and required that we work steadily to get everything done. We'd leave Prince George early in the morning and reach the woodlot within a couple of hours. Our backpacks were full of supplies: snow measurement tools, a field notebook, a laptop, plus lunch and extra warm layers. We'd strap on our snowshoes, then head down the snowy road with Tsuga.

At each stand I downloaded the weather station data, recorded that day's weather conditions, and looked for evidence of what the weather had been like since my last visit. Sometimes fresh snow had to be cleaned off the radiation sensor. If snowmelt had occurred, I would have to clear ice layers off the sensors, especially the wind sensor, which could freeze in place.

I also dug a snow pit at each stand to observe snowpack development and measure snow density, then took snow depth measurements in the cardinal directions from each pit. I used the average of these depth measurements and the snow density value from the pit to calculate each stand's snow water equivalent: the depth of water the snow would produce if it all melted at once. Digging pits at this research site was a lot easier than it had been in the Arctic—the snow was less than a quarter as deep.

The structure of the snowpack differed between visits. As the season progressed, new layers accumulated, with different crystals within them. The snow pits served as archives, providing information on what had happened in the forest when I wasn't there to see it. Sometimes there were layers of needles within the snow, suggesting that wind or heavy snowfall had knocked them to the ground. In all of the stands, a midwinter rain-on-snow event or even a brief melt event would create a melt-freeze crust in the snowpack, which was then covered by a fresh snowfall. But in the clearcut stand in particular, a thick layer of ice also formed at the base of the snowpack. When I took snow depth measurements at that stand, I had to account for the ice layer because my probe couldn't punch through it to easily reach the ground below.

It was pleasant and enjoyable work, observing the snowpack and thinking about what processes formed the layers and crystals I measured. Looking at the way sunlight dappled the snow surface in the forested stands versus the full-on sun that shone on the clearcut. Observing how each forested stand intercepted snow: how it was particularly well intercepted in the live stand, where the needles were green and healthy, and how in the dead stand the red needles dropped onto the snow surface as the snow weighed them down and they lost their grip on the branches. Every visit there was something different to see, and I made sure to record as many observations as possible.

Working outdoors in the winter, I especially liked seeing the signs of passing animals on the snow. Bounding snowshoe hare tracks, light wing brushes where birds briefly touched down, and the cloven hoofprints of deer passing through. Traces that are invisible in summer. The winter forest was beautiful, the evergreen tree branches limned with fresh snow.

Dave and I would stop at 1:00 p.m. for lunch, then complete our last measurements for the day. I looked forward to our lunches in the woods, the hushed silence broken only by the hammering of woodpeckers looking for beetle larvae under the pine bark. It was satisfying to have done the work to earn this small break. Snacks, a thermos of hot tea, and a quiet moment with my family in the wilderness—what could be better? This routine was less stressful than some of the marathon work days I'd endured in the Arctic, but I still missed the mountains. Forest research wasn't quite the same.

When we'd finished at the last stand, we would make our way back to the SUV and head home. The daylight hours were short during the winter months, and the highway was often slick with snow and ice. After sunset, fog rolled off the cold fields and onto the road, reducing visibility and adding time to our trip as we slowed down to avoid wildlife and other vehicles. Sometimes the two-hour drive felt like a lifetime as we strained to see through the dense fog. We were always relieved to pull into our driveway, having made it safely back from the field site again.

✷ I chartered a second chopper flight in late March. I wanted to verify the canopy composition of my forested stands, and to get an aerial view of the snowpack across the region at the onset of spring melt. This time I left my map behind and focused on the forest below me. It covered the land in all directions, a mosaic of dead, live, and clearcut stands. Patches of red and grey marked where the infestation had taken hold, while bare patches indicated the aftermath of salvage logging. There was very little green. This flight provided a much-needed perspective beyond the limited scope of my three study sites, and confirmed that my stands represented the larger regional landscape. It also let me see that my live stand was beginning to succumb to pine beetle; in a few months its trees would die and turn completely red.

Field measurements and observations were only part of the equation. I also applied some of my numerical modelling skills from my PhD work. For this project, I used the energy balance model I used in my PhD chinook paper. My starting point was the maximum snowpack measured in each stand; I modelled snowmelt after that maximum date using data from my weather stations and tree measurements. The modelling was a success: the output matched the dates of snow disappearance that I observed in the field.

My results showed that the forest created differences in microclimate between the stands, which led to obvious variations in snow accumulation and melt. The clearcut stand, for example, got the most snow because there were no trees to intercept it. This snow was like the glacier snow I'd studied in the Arctic: it fell directly to the ground without passing through a forest canopy, and melted as expected in spring due to sunlight exposure and warm air temperatures.

As I'd guessed, the dead stand was an intermediate stage between the live one and the clearcut. It accumulated a bit more snow than the live stand because the trees couldn't intercept as much. This meant there was more snow to melt in spring than in the live stand, but it melted slower than both of the other stands. This was unexpected: I had thought the dead stand would melt faster than the live stand, but slower than the clearcut. While my results had some implications for regional water supply, this was just a one-year study: I needed more data to draw any substantial conclusions.

This project reminded me that I enjoyed fieldwork and, despite working in a new-to-me field, I knew what I was doing and was confident in doing it. I had taken the time to do my background research, and had acquired the right knowledge to be able to provide useful information about how snow processes respond to forest disturbances like insect infestation. I relied on what I'd learned in my PhD courses on surface water hydrology and snow processes—the courses I had excelled in and had enjoyed the most. What I didn't realize at the time was that I was making a niche for myself in the research world, something I hadn't accomplished with my glacier research. I was building up my future research career, one forest stand at a time.

✳ My work wasn't all about forest hydrology, however. In early 2006 I responded to a message that came through an Arctic email listserv. The sender was looking to hire someone to write for a newsletter put out by Alaska-based VECO Polar Resources, about research projects the company was supporting in the Arctic. I applied and got the job right away, and divided my time between snow research, teaching, and writing. It felt great to get back into writing, as I was hardly even journalling at the time—there was just too much to do between teaching and research.

The work for VECO was a satisfying blend of science communication and creative writing. Every few weeks I'd get an assignment from my editor to write about a particular research project. This usually involved interviewing scientists whose work I was familiar with; in some cases I'd even cited their research in my own papers. I would put together some background on their project and come up with a series of questions, then arrange a phone interview and get ready to write down their responses as fast as I could. Most scientists were happy to answer questions about their work, and I enjoyed hearing their stories about the research process rather than just their study results. I pressed them for the human-interest side of things: what they did in camp or what they thought about while walking to their field sites, the aha moments that made fieldwork worthwhile. Through their eyes, I became a temporary expert in their discipline, be it geology, remote sensing, or ecology. I lived vicariously through them, enjoying their field adventures as they relayed them to me.

✳ Mindful that I was only in an eighteen-month position, I continued applying for permanent academic jobs. In January 2006, I interviewed for a job at Simon Fraser University in Burnaby, near Vancouver. As I found out later from colleagues in the Canadian hydrology community, all three candidates for the position were women, which was a nice change from the status quo.

I had a jam-packed single-day interview—unlike most academic interviews, which can stretch over several days. It started with the geography chair welcoming me to the department, after which I gave a mock teaching lecture to the faculty based on a topic of my choice. Audience members acted as students, asking bizarre and sometimes confrontational questions, trying to simulate what I might experience in a real classroom. After meeting with a few individual faculty members to talk about our research and get their thoughts on the department, I gave my research presentation. I covered the research I'd done, stated what I was planning to do and why it was important, and identified potential collaborators—both within the department and across the university as a whole.

I also had a one-on-one meeting with the chair, who outlined the department's expectations of faculty. "We expect that you'll publish at least two papers a year," he said. "You'll teach three courses a year and contribute to department and university committees." That sounded reasonable to me, though I didn't know how much time committees could suck up.

Finally, I met with the dean of the faculty. "What kind of resources do you need to get your research program off the ground?" he asked. No doubt he was weighing the cost of hiring me versus the other candidates, to see who might be a better deal. I was glad I'd done my pine beetle research, as it gave me a sense of the funding I'd require to kickstart a long-term research program.

As exhausting as it was, the day-long interview went okay and I thought I'd done well. Not well enough, I guess, because I didn't get the job. That was fine, though, as I'm not sure I would have survived in a big city like Burnaby. Nevertheless, the day did have a positive outcome: I became friends with the other two candidates. We had a lot in common given our hydrology backgrounds, and would later commiserate at conferences about our respective job experiences and dealing with difficult faculty members.

Just when I started to question whether or not I was marketable, I had a third shot at an academic job—this time at Trent University in southern Ontario. I solicited a lot of advice from Dan about interviewing for this position because I wanted to make the best impression possible. As with my experience at Simon Fraser University, I spent the day giving a research presentation, talking with individual faculty members and the dean, and talking with graduate students. They weren't interested in my skill set, however.

"This all seems pretty basic," the department chair said after my research presentation. "What techniques will you use that are new and unique?" I interpreted this to mean that my field-based research was too elementary for their liking, and they wanted to see me complement my field studies with more numerical modelling, remote sensing, or chemistry. Apparently I didn't do a good enough job of describing my modelling experience from my PhD work and pine beetle project. They ended up hiring a hydrochemist, someone who was much more lab-based. It sounded a bit too much like my summer in the clean lab running the ion chromatograph—that definitely wasn't for me.

✳ My research confidence was tested in the spring of 2006, when I was due to give a presentation at a meeting of the western division of the Canadian Association of Geographers in Kamloops. Not only would this be my first time talking about a research project that I'd seemingly conjured out of thin air, but Rita Winkler, a provincial government hydrologist, would be there. We would be presenting in the same session.

Rita was the only female researcher I was aware of who studied trees and snow, and the only other person who was studying the impacts of mountain pine beetle on snow. I was keen to meet her, but worried that—since she knew much more than I did—she'd spot the holes in my research, ones that I failed to catch thanks to my recent entry to the field. And, even though Rita worked in government, given my experience with academia, I assumed she'd be protective of her work and dismissive of mine.

The geography department at UNBC sent a busload of professors and students to the conference. I stepped off the bus and into a real city; Kamloops made Prince George seem like a backwater town. Restaurants and big-box stores lined the main strip, and art galleries and cafés were tucked into small spaces around the downtown core. Once I'd finished gawking at the sights, I settled into my hotel room and nervously checked over my presentation to make sure everything made sense and was well supported by my data.

When I arrived at my conference session the next day, I noticed a long-haired, slight woman about my height at the registration desk; her name tag identified her as Dr. Rita Winkler. This was my moment. I put out my hand and introduced myself. I needn't have worried about being "brought down" by Rita. She was kind and chatty, and asked about my research while talking very little about her own—something that many academics don't do because they have to make sure everyone knows what they're working on and how great they are at it. She presented her research on snow in forested versus clearcut stands, and I shared my work on snow processes in beetle-killed stands. We talked a bit after the session about my research learning curve, and about our scientific life histories. She was easy to talk to and I was glad we managed to meet up in person.

When I interviewed Rita for a Women in Science series I wrote several years later, I learned that she did her MSc in forest hydrology in 1980 but wasn't initially employed as a forest hydrologist. This was because, at the time, water wasn't considered an important factor in forest operations; the water supply was assumed to be limitless. She worked in ecological classification for the BC provincial government, but was laid off during the cutbacks of the 1980s, so she started work as a forestry and hydrology consultant. One of her quirkier projects involved shooting cones out of trees with a rifle to test their viability. In 1991, she joined the BC Forest Service as a research hydrologist. She returned to university part-time in 1994 to pursue a PhD in forest hydrology, which she completed in 2001.

Now retired, Rita was a field hydrologist through and through. Both of her graduate degrees were based on fieldwork, and her work with the BC government was also fieldwork-heavy. Some would argue that her research methods were dated and out of touch. However, she collaborated with other researchers who did numerical modelling and remote sensing, using her data as field-based verification of their outcomes. This was what I aimed to do in my research: collect field data then use it in numerical models to better understand larger-scale processes.

Rita did run into problems securing funding for her fieldwork, however, specifically since much of it relied on multi-year datasets. She noted that scientists (and funding agencies) needed to avoid "the cult of instant gratification," and instead champion long-term research projects that don't have an immediate payoff, but are important for understanding landscape-level processes. I fully agreed with this sentiment, having benefitted from collecting long-term data during my Arctic research.

Rita is an excellent example of a strong woman in science, in the same field to which I had transitioned: forest hydrology. She worked her way up the ranks to become the forest service's regional hydrologist for the BC Interior. Along with the challenges, Rita found some major rewards in her work, particularly the satisfaction she felt when her research changed an environmental management practice or policy for the better. She was open to new collaborations and worked with researchers from a range of backgrounds. She was also a good model of how to integrate my personal and professional lives: unlike an academic, she didn't take her work home with her. She was a fellow field scientist at a time when field research was considered a dated form of scientific exploration, less useful than more flashy science like remote sensing or hydrochemistry.

After that conference in Kamloops, Rita and I stayed in touch. In meeting her, I found a like-minded mentor who became a good friend—someone with whom I could share the trials and tribulations of academic life and science. We ended up collaborating for the next fifteen years, studying all manner of things relating to snow in beetle-killed versus healthy forests, and the effects of logging on snow-dominated streamflow.

✷ In December 2006, Dave and I travelled to Monarch, Alberta, forty-five minutes west of Lethbridge, to pick up Jasper, our new flat-coated retriever puppy. It was a grind of a drive from Prince George to southern Alberta, four days before Christmas. We took the Icefields Parkway and had to navigate through huge snowdrifts on the stretch near the Athabasca Glacier. On the way back, we stopped at Big Bend to let Jasper out to pee. He was a trooper and did his business in the cold at the side of the road, shivering in his sparse black coat.

Curiously enough, it turned out that Jasper's breeder was also a professor at the University of Lethbridge, where a tenure-track faculty position had just opened up in the geography department. I told him that I was thinking of applying for it, and asked his opinion about the university. His reply wasn't what I'd expected: he didn't have a lot of positive things to say. He was bitter about a number of administrative gaffes, and grumbled about faculty not being treated well in the university hierarchy. Morale was low and the university didn't support key initiatives as much as it could have. I should have paid more attention to his points, but was overwhelmed by the two-day drive from Prince George, the animated puppy wriggling in my arms, and a terrible head cold pressing on my sinuses. I applied for the job anyway, regardless of his warnings, as there weren't many available academic jobs in my field.

✷ By April 2006, I'd finished one pine beetle and snow project, but it only gave me a window into what was happening during a single winter season. I needed more years of data to really understand how snowfall and snowmelt worked in beetle-killed forests, and to determine the potential impacts on regional water supply. So, in the summer of 2006 I submitted a second grant proposal—this time to the federal government. I planned for a two-year project (winter 2006 to spring 2008). When added to my first project (winter 2005 to spring 2006), I would be able to find out if the results from that first study held true over three years with different weather. The project was successfully funded, so I set about finding my study sites.

I couldn't use my previous forest stands because the live stand had succumbed to pine beetle. I ended up selecting a research site farther out in the bush, near François Lake, 250 kilometres northeast of Prince George. Rita had played a part in this choice: she had connected me with another provincial government hydrologist who had a field site there. He had set up a grid of thirty-six measurement stakes in each of three forest stands. The stands included a clearcut, a young pine stand, and an older beetle-killed stand that was in the grey phase of infestation, rather than the red phase of my first study. He measured the snow water equivalent at each stake, and compared the data between stands to understand how beetle infestation and clearcut logging affected snow accumulation and melt. I collaborated with him by setting up my weather stations in his stands and taking my own snow measurements of each grid.

Dave and I stayed at a small, rustic cabin on François Lake during our weekend field visits—this project required two days of measurements instead of the single day we needed for my previous project. The cabin was almost on the lake itself, which was frozen solid and glimmered slightly in the weak winter sunlight. Jasper and Tsuga loved running on the lake, chasing each other and getting the heebies out of their systems before settling into the truck among a pile of research equipment to accompany us for the day.

We drove an hour on logging roads to get to the field sites. On the few weekdays we travelled there, logging trucks were running fully loaded on the narrow roads. It was a white-knuckled drive that had us radioing in our position at every call sign and using roadside pullouts to avoid oncoming vehicles. We watched for "sweepers"—long logs that hang off the back of trucks that could swing into the oncoming lane and sweep cars off the road. Thank goodness most of our work was done on the weekend, when traffic was minimal. Another plus: the logging roads were better maintained for winter conditions than the highway. It was beautiful, remote country. On one trip, three lynx padded beside the road on their broad, soft paws before turning and melting back into the forest they came from, leaving only a memory of the fur tufts at the tips of their ears and their haunting, yellowish eyes.

I used my simple weather stations from my previous forest-snow project in the forested stands, and bought a new, high-end weather station, like the ones from my PhD days, for the clearcut stand. Having been out of the loop for a few years, however, I didn't realize that not only had the scientific equipment company changed the data logger model, they'd also changed how it was programmed— and I'd have to learn how to do it from scratch. Of course, I'd left this step to the last minute as I'd been certain I could use the same programs I'd used at John Evans Glacier. That was a mistake. I was up late the night before we first went in the field, complaining bitterly as I taught myself how to program and wire the new data logger.

As with my simple weather stations, I'd use this new station to measure weather variables, and also to measure snow depth with an automated sensor. I installed a time-lapse camera that took two photos per day of the clearcut stand. This would show when fresh snowfalls occurred, and precisely date the timing of snowpack disappearance.

After setting up my weather stations, I started my snow measurements in December 2006. I went out at the beginning of each month until April 2007. As with the previous year's project, I dug a snow pit in each stand and measured snow crystals, temperature, and density. Then I measured snow depth at each stake in the grid and multiplied it by the density in the snow pit to get the snow water equivalent.

While I worked, the dogs had to sit quietly beside each stand's weather station so they wouldn't disturb the snowpack in the sample grid and mess up my measurements. Jasper was still young when we took him in the field, and got cold sitting in the snow. So I dressed him up in my puffy insulated jacket, the empty sleeves hanging down in front of him and the zipper done up to his neck. It worked, but he sure looked funny and a bit pathetic.

Measuring each stake was fine in the clearcut and dead stands, as it was easy to see the stakes laid out in even lines and make my way between them. In the live stand, however, the scene was like a giant game of pick-up sticks, with fallen trees lying across live trees and no clear sightline between grid points. I often got lost, not sure which way to walk to get to the next stake in the grid. I checked my GPS regularly to orient myself, fearful of getting turned around and missing a stake or measuring one twice.

Doing field research with my family was always a great experience. The dogs got to burn off energy by bounding through the deep snow to reach each stand, and Dave and I got to enjoy a weekend outdoors with a warm cabin to come back to, where we could relax and dry our gear. The cabin itself was pretty basic, with two single beds with thin foam mattresses, but it had a kitchenette in which to make a hearty dinner and a hot shower to warm us up from being in the field all day.

That winter, we also measured forest stand characteristics in much more detail than for my first pine beetle project. This was where Dave's field experience in forest science came into play. At four locations in each stand, he outlined a measurement circle using a stake from the snow survey grid as its centre. Within that circle, he measured a range of tree variables to figure out how the canopy interacted with snowfalls and affected snowmelt.

In the summer of 2007, I braved the mosquitoes and blackflies and went out to the stands to take upward-looking canopy photos at each weather station. Sporting a camouflage-green bug net ringed with hoops to keep the mesh off my face, I set up a camera tripod on the mossy ground, levelled it, and attached a digital camera with a fisheye lens. The insects might have stayed off my face, but they were voraciously biting at my hands. When not busy shaking my hands to get the bugs off, I tipped the camera back so that the lens was pointed straight into the sky, put a level on it to make sure it was parallel to the ground, and then shot a few pictures. I did this at every weather station to capture what the forest canopy looked like over each one. Back on campus, I fed the photos into a computer program to calculate what percentage of the sky was covered in canopy. As expected, the live stand had the highest canopy cover, the dead stand intermediate cover, and the clearcut stand no cover at all. I used the canopy photos to help understand snow processes and to model melt in each stand, using the energy balance model I used in my first pine beetle study.

✳ My research results for my two-year project (winter 2006 to spring 2008) were more interesting than those in my initial study (winter 2005 to spring 2006). The dead stand was a bit of a chameleon—in one year it behaved more like the live stand and in the next it behaved more like the clearcut. Weather was a major driver of these differences—particularly the size and timing of snowfalls. In the first year, heavy snowfalls overwhelmed the ability of the forested stands to intercept snow, so the snow fell off the branches and needles and accumulated on the ground. This meant that the snowpack in the two forested stands was very similar. The next year, however, more light snowfalls occurred that were intercepted better by the live than the dead forest. This caused bigger differences in snowpack between the two stands: the dead stand had more snow on the ground than the live stand.

My research had tangible answers for an important forest management question—namely, do dead stands behave the same as clearcuts? The provincial government argued that, if they did behave the same, there would be no reason not to harvest the timber from the dead stands. But my data showed that dead stands were a different entity than both live and clearcut stands, and logging them could have serious impacts on snowmelt runoff.

Before salvage logging, snowmelt happened in fits and starts across north-central British Columbia. This was because there was a patchwork of forest stands—healthy, dead, logged—that melted at different times. By adding more salvage-harvested clearcuts, however, snowmelt could become synchronized across all the logged stands, with all the snow from the clearcuts melting at once. And, because clearcuts accumulate more snow, and this snow generally melts faster than in dead stands, spring snowmelt could happen earlier and at higher volumes. This could cause downstream flooding and subsequent ecosystem and property damage. While salvage logging might have been a good idea from the economic side of things, it wasn't a great idea from the hydrology side.

What was frustrating was that, even though I and other researchers knew that dead stands affected snowmelt differently than clearcuts, salvage logging continued to be approved by the government. One of the arguments to support the practice was that beetle-killed forests were a wildfire hazard—and it was certainly true that some wildfires burned more rapidly in dead stands. However, the research was conflicting, with some studies saying that beetle-kill didn't affect forest flammability. It seemed to depend on the stage of infestation. Cities like Prince George weren't taking any chances, though. They took things one step further and required that all homeowners remove beetle-killed trees from their property. We lived on a third of an acre, and took down more than twenty trees in our backyard. There were still trees standing, but we were heartbroken to see so many cut and piled on the ground.

* My assistant professorship at UNBC ended in December 2006, but I remained an adjunct professor and did my pine beetle research under the university's umbrella. I also continued looking for academic jobs, feeling that I wasn't qualified for anything other than being a professor. Even though my writing for VECO was going well, I still didn't consider writing a viable alternative to an academic career.

In February 2007 I interviewed for a job as an ecologist with Parks Canada. While it wasn't an academic job, I'd always dreamed of working in the Rocky Mountain parks, and this sounded like a great opportunity to do so. I flew down to Vancouver for the interview, which started with me giving a presentation on a topic they had provided beforehand. I had to discuss how I would develop a research program to monitor the effects of wolf reintroduction in a national park. I also wrote an exam that covered basic ecology and scientific techniques, and did a formal in-person interview with three men from Parks Canada. I was exhausted when it was over, and wasn't sure how well I had done on the written test. They sent me on my way with a promise to get back to me, and a warning from the administrative-assistant-in-tow that "government hiring can take a long time." After dealing with the stress of the presentation, exam, and talking to strangers about how well-suited I was for the position—all of which took place within a three-hour period—I fled to a nearby coffee shop for a chai and biscotti to calm myself down. It seemed highly unlikely that I'd be hired, particularly because my scientific background only recently focused on forest ecology, and I had no experience with wildlife ecology.

In March I interviewed for the geography faculty position at the University of Lethbridge, where I spent two days performing the usual academic song and dance: giving a research lecture and a guest teaching lecture, meeting with faculty and with the dean, meeting with graduate students. A new twist on the interview process was the breakfast meeting. Both mornings of my stay, a faculty member came to my hotel for breakfast, then we drove to the university together. The faculty member who picked me up the second day wouldn't stop talking about how terrible the university was, how hard it was to get a federal research grant at such a small institution, and the problems with graduate student education.

* I didn't twiddle my thumbs waiting to hear back from the University of Lethbridge and Parks Canada. Instead, I accompanied a group of UNBC undergraduates and two other faculty members on a field school trip to South Africa in late April 2007, just after my last pine-beetle site visit for the season. It was great to be part of a field program again—one I also learned from because it included social science field techniques. Students would not only sightsee, but they would also do research projects in both human and physical geography to better understand the country and its people. I supervised one student's project in fluvial geomorphology, for which she studied river channel size and shape in the Injisuthi Valley of the Drakensberg Mountains. I loved working on this project: it allowed me to share my passion for fieldwork with a keen student, and it fed my affinity for rivers and the stories they told as they rushed over rocks and pulled at their banks.

We travelled through poor towns where funerals took place daily for those taken by the AIDS epidemic, and through gorgeous Tolkien-like landscapes. When visiting wine country, we noted the huge wealth disparity between the wine growers and the people in the outlying towns. We enjoyed many barbeques (*braai*s in Afrikaans)—in fact, I gave up ten years of vegetarianism on that trip as vegetables were few and far between.

One of the best parts of the trip was when we hiked fourteen kilometres round-trip to visit rock walls covered with Indigenous art in the Drakensberg Mountains. The art, some of it centuries old, was amazingly detailed and realistic, with 3-D effects created using complex shading techniques. Despite being besieged by a long-lasting cold that shrank my lung capacity and kept me coughing and hacking late into the night, on the way to see the art I rediscovered the joy of leaping from rock to rock to cross a stream, and the satisfaction of finding my footing on a rubbly mountain trail—I was strong and competent. I hadn't been doing enough challenging hikes in the blur of teaching, research, and writing, something that should have alerted me to the limitations of being an academic.

The other amazing part of the trip was the visit to the game park of Mkhuze, where we stayed in safari tents built on wooden platforms. One evening we went on a wildlife ride and startled an elephant with a large clump of greenery in its mouth. In the middle of the night my tent-mate and I were awoken by a hyena drinking from our dripping water tap. The next day we all sat in a hide next to a watering hole as warthogs, wildebeests, nyala, impala, and daika wandered by, and watched with quiet whispers as they peacefully shared the water.

That same day we went to a local lake harbouring three hippopotamuses. This wildlife-viewing opportunity became even more exciting when one of them heaved itself out of the water and ran at three of us who had separated from the main group. "Run the other way!" yelled one of the other professors. But when we ran in that direction the hippo did, too, so we had to run back, all the while keeping an eye on the two other hippos who were slowly moving towards the lakeshore. Only after we got back into the van did we realize how lucky we were to have escaped major harm, as hippos can run up to thirty kilometres per hour. On the way back to our tents several giraffes appeared next to the road—so stunning in person, drifting gracefully across the grasslands with their long necks and relatively small heads.

We also visited the Sterkfontein Caves, part of the region known as the Cradle of Humankind. It was fascinating to see the early hominid remains that had been found at the site, and to get a sense of how long our human lineage is, how long people have been on the planet, and how they travelled across it. I've never been good in confined spaces, so was worried I'd get claustrophobic in the cave system. But it was high and wide enough that I didn't have to worry about not being able to get out if I needed to.

Going to South Africa wasn't just a once-in-a-lifetime trip, it also brought me two new mentors on the academic path. Both of the UNBC professors who had directed the trip gave me all sorts of advice on being an academic. Their most compelling suggestion was to think more about what kind of person I want to be than how to be a great researcher: people often have a stronger memory of and connection to a person rather than that person's research. Too many academics ignore this piece of wisdom, wanting to be remembered for their prolific and groundbreaking work. They also suggested I keep a long-term research vision in mind when working on projects, so I could make informed decisions about the suitability of new project opportunities in the larger context. And that I write rough drafts of several papers over the summer that I could edit and revise during the teaching term, when time for new writing was limited.

Their biggest piece of advice, though, was to scrap the science writing and focus on research papers, because publishing those would be critical for moving my career forward. I knew they were right, but I had a tough time with this suggestion. Science writing kept me somewhat sane amid the constant drive to excel in academia. It fed my writer's soul. Though I may not have agreed with them, it was still helpful to feel supported and mentored by colleagues who were genuinely interested in seeing me succeed—something I would miss in the future.

✷ I returned from South Africa to find an email from the University of Lethbridge offering me the job. A wave of relief washed over me because there were no other academic jobs on the horizon. It was Lethbridge or nothing. Though excited about the prospect of starting a new chapter in my academic life, I still held out hope for a Parks Canada position. When I contacted them, however, they said that I'd passed the interview but they were in the process of deciding to which park to assign each successful applicant, and wouldn't have that information for another month. I didn't have that kind of time to wait: the Lethbridge job offer came in May, and I'd have to start in early July. So, I declined to be considered for the Parks position—a decision I sometimes regret.

Even though I'd heard some negative comments about the university, accepting the job at Lethbridge was the right thing to do given the dearth of faculty positions in Canada. As an academic "on the market," you are expected to take a chance on any tenure-track job. Still, I didn't consider all the factors I should have, like the culture on campus, whether I would get along with my colleagues, and what the workload would be like for both teaching and research.

I had based my knowledge of what the job would entail on my UNBC experience—which didn't make sense because my temporary position there was more like a postdoctoral fellowship than a tenure-track faculty position. I'd had almost none of the administrative responsibilities of a faculty member, such as sitting on student thesis committees, department curriculum committees, or university-level governance committees. I had worked on one research project at a time, whereas most professors work on several at once. I had supervised one undergraduate student, and only for four months, instead of multiple graduate students over several years. And I had been teaching in fields I was familiar with, which doesn't always happen in a faculty position.

When weighing the pros and cons of potentially living in Lethbridge, I also didn't consider possible differences in community mentality between northern British Columbia and southern Alberta. I imagined that life in Lethbridge would be much like life in Prince George—a combination of teaching, research with my family, and writing on the side while enjoying the outdoors with Dave and the dogs. I focused on the positives: Lethbridge was a relatively small city, similar to Prince George, which made it more attractive than large urban centres. Plus it was closer to the Rockies—only a two-hour drive—which was a huge bonus.

How different would life have been if I hadn't become an academic? What if I had heeded the warnings from Jasper's breeder and other Lethbridge faculty and decided not to accept the offer? I wrote to VECO to tell them I had to bow out of my writing job because I was starting a new position that would take up most of my time, especially for the first year.

Little did I know that I wasn't just bowing out of a writing job, I was potentially abandoning a writing life altogether.

9

WOMEN IN SCIENCE

BELONGING TO ANY KIND OF MARGINALIZED GROUP can be difficult, and being a woman in science is no exception. According to the Council of Canadian Academies,[1] women tend to occupy fewer high-ranking academic science positions than men, and their numbers steadily decrease as rank increases. While many people suggest that this is a "leaky pipeline," with women dropping out of academic science as they reach higher career stages, the reality is much more insidious. Women are making it to the faculty level, but they're coming up against long-standing issues that centre on a lack of diversity, equity, and inclusivity. It's not necessarily a glass ceiling, but some have characterized it as a glass obstacle course, where women are tripped up by interactions with others in their lab or department. The glass ceiling represents a hierarchical level beyond which women often face difficulty progressing, while the glass obstacle course is made up of barriers that are not "static, one-time experiences that can be permanently conquered...they may appear with little warning or reappear even after being overcome once."[2]

(Top) Mount Coulthard, as seen from the burned forest stand in the southern Rocky Mountains, Alberta, January 2008. (Photo by the author.) (Bottom) A graduate student (right) and I take a quick break from searching for research sites to instrument, Crowsnest Pass, Alberta, September 2008. (Photo by S. Euler, deceased)

Researchers have written about how female faculty are treated as less than equal:[3] they receive less pay than their male counterparts, their ideas and opinions are less valued, they get less respect from students, they are less successful at obtaining research funding, and they have less time to do research because they are often expected to take on more service duties. Despite my research field being male-dominated, I'd had largely positive experiences throughout my career thus far. I assumed that, by 2007, people were generally more cognizant of the challenges faced by women in science and were working to rectify them. That assumption would change now that I was at the faculty level.

✲ I arrived on the University of Lethbridge campus in the second week of July, though my official start date was July 1. "You're here," said the department chair. "We were wondering when you'd show up."

It wasn't the most auspicious of beginnings. I had been hired at the same time as Keith, another new faculty member; he'd moved to Lethbridge from only two hours away, and had been on campus for a few weeks already, making a good impression. I explained about the short notice for moving the fourteen hours from Prince George, given the late timing of my final contract with the university, but I'm not sure it made any difference.

There was another reason for my delayed arrival: I had been at a workshop in Kelowna about the mountain pine beetle in western Canada. There I met a researcher from the University of Alberta who was interested in my work. He directed an extensive research project studying post-wildfire hydrology in the southern Rockies, just two hours west of Lethbridge. He was looking for someone to join the project to study snow hydrology. This sounded perfect for my skill set, so I agreed to come on board. I thought it would be a smart way to launch my career at the University of Lethbridge.

At my new job, though, it soon became clear that I'd stepped into an academic minefield. Every new tidbit I gleaned from my colleagues made me realize that I was far from a straightforward hire. The human and physical geographers had each wanted my position for themselves, so the former were understandably upset that it had gone to physical geography. The previous person in the position had quit, having been told she'd never get tenure. On top of that, several faculty let me know that I was the third-choice candidate for the job (out of three), so I didn't exactly feel welcomed by my new department.

Not only was my appointment contentious, the department was plagued by political problems that slowly revealed themselves during that first term. The department chair had very reluctantly taken on his position and was quite bitter about it. In a thirteen-person department there were only two other women, one of whom taught more courses than the other faculty just to keep her sub-program going. I was a long way from the friendly and accommodating department at the University of Northern British Columbia, where we sometimes went for coffee together and held potlucks where even warring faculty put aside their differences for an evening. I was navigating without a compass through a maze of past injustices and office politics, unable to see whose toes I was likely stepping on.

I made myself at home in my office at University Hall, a building designed in the late 1960s by architect Arthur Erickson, who had also designed the Simon Fraser University campus in Burnaby. Local folklore had it that the latter's concrete, bunker-like structure had once led to the highest university suicide rate in the country. Whether this was true or not is another story. Lethbridge's University Hall is also bunker-like, but it's strikingly offset by the undulating landscape of the river valley coulees, and nestled in among their curves. Apparently Erickson was inspired by the nearby train trestle, the High Level Bridge, which crosses the Oldman River valley and is the largest railway structure in Canada.

My office door opened into a busy hallway that, at 240 metres long, had the dubious distinction of being the second-longest hallway in North America, after a slightly longer hallway at MIT. It was loud and raucous during course changes, with students pouring out of adjacent classrooms on their way to their next class.

Thanks to Arthur Erickson's architecture, my office window framed a beautiful view of the coulees, those gently rolling hills in the river valley that almost made up for the otherwise flat landscape around Lethbridge itself. Deer and coyote passed by regularly, and tall grasses waved in the chinook winds that howled frequently from the mountains to the west—winds that drove sub-zero winter temperatures up into the double digits within hours.

Dave and I had made a rookie mistake in buying a house on the west side of town, within walking distance of the university. We bore the brunt of those chinook winds, while my colleagues who lived close to the city centre hardly noticed them at all. On particularly bad days, the wind whistled eastward across the grasslands and through a field behind our house, rushing into our backyard and wailing over top of the chimney. In winter it created huge drifts in the driveway, so much so that part of the concrete would be completely snow-free while the rest was obscured by a wall of white. Sometimes I found it difficult to inhale because the wind pushed so hard against my chest and mouth. One of my undergraduate students warned me that I'd soon grow tired of it. "I'm glad I'm only here for four years," he said. "I can't wait to leave the wind behind." Another student of mine arrived on campus for his first day, got out of his car, and was hit by a pebble flung at him by the wind. "I wondered what I was getting into," he said, wryly.

We figured the wind was a small price to pay for being close to the Rocky Mountains again. It was only a two-hour drive from Lethbridge to Waterton Lakes National Park, where the mountains rose up out of the plains at the last turn in the road, with no foothills to soften their arrival. We went every weekend we could, taking the dogs swimming in Waterton Lake, and visiting the ochre vistas of Red Rock Canyon. We also walked partway around Cameron Lake once, before deciding it was likely grizzly territory and we should probably head back to the parking lot. We snowshoed with the dogs in winter and hung out at our favourite place along Cameron Creek in summer, just up the road from the hamlet of Waterton itself. It was worth it to drive out there as often as possible, to soak up the mountain air and enjoy time together as a family.

✲ I was assigned a mishmash of courses to teach, none of which were in my field of hydrology and cold regions science, but my colleagues were kind enough to share their resources. One of the other women in the department, Heather, loaned me her lecture notes and coursepack for my fieldwork class—at least I was comfortable teaching that course, thanks to my background in the topic. A colleague from the University of British Columbia loaned me lecture notes for my resource management class, which I had no idea how to teach. I also taught a large introductory environmental science course. It was similar to a course I'd taught at UNBC, but tougher because students in this class were from a range of disciplines and many of them thought it would just be an easy science credit.

Meanwhile, Keith—the other new faculty member—was given three courses, all within his research specialty. Since I wasn't working in mine, it took me longer to prepare my classes, and I had to work twice as hard as he did just to get to the same place. I was starting to see how the glass obstacle course worked.

Just before fall classes began, the department chair called me and two other faculty members into his office. He wanted us to decide, at the last minute, who would teach a course in soils. Unsurprisingly, Keith was not present. I was extremely uncomfortable being put on the spot like that, especially since I had absolutely zero experience in soils. Usually new faculty are given a breaking-in period, which includes a reduced course load in the first year to allow them to get up to speed on teaching and get their research program going. I couldn't afford to be subsumed under more new course preparation; I was swamped enough already. So I refused to take it on, risking alienating the other two faculty members in the room and turning the chair against me. I suspected my refusal was seen as an affront to the department. Was my "strong will," as Martin had outlined in one of his reference letters about me, a liability in this position? Was it my fault that things seemed to be going off the rails? Or was it to do with the university's academic culture? I had a sneaking suspicion that it had less to do with me than it did with the institution.

To make matters worse, the Dean's Office asked me to hold off on applying for a federal grant that all academic scientists apply for—the Natural Sciences and Engineering Research Council (NSERC) Discovery Grant. This grant covers up to five years of research and is designed to kickstart and maintain a research program from the beginning of an academic career. Receiving a Discovery Grant is a sign of your credibility as a researcher: if you have one, you're automatically part of "the club." The rationale for asking me to put off my application was that Keith would have too much competition. At the time I agreed, mainly because I didn't think I'd be able to pull together a research proposal in the short time I had before the September deadline. I also didn't want to rock the boat, and figured that an extra year to complete my research proposal would be beneficial.

I came to regret that decision when I applied the following year. By that time, NSERC had completely revamped their evaluation system, and my application was unsuccessful. In fact, it took me four attempts before I was finally funded. Even seasoned researchers in my field were worried about their chances of success with the new Discovery Grant system, especially because we were at a small university, and that put us at a disadvantage. We had higher teaching loads and thus fewer graduate students.

Not having a Discovery Grant also worked against me when it came to joining collaborative projects; one professor asked me to step back from a program that I was part of—he said my lack of a Discovery Grant reflected badly on the research team. Stunned and furious, I couldn't believe I was watching my research opportunities dwindle just because I had agreed not to submit an application at the same time as Keith.

That wasn't the only time I was asked to step aside for Keith. A year later, the Dean's Office asked me not to apply for a provincial government grant for new researchers, again to reduce Keith's competition. By the time I applied the following year, the program's funding had been slashed and I was unsuccessful. The granting committee told me that, had their funding stayed at the previous year's levels, my grant application would have been approved.

I was incensed that, thanks to the university's machinations on Keith's behalf, I was always in the wrong place at the wrong time, striking out on major research funding opportunities simply because the funding climate had changed. I failed to build the stepping stones I needed to forge my path as an academic—without a Discovery Grant or funding from the province, I had to find other sources of research support. These were mainly smaller, short-term grants from funding agencies that requested annual reporting, which meant that I was always either writing a new grant application or putting together an annual report. I had to run around the block twice just to keep up with Keith, who was confidently striding down the middle of the straight path the university had smoothed for him. It wasn't his fault, but it sure didn't make things easier for me.

One good thing was that the university had decided to invest in water-related research, and had recently opened the Alberta Water and Environmental Science Building. I was given a new office in that building, along with the rest of the physical geographers and a group of biologists. It was much quieter than my old office; no students boisterously passing by in the hallway at every class change. I was also able to buy a lot of field equipment for my research program, courtesy of a large grant the university had acquired for faculty in the new building. The first purchase I made was a snowmobile. This generated bemused interest from the Dean's Office. "Did you submit a purchase request for a snowmobile?" the dean's administrative assistant asked. "Yes," I replied. "Is there a problem?" "No, we just had to confirm that this is for your research," she said. No one had purchased something like that before. Research vehicles, yes. Snowmobiles, no.

I also used the start-up funds I'd negotiated from the university to pay for conferences, where I networked with colleagues from different universities and government labs and shared the research

I was working on. I found community at these meetings, with people who respected me and my work. This respect was completely opposite to the atmosphere in my department, where I suspected my colleagues considered me an uppity junior faculty member who wasn't following the unwritten rules of the academic hierarchy. At one of our departmental meetings an older faculty member had even called me "kiddo." I had to bite my tongue not to reply "old fart."

The biggest problem I had, though, was with lab space, which the dean had promised in my initial contract. Most faculty had a space where they did work that wasn't office-based. My requirements were relatively simple: I needed a sink to test hydrologic sensors and to clean equipment, counters with computer stations for students and space for assembling and testing equipment, and lots of cabinets to organize and store field gear. I also needed windows to test my radiation sensors. Unlike other colleagues, I didn't need a fume hood, or a place to store dangerous chemicals, or a room full of aquariums in which to raise fish.

At first, the Dean's Office gave me a small room in the basement of the physical education building, a twenty-minute walk from my University Hall office. The elevator didn't work, so we had to carry equipment up and down stairs. The room had small windows near the ceiling, 1960s-era yellow cinderblock walls, and flickering fluorescent-tube lights. There were no cabinets, so everything was piled willy-nilly on the room's black resin countertops.

Once I moved into the new building, I was eventually allocated a small meeting room with one wall lined with shelves; tables and chairs took up the rest of the floor space. My equipment pretty much filled the shelves and I had difficulty finding some of it, having expertly packed it away to make the most of these cramped quarters. The limited space meant that my students and I had to set up and test equipment (like weather stations, for example) in the hallway before taking it out in the field. It's a good thing the halls were wide and sparsely populated! The one saving grace was that my so-called lab space was across from my office, so I could easily pop in and grab whatever I needed—once I found it, that is.

Keith, on the other hand, had been given a lab space as soon as we moved to the new building, complete with desks for his students and a separate area for storing gear. The argument was that he'd accepted an interior lab space without windows, while I had requested an exterior space with windows. The design and construction of his lab had been completed before mine, but there was no real reason it should have been. In fact, other lab spaces had been built on either side of mine; addressing my requirements just hadn't been a university priority.

Had I taken a wrong turn into academia? Everything I did was an uphill battle. Funding, teaching, and lab space issues took up a lot of time and effort over my first few years, and I did absolutely no creative writing anymore. Meanwhile, Keith's career was progressing nicely, with funding from major granting agencies, courses in his research specialty, and a well-appointed lab space to work out of.

✳ The year I started at Lethbridge, the university had introduced a trial mentorship program for new faculty. I signed up for it right away, and asked to be linked with a female faculty member in the sciences, but not in my department. That's how I met Sherry. She had been at the university for close to twenty years and had a lot to say about women in science, backed by her own experiences. She had been talked over in meetings and harassed by other faculty. In fact, it was so bad in her department that, in the second year of our friendship, she left to join another department that was more supportive of her teaching and scholarship.

We met for lunch regularly and talked about the struggles of being an academic and balancing work and home life. We commiserated about bullying by male colleagues and being asked to "get along" with other faculty members when there was no suggestion that they try to get along with us. Sherry had dogs, too, so we met up almost every weekend to walk the coulees behind her property, where we made our way down to the Oldman River and let the dogs swim before the long climb back up to her house. In winter we walked between snowdrifts left by the relentless wind, and were extra careful around the river because of the tricky ice cover, not wanting one of the dogs to step onto the ice and fall in.

Dave was doing some tree-ring contracts during this time, but mostly he was a house husband so that I could focus on my career. While we had made a few friends on-campus, having dogs admitted us to a community of dog trainers and owners that provided a welcome break from academia. We took our dogs to doggie daycare once a week and got to know the proprietor and her employees. Jasper's breeders lived west of Lethbridge, on a large acreage on the river, and we often got together in summer to do field training in preparation for hunt tests and hunting itself. Despite the glass obstacle course of academic life, there were some benefits that came with living in Lethbridge.

* Aside from dealing with issues on campus, I was busy getting the lay of the land of the Southern Rockies Watershed Project (SRWP), which I had joined at the pine beetle workshop I attended in July 2007. In 2003, one of the worst wildfire years on record in western Canada at the time, the Lost Creek wildfire had raged through the Crowsnest Pass in the southern Rocky Mountains. This was a major disaster, not just for residents of the region, but for downstream water supplies. Water from the eastern slopes of the Rockies flows east and is parsed into residential, agricultural, and industrial use. Cities like Lethbridge rely on this water because they're in a semi-arid region: they can't count on summer rainfall for their water supply.

After the fire, Dr. Uldis Silins from the University of Alberta set up a network of monitoring stations in seven local watersheds: three burned, two unburned, and two burned then salvage logged. He had weather stations and stream stations in each watershed, and did additional sampling of fish, algae, invertebrates, water quality, and more. He measured the impact of both wildfire and salvage logging on stream sediments, post-wildfire vegetation recovery, and precipitation. To do this, he had a full-time field crew working for him: one crew boss and three crew members. They did all of the field-based research in the catchments, and were responsible for the day-to-day maintenance of the research infrastructure.

This was a very different setup than I was used to. I had always done solo research, usually just with Dave's help. It started with my Hilda Glacier work and continued to my PhD, where I had to prepare for the field season and design my field program largely on my own. While I did have the help of my supervisor, Martin, for my first summer field season, my fellow students and I served as one another's field assistants in later years, which made it difficult for everyone to get their own research done. At UNBC, I had set up two pine beetle and snow projects by myself—the second involved collaboration with another forest scientist, but we mainly compared measurements and talked about differences we observed in the forest stands we were both monitoring. I had never worked on a field project at such a large watershed scale. Though I had modelled large watersheds, I hadn't instrumented them.

In the fall of 2007 I went on a tour of the SRWP research installations that had been organized for research funders and the government. It was my first glimpse into the field aspects of such a large project and I was duly impressed. A bunkhouse with a large garage served as the project's field base. Next door to a graveyard, the bunkhouse was an old mining-company house with four bedrooms, a bathroom, and a small galley-kitchen-and-living-room combination. It was perfect for the field crew, especially when they were in full summer mode. A task board in the garage outlined what needed doing and when, and what problems needed to be solved. A squadron of ATVs stood by, ready to transport people to the field sites.

The SRWP field crew worked like a well-oiled machine. They had organized a large part of this field trip, and were cool, calm, and collected about shepherding a group of bureaucrats and me through the mountainous terrain by ATV, making sure everyone was safe and able to see what they needed to see. I felt out of place among the bigwigs on the tour, and was easily drawn into the banter of the field team and their obvious camaraderie. I belonged more with them, the ones doing the fieldwork, rather than with the principal investigators who largely directed the fieldwork and maybe did a little bit of it themselves when they had time. It reminded me that I'd once believed I would prefer to be a field technician or a research assistant, not an academic once-removed from the field.

We visited field installations that measured streamflow and other stream variables, and others that measured weather variables. When I saw a burned forest for the first time, I was struck by how oddly beautiful it was. I had expected the acrid scent of ash and charred wood but, four years after the fire, the air was fresh and crisp and the trees had been polished to a silvery hue by wind, rain, and snow. Bright pink fireweed grew knee high and mingled with the tender green of pine seedlings. The fire had burned into the soil layer, leaving many dead trees perched in the air, the ground surface now half a metre below their exposed roots. Some of the burned trees also had relict pine beetle galleries: wiggly lines between the bark and the tree itself where beetle larvae had eaten their way out of the tree.

The scene had a certain bleak majesty, a lingering reminder of the perilous Lost Creek wildfire. Facing northwest on the road that traversed one of the watersheds, I saw nothing but hills of standing dead trees rolling off into the horizon. Burned trees had fallen across creeks, which were babbling their way past collapsing stream banks. We trundled our way by ATV up into the alpine area of one of the catchments, checking out a 1946 plane wreck along the way. The alpine bowl was home to a remnant snow patch, which contributed to streamflow throughout the summer season without disappearing completely—evidence of the complexity of the hydrologic system in these watersheds.

This project was already big, and Uldis was making it even bigger. He was collaborating with researchers from the University of Waterloo to test downstream drinking water quality, and to measure the downstream transport of contaminants. These contaminants stuck to sediments that were transported in the rivers draining both the burned and salvage-logged watersheds. My short visit to the field sites hardly scratched the surface—there was just too much to see in one day. I was joining a juggernaut of a research program and would contribute a small part to what was a monumental endeavour. It was fortuitous that my pine beetle research had allowed me entry into this established project; I was keen to get started on snow fieldwork in the burned stands.

✻ Before I could commit to the SRWP, however, I had to finish the last year of my pine beetle project. Dave and I and the dogs drove the fourteen hours from Lethbridge to the field site at François Lake in December 2007. We stayed at the same rustic cabin we had previously, and let the dogs run on the lake ice to stretch their legs. At the three forest stands we made sure the equipment was working as it should; we took snow measurements and downloaded the weather station data. It was good to be back in the forested terrain of central British Columbia, a welcome change from the flat, dry grassland around Lethbridge.

Throughout the winter term, while I was stuck in Lethbridge teaching, Dave filled in for me. He flew back to Prince George at the beginning of January, February, and March 2008 to take the snow measurements and check the weather stations. He took our former next-door-neighbour from Prince George into the field with him as an assistant and for safety reasons. I was glad to have such a dedicated partner who knew everything about the project. However, it bothered me that I wasn't able to collect those final field measurements myself: I had started the project and wanted to see it through to the end. As with my Hilda Glacier project and my first field season at John Evans Glacier, I was forced to transfer responsibility for my work to others, and wasn't able to make crucial first-hand observations. Is this what life as an academic was like? Not doing your own fieldwork because you're bogged down in teaching and administrivia? That wasn't what I'd signed on for.

Even though I couldn't go in the field as often as I'd like, things weren't all bad. I travelled to Prince George again in late March 2008, and chartered a chopper to take me out to François Lake to do a forest survey; I wanted to make sure the stands I was working in were representative of the larger landscape. My survey showed that they were, so I was confident that my results could be scaled up to address watershed-scale snow processes. I later collaborated with a colleague from the University of British Columbia who used my field data to calibrate his model to calculate runoff from watersheds with beetle-killed stands. I also collaborated with a departmental colleague who used my tree measurements to successfully test a remote-sensing technique to gather the same tree metrics from satellite imagery. It was the best of both worlds: I did the fieldwork I enjoyed, while my results were used more broadly to show what was happening at the watershed scale. I was proud to be part of a growing community of researchers who shared field data and modelling results to get a handle on the pine beetle epidemic at various landscape scales.

✳ During the busy winter term, I was also preparing for a return to Arctic research—in July 2008 I'd be heading to Belcher Glacier, an outlet glacier of the Devon Island Ice Cap. The ice cap is on the east side of Devon Island, which sits in the northwest part of Baffin Bay and is about four hundred kilometres south of JEG. Belcher Glacier is different from JEG, not only because it's bigger and part of a large ice cap, but because it's a tidewater glacier, which means it terminates in the ocean instead of on land.

Planning for this 2007–2008 International Polar Year (IPY) project had begun when I was still at UNBC. There have been four IPYs since the 1800s: the first was in 1882–1883, the second in 1932–1933, and the third in 1957–1958. The 2007–2008 IPY would involve an international program of over fifty thousand researchers focused on intensive study of the polar regions. Ours was one of a suite of projects that were studying glaciers across the North.

I would be working with my former PhD supervisor, Martin, and a team of researchers to measure melt, runoff, and calving from Belcher Glacier, and then use that data to model the effects on glacier flow. Though this was a multi-component, multi-person project, it wasn't nearly as sprawling as the SRWP. It was focused on a single goal: to model the flow of the glacier and determine its possible response to climate change. Each team member had a distinct and equal role to play in providing data for the modelling effort, and there was no danger of stepping on one another's research toes. I would be in the field with a graduate student from the University of Alberta whom I was co-supervising with Martin, and whom I had yet to meet in person. We would be a two-person field team, as Martin wouldn't be out on the glacier that summer.

As I wrapped up my final report for the federal pine beetle project, I emailed back and forth with Martin and our team about Arctic field logistics. It was a strange juxtaposition of research worlds, from forests to glaciers. I was happy to be working with Martin again as a fellow scientist rather than as a student—we had a good working relationship that helped move our project along. But it had been six long years since I'd last done Arctic fieldwork and things had changed significantly. Now flight logistics and daily check-ins were done by satellite phone, and students brought digital music and movies to keep themselves entertained. Gone were the two-way radio, the Discman, the card games, and just shooting the breeze while waiting out a storm in the igloo. My Arctic experience was a relic from another era.

I flew up to Resolute in the third week of June 2008, feeling a bit distracted and underprepared for the upcoming five-week Arctic field season. For one thing, I couldn't stop thinking about the work I had left behind and how much would pile up while I was gone. I wondered if that's why Martin behaved so strangely during our 2002 Arctic field season: perhaps he was swamped by university work and couldn't really afford the time away.

In the weeks leading up to this trip, I had briefly brushed up on my crevasse rescue skills with my colleague Heather, who also studied glaciers, and I made sure to take a first aid course to keep my certification up to date, even though it wasn't a wilderness first aid course. I hadn't practised my shooting skills, but I still had a firearms licence. And I still had all of my Arctic field gear: windproof jacket, down jacket, down booties, plastic boots, down sleeping bag, and more. I was the critical second person in camp for occupational health and safety reasons, and would mainly provide guidance to my co-supervised student as he carried out his on-ice research. He was studying glacier hydrology in much the same way I had on JEG.

I travelled north with another one of Martin's students. She was going to the upper camp on the glacier while I was going to the lower one; our camp-mates had already been in the field for several weeks. What would be different for me is that we were camping directly on the glacier for the entire season, from spring to the end of summer. We'd have to deal with snow and ice melting around our sleeping tents and the mess tent. This meant we'd have to shift the tents regularly, or they'd end up on an ice platform that melted more slowly than the surrounding ice. I worried about how wet my tent would get, or if it had enough waterproofing on the bottom to stay somewhat dry.

We left Resolute for Belcher Glacier two days after arriving, sandwiched in a Twin Otter between two drums of jet fuel and five hundred kilograms of gear. We were switching places with two researchers who were scheduled to head back to civilization; it required some complicated manoeuvring to get everyone and their gear either to the correct camp or back to the base. The Twin Otter flew us to Dundas Harbour on Devon Island, where we unloaded the jet fuel and reloaded four empty drums. It was an iffy landing; the pilots flew over the airstrip three times before setting down. The chopper was already there and ferried us to our respective camps. As the thrum of the departing chopper faded, I stood on the ice among a pile of gear and fresh food for the camp, smiling at the scruffy-bearded student who was staring at me. "Hi Derek," I said. "Nice to finally meet you."

Derek gave me a guided tour of camp: the sleeping tents; the mess tent (a red, yellow, and blue Slinky-like structure with a side entrance); the toilet tent; and the equipment pile. The day was bright and sunny, and the snowpack had just about hit that awful soft phase, with a few surface lakes starting to form. Our camp was set up near a medial moraine, which forms when two glaciers join up and push debris along the seam between them. This moraine was relatively wide, made up of small pebbles and gravel, with metre-long rocks scattered on top like the footsteps of a travelling giant. The moraine made for a good landmark when we were out on the vast ice and all we could see was white in every direction.

We spent the next few days visiting Derek's field sites; he showed me what he'd set up and what we'd be monitoring during the melt season. As we travelled along the glacier, we heard a symphony of creaking and cracking coming from crevasses, and the sound of water running below the surface. Things were starting to happen in the glacier's plumbing system—the glacier was waking up.

Derek was particularly interested in four surface lakes that he thought would eventually drain into the glacier. He'd instrumented two of them to capture water level changes due to filling and drainage. The other two lakes would be monitored by the upper camp team. To avoid the problems I'd experienced with data logger flooding at JEG, Derek had installed his logger enclosures on tall poles drilled into the ice—the water depth, electrical conductivity, and water temperature sensors dangled down to the glacier surface. He had enough tracer dye to do intensive water flow measurements in the monitored streams and measure both low (early melt) and high (late melt) streamflows. He'd also installed Leroy and Elmer, the time-lapse cameras from my JEG days, to monitor surface melt and lake drainage. He was well prepared, and we looked forward to observing and measuring changes in hydrology over the next five weeks.

Part of our routine would involve collecting data for one of the upper camp members. We were in charge of his weather stations, and we'd be continuing the snow measurements that he had started while he was in the lower camp. We'd dig a line of snow pits every second day and measure snow depth along the same line every two weeks. There was plenty of work to keep us busy for a solid five weeks, and it was nice to get a sense of what we'd be up to during our time in the field. I was glad to be in a supervisory role, to not stress about my own data collection and just help my student with his.

But I was also lonely. Even though I'd familiarized myself with camp and my student's research stations, I was out of my element on this unfamiliar glacier with someone I knew nothing about. I missed doing pine beetle research with my family, the familiarity of working with Dave, and the fun of taking the dogs in the field. I wasn't as keen on remote fieldwork anymore; I much preferred heading out into the bush for a couple of days and then going home again. That routine had fit best into my academic career, as I could do fieldwork on weekends and university work during the week. I was prepared to make the most of it, though, and planned to enjoy what was likely to be my last Arctic field season. I didn't have the research funding to support this type of work, and wasn't sure I'd be invited to collaborate on other Arctic projects given that I was no longer at the forefront of Arctic glacier research.

The field season was destined to be unexpectedly short, however. After a long day of checking instrumentation, we came back down-glacier just before 10:00 p.m. to discover that we were cut off from our camp by raging rivers of slushy water. Derek crossed one of them but it almost sucked him in like quicksand, leaving him soaked from the waist down. He was stranded across the slush flow from me, on an island of ice between that and another slush flow, in full panic mode. Wrapped in the foil blanket from our first aid kit, he kept saying "I don't want to die, I don't want to die." The situation was dire, and we ended up having to be evacuated by chopper back to the Resolute base at two o'clock in the morning. A mere five days in the field and four days in Resolute and I was heading home again.

Should we have just waited out the slush flows overnight and seen what conditions were like in the morning? Would things have been different if I was in the field with someone I knew and trusted implicitly? We might have been able to reach our camp once the slush flows had run out and each consolidated into a single stream channel. But there was no way of knowing if that would happen in a matter of hours, or if it would take several days. We also didn't know what the streams would be like once they were slush-free—if they were deep, fast-moving channels, we wouldn't have been able to cross them anyway. Plus, Derek was soaked, so it didn't seem prudent to have him stay on the ice in that condition. Then there was the problem of my bad knee, which had swelled to epic proportions and couldn't bear weight—echoes of my first season at JEG.

It was heartbreaking to have to abandon my International Polar Year field program. Even if I was initially a little hesitant, I knew I would have settled into the day-to-day of camp life and the routine of regular field measurements. It was doubly disappointing to be a field researcher and have that research fail so spectacularly. I was swimming upstream; academia wasn't working out the way I'd expected.

* I returned to Lethbridge that July with a rough field season behind me and a grant application to write for NSERC. I proposed to do my work as part of the SRWP, continuing my research on disturbed forests—from pine beetle to wildfire. One of my points was that forest disturbance might have a bigger impact on snow processes than the effects of climate change. This didn't absolve me from studying climate change. But I was looking at its secondary impacts—shifts in snow processes because of how climate change had affected the forest. Pine beetle ran rampant because of drought-stressed trees in summer and warmer winters, while wildfires were increasing in size and severity because of higher air temperatures and longer summer seasons.

I took a break from my grant application in August, when I went to the Crowsnest Pass for another trip into the SRWP field sites. This time I went with Uldis—one of the two principal investigators on the project—and another researcher, Mark. We travelled to a number of instrumented sites by ATV, bumping and rumbling over rough, steep trails that were washed out in some places by deep puddles. The trip gave me a better sense of what the SRWP was designed to measure, and gave us a chance to check out Mark's field installations. At several sites we emptied Mark's sediment samplers into a bucket, glad to see that they were working as they should. The outing was also an opportunity to relax beside a gurgling mountain river—and for me to chat with Mark while Uldis fished for trout.

Mark had a lot to say about academia and succeeding in it. While I appreciated receiving advice from someone much farther along in their academic career, I got the sense that he didn't consider me an equal collaborator in the research program, ignoring my history of solid solo research. At a group meeting a few months later, the other principal investigator told me—out of the blue—that I should feel lucky to be part of the project so early in my career. I knew the other researchers were more experienced than I was. But I wanted to be treated the way I'd expected to be when I first signed up to join the project—as a peer, working side by side with them. Such comments were my first inkling that my experience with this research group might not be as positive as I'd hoped. Even the fieldwork I enjoyed was being spoiled by academic politics; the SRWP wasn't much better than my university department. I suspected it all had to do with academic hierarchies, something I'd never been a fan of and often unintentionally failed to observe.

✷ In fall 2008, my first MSc student arrived on campus. Janice had completed her BSc at Thompson Rivers University in Kamloops, BC, and knew Rita Winkler, who had recommended me. Janice came fully funded with an NSERC postgraduate studies grant: a feather in her cap for future academic work. She would be working in the SRWP catchments comparing snow processes in burned and unburned forest stands, which meant we had to find her some forest stands to set up in.

We went out to the Crowsnest Pass with Uldis in early September to scope out field sites. Janice and I shared an ATV; she drove while I sat on the back. I never did get used to driving ATVs in such hilly, potholed terrain, even after taking a safety course that was designed to get me comfortable with them. I was always the passenger, never the driver. In one instance, that decision backfired on me. The ATV I was riding on slipped while my PhD student was driving it up a steep hill and I fell off the back. He flipped the ATV, but landed safely on the ground. The vehicle itself twirled through the air above my body, landing on the steel shank of my hiking boot. The fact that it didn't land on my head was about the only positive thing about the whole incident—which left me with only a sprained ankle, thanks to my sturdy boots.

We found two suitable forest stands for Janice's work in the shadow of Mount Coulthard, one of the higher peaks in the area that marks the boundary between Alberta and British Columbia. The mountain served as a gorgeous backdrop to our burned stand, rising snow-covered and majestic against a foreground of black and silver stems. The unburned stand was in the adjacent watershed, at a slightly lower elevation than the burned stand, and was so dense as to be almost impenetrable. The trees were second-growth spruce and pine. Some had fallen and were covered in moss, while others leaned gently into the wind that ruffled the tree tops but barely made it down to ground level. When travelling between the stands, we crossed a nearly straight line that demarcated the transition between live and burned trees. Finding the field sites was the easy part—the hard part was going to be installing all of our instrumentation, which was much more complicated than the equipment I'd used in my previous research projects.

On the October Thanksgiving weekend of 2008, Janice and I loaded up a cargo van with a massive pile of research equipment and drove the two hours west to the Crowsnest Pass. We had sensors to measure weather conditions, plus the hardware we needed to set up the weather stations, courtesy of a shopping spree at Home Depot. We had all the tools we needed to install the sensors, and a fat binder stuffed with documentation: manuals for each sensor, manuals for the programs we would load into the data loggers to run those sensors, and a wiring diagram to show how each sensor had to be attached to the data loggers. We were ready for action. There was just a skiff of snow on the ground, reminding us that winter was coming, and I was glad to have help from an experienced group for this first installation.

We met up with Uldis and two members of the field crew at the bunkhouse, and we all drove to the ATV staging area to access the York Creek watersheds. We filled an ATV trailer with as much gear and tools that we could safely (and maybe not-so-safely) cram in, strapped the rest to the three ATVs themselves, and headed up the trail to the field sites. On one particularly steep section, the front wheels of the ATV I was doubling on lifted off the ground because of the heavy load it was carrying. The driver turned to look at me, her eyes wide, then stood up and leaned forward to keep weight over the front tires.

This was the biggest and most complicated field installation I'd ever done. Instead of the weather station tripods I'd used for my federal pine beetle project, I had nine-metre towers that I'd never worked with before. The towers were assembled from three pieces; each piece was three metres long, and each was smaller in diameter than the one beneath it. They were shaped like triangles connected with crossbars, so they wouldn't sway in the wind. In each stand we cleared a level spot for a square concrete paver, sixty centimetres wide. We put the tower together, then set it on top of the paver. Three guy wires were attached to each tower, which we pulled taut and secured in the ground some distance away, making sure that the tower was stable and safe to climb.

Climbing the tower was like ascending a very narrow ladder, and we needed safety equipment so we wouldn't fall off and break a leg, or worse. We wore harnesses and clipped in to the tower when we were on it. A bit different from how we'd used harnesses at JEG! I'm not a big fan of heights—even two metres off the ground creeps me out—so I let the field crew install the solar panel at the top of each tower. I installed the data logger enclosure and a metal box containing the deep-cycle battery that the solar panel would charge, which would then power the data loggers.

On the second and third days we installed the data loggers and some of the weather instruments on the tower. Cardboard boxes, polystyrene foam, and bubble wrap were strewn around the field sites as we unpacked. Scattered among the mess were our personal things: lunch, water, thermoses of coffee, and extra outdoor gear. I wasn't used to working in largely snow-free conditions, and found that I got a lot dirtier in the field than I did in winter snow or on a glacier in summer! I managed to get over my fear of heights and climb six metres up the tower with my harness firmly clipped in. The views of the surrounding snow-capped peaks were fantastic. The birds-eye view, although somewhat terrifying, also gave me a bigger-picture understanding of what was happening in each stand.

That Thanksgiving Monday we headed back to the bunkhouse, exhausted, for a well-deserved dinner of turkey, potatoes, and vegetables. It was strange to spend the holiday in the field rather than at home with Dave and the dogs, but the company was still good. I got along better with the field crew than with my academic colleagues, perhaps because we were of similar age, or because they did the very thing I liked the most—fieldwork—as their everyday job.

On a second trip to the stands in late October, we installed and wired up the rest of the instruments. Since there were so many of them we needed two data loggers at each weather station. We also built a wooden platform to hold a precipitation gauge, which was basically a large-diameter piece of sewer pipe mounted vertically on a PVC base. It had to be hooked up to a separate data logger that would measure water level from the rain and snowfall it captured. Our biggest problem was that the instrument that measured water level had to be attached inside the gauge, at the bottom. Janice and I tried hard to attach it, but it took one of the smaller field crew members to climb inside the pipe and connect the instrument. All in a day's work for him.

A few weeks later we went out again and installed a grid of thirty-six stakes in each stand, like the grids at François Lake. Once the snow fell, Janice and I would measure snow depth and snow water equivalent at each stake. We used a compass to mark a straight line through the trees with a tape measure, then pounded in a piece of rebar every ten metres. We put a bamboo stake on top of each piece of rebar, with a bright piece of flagging tape on it so the stakes were easy to find in the middle of winter. It was also time to critter-proof the weather stations by installing chicken wire over the base of each tower and putting any exposed instrument cables in plastic protectors. For some reason, mice, voles, and squirrels all like to munch on fresh cables.

The installation took close to a week, over four field visits, with lots of help from the SRWP field crew. The job was both physically and mentally exhausting, though the bonus was that it only took two hours to reach the Crowsnest Pass from Lethbridge. By the time setup was complete, snow was accumulating and it was almost time to switch from ATVs to snowmobiles. The stations were as finished as they were going to be, and there wasn't much more to do except wait for February 2009, when we'd take our first winter measurements.

But in April 2009, after just two visits to the field sites, my fieldwork was cut short by a freak accident. While packing up to go in the field, I slipped on the only patch of ice in our driveway and dislocated and fractured my kneecap. To add insult to injury, this was my good knee. Dave was inside the house at the time, and thought he heard a dog in distress—but it was me, screaming in agony on the concrete. The paramedics who took care of me on the way to the hospital said they'd never heard someone swear so profusely. "This can't happen now!" I said. "I can't fucking believe this is happening to me!"

I was in hospital for three days. I needed surgery to tighten up the tendon that got stretched by the dislocation, and to find the piece of bone that had broken off my kneecap on impact. On day two, my colleague Heather came to visit and we talked about the procedure and when I'd be released. I wondered if I'd also see the department chair. He'd made a point of visiting Keith in the hospital after a minor cycling accident, so I assumed he'd stop by to see me. I'd never seen him outside the confines of the university.

In the end, he didn't show up. I was disappointed but not surprised. I did get a nice bouquet of flowers from Uldis and the team, which was a welcome gift. It helped me feel less despairing about my lack of mobility.

Even though it wasn't the same knee I'd had surgery on during my MSc, this knee didn't heal properly either, and wouldn't bend past a certain angle no matter how much physiotherapy I endured. I had to find a field assistant for Janice, since I was out of commission and Dave wasn't involved in the SRWP fieldwork. For the rest of 2009 she visited the stands with someone from the field crew, and in 2010 I hired an undergraduate who also worked on his own research while he and Janice were in the field. I made the same mistake that Martin had made during my PhD—sending two students into the field who both had their own projects and weren't fully present to help each other out. The student I hired should have been strictly a helper, nothing more. That would have been easier on Janice, who had already been saddled with a lot of hard work setting up the weather stations and snow survey grids.

✳ Grad student supervision took up more of my time than I'd expected. In 2009 I got provincial government funding for a new research project to determine how pine beetle infestation would affect snow accumulation at the watershed scale, so I brought on a second MSc student to do that work. Liam did his fieldwork in a watershed adjacent to Janice's in the spring of 2010 and 2011, after doing some computer analysis to characterize the vegetation and topography of the watershed itself. Thanks to my knee injury and full schedule, I wasn't able to go in the field with him until his second-last field visit. While it was far from an ideal situation, he went with my third MSc student, Jared, and I had to trust that the advice and guidance I provided on campus would be applied in the field. Liam did just fine without me there—although, having been a grad student myself, I suspect he and Jared goofed off a lot.

Jared was modelling a watershed in south-central British Columbia that Rita had been working in for twenty years. He was using a Canadian hydrological model along with input data from the watershed itself to model snowmelt and runoff response to both climate change and forest disturbance. He was a challenging graduate student, slow to take initiative and more interested in indulging his weird sense of humour than getting his work done. I remember sitting with him in the lab, running the model and asking him to explain what the components were. He was able to explain it all to me, which made me glad that he'd got something out of a year of working on the project. But I still wasn't sure he'd pass his thesis defence.

Finally, there was Roger, a PhD student whose decision to work with me caused a bit of controversy. He had been meant to work on a modelling project with the department's recently appointed new chair. But Roger wanted to work with me for the field aspects of the research. In the end, the chair and I co-supervised him for an ambitious combined field and modelling project studying water temperature in mountain streams. Unfortunately, the chair couldn't pay his half of Roger's salary because his funding was earmarked for other projects, so I ended up covering most of it. This left me feeling that I was just a source of money for the project, not an active participant in the hands-on research itself. Especially since I wasn't able to go into the field with Roger until he had everything set up and had been working on it for a year. Regardless, he did great work that kickstarted his post-PhD move into scientific consulting.

∗ Then there was the SRWP. Starting in the fall of 2009, Uldis organized a series of intensive all-researcher meetings to talk about expanding the project. As the project's focus shifted towards downstream drinking water and contaminant transport, the basic field measurements that we needed to understand how upstream conditions affected these variables took a back seat. The priority was to find funding for the new research topics. The meetings were intense: we stayed together in a cabin in the Crowsnest Pass, talked all day about research and how to fund it, ate all our meals together, and spent all our spare time together. Our goal was to come up with a common language among forest scientists, drinking water treatment engineers, and geographers. Once we had that language and could clearly articulate what the next phase of the project was about, we put together a research proposal that successfully sold the project to a funding agency. We also spread the word about the expanded SRWP through public presentations to neighbouring municipalities, and presentations to the provincial government, who were funding a large part of the field research.

But I wasn't sure I wanted to continue my involvement with the group, given the direction it was going. One of Uldis's ultimate goals was to apply a variety of logging treatments to the Star Creek watershed to see how they enhanced or reduced water supply from the sub-watersheds within it. This was similar to another experiment conducted in Colorado in 1956. While I originally thought it was an interesting idea, Star Creek was an important community recreation area that was also habitat for an at-risk fish species. It didn't seem wise to log it solely for a research program. I also wasn't that interested in the snow measurement part of the research—I wanted to work on something more comprehensive. Being a minor cog in the wheel of a larger project had lost its appeal.

It wasn't just the research, however. It was how Uldis denigrated Janice when she won a student presentation award at a conference, grumbling that she didn't deserve it. It was how he regarded another research group—a group that was trying to answer some of the same research questions—as competition, not collaborators. It was how he talked about his graduate students, putting some of them down regularly at our meetings. It was how he dominated the field side of the project, leaving no air for me to breathe or room for me to contribute. It was his assumption that I would gladly go along with whatever was proposed and do my part. It was the fact that he told me not to call Dave when the ATV landed on my ankle, saying he wouldn't have "bothered" his wife about it.

✽ Also in the fall of 2009, Rita and I were working on a project examining the impacts of forest litter on snow reflectivity in beetle-killed versus healthy forest stands. It was fun to work with her—we were both field researchers and had similar ideas of what was important to study. I enjoyed our talks about being women in science and empathized with how poorly she was treated by some of her colleagues and collaborators. Hearing her stories, I didn't feel as alone in my struggle at the university and with the SRWP, though both were becoming difficult to handle.

I was putting my all into the job, but I was constantly treated like a second-class citizen and wanted to find a department that was more collegial and appreciative of my strengths. I applied for a number of positions and was invited for interviews, but the successful candidate was always a man. In one case, I was sure that my credentials gave me an edge over the competition. I had more than enough research papers, and a robust research program. Yet they hired a male colleague who had one published paper and no research program to speak of. In the end, it was just as well that I wasn't offered any of those jobs, as they weren't necessarily in places where Dave and I wanted to live. Even so, I couldn't help feeling undervalued and overlooked.

All the job applications, teaching, student supervision, administrative duties, the knee injury, and applying for grants was starting to wear on me. My department still didn't feel welcoming, I had very little spare time, and I was getting farther away from both fieldwork and writing; my soul felt that gap widening. I wasn't getting enough time at home with my family, and when Jasper died of cancer in June 2011 at only four years old, I just didn't have the bandwidth to cope with it all. I pulled back from work and spent the summer growing tomatoes and potatoes, and sitting on the deck in the sun, wondering what I was doing and how I'd gotten so far down the academic road in the first place.

✳ In the summer of 2010, a colleague from the University of Calgary invited me to visit his field site at Lake O'Hara, in Yoho National Park. Matt was studying groundwater processes in an alpine headwater basin. The location was gorgeous: a sapphire blue lake in an alpine bowl, surrounded by stunted alpine forest, with the debris-covered Opabin Glacier retreating up to Opabin Pass. Dave and I drove to the site from Lethbridge, and had a fantastic day in the field seeing all of Matt's weather and water installations, and discussing what processes might be driving the groundwater hydrology his team was measuring there. Matt was an excellent mentor who championed me by inviting me to give a talk at his university, and to be an external examiner for one of his students' theses. He talked candidly about how hard it was to balance a home life with an academic life. I wished we had connected earlier because he bolstered my confidence, both in my work and my academic value.

After going to Lake O'Hara and seeing how Matt's research project explored proglacial hydrology, I decided to go back to Hilda Glacier and do the project I'd dreamed of doing after working there over a decade ago. I now had the knowledge and skills, and the right kind of field instrumentation, to better answer my original research questions there. I also had a mentor "just down the road" at Lake O'Hara. My background knowledge of the site would help me design a quality field program to understand how hydrology works in catchments where glaciers have retreated.

In 2011 I submitted a proposal to the university's research fund that was designed to get new projects off the ground, and applied for a research permit and in-kind support from Parks Canada. Both were successful: I was going back to Hilda Glacier! My field assistants would be Dave and Tsuga, just like with my pine beetle work. We'd hike in with gear on our backs, and set up whatever I needed to, wherever I wanted to. This was also a smart career move, as I needed to direct my own research project instead of working as a junior collaborator on a larger program. While I was thankful I'd been given the opportunity to participate in the SRWP, I needed to get back to the mountain glacier environment. I'd finally figured out what I should be doing and was heading in the right direction for the first time since I'd arrived at Lethbridge.

10

OUTSIDE SCIENCE

DRINKING WAS A BIG PART of the academic research culture. In the field, SRWP crew members worked hard during the day and drank hard when the day was done. When I was there, I joined in. We spilled out of the bunkhouse into the night and wandered through the adjacent graveyard, cups in our hands, the sky bright with stars above us. At conferences, my colleagues and I went to the pub to socialize. It was easier to connect with them if we had all had a few drinks and were sufficiently relaxed to talk not only about new research ideas and collaborations but about university politics or funny field stories.

I hardly drank at home. But there was something about being lonely, away from my family, and wanting to build rapport with the field crew and fellow researchers that made me go along with the drinking culture instead of saying "No, I've had enough, I'm going to bed now." Academic life can be isolating for those who don't drink. If I didn't go to the pub, I wouldn't get that valuable inside information on job openings, research grants, and funding sources, and it would be harder to develop a network that would help me

(Top) With a snowcat, H.J. Andrews Experimental Forest, Oregon, January 2012. (Photo by G. Downing, used with permission.) (Bottom) Cedar and Cosmo pose near the swimming hole at our rental house in Black Creek, Vancouver Island, British Columbia, December 2013. (Photo by D. Lewis, used with permission.)

throughout my career. It's like being a woman in business who doesn't play golf. Deals are discussed on the course and finalized at the so-called nineteenth hole, and if you don't participate—or partake—you lose out.

It wasn't just the drinking that was out of character, though. I started to notice that I was having problems teaching. I would get nervous in the half hour before the class started, and by the time class began, my palms were sweaty, my pulse was racing, I was getting chills, and my voice sounded like it was being squeezed out of the stretched neck of a helium balloon. If I wrote on the board, it was hard to keep my hands steady enough to write legibly. I dreaded my evening environmental science course—one hundred students, all expecting me to entertain them for three hours. I was so exhausted. All I wanted to do was curl up in a ball and go to sleep.

I was also struggling with my science. I would experience bursts of energy and feel invincible for weeks at a time. But then there'd be weeks where I would shut down, hardly getting through the everyday tasks needed to keep things running smoothly. I had so many great ideas during my energetic phases, but those phases didn't last long enough for me to implement them. I began to find it difficult to do my research analyses and extract key results. Sometimes those results read like Latin to me, making it impossible to wrap my brain around the concepts I was trying to study. I was also losing some of my field skills—specifically the ability to make snap decisions and deal with adversity. One day I burst into tears because Janice and I couldn't get the snowmobile up a side slope in half a metre of fresh snow. I didn't know what was wrong with me, and feared that I was no longer able to do my job properly. I hoped it was temporary, whatever *it* was, and that if I just started working at Hilda Glacier and had some quiet time to myself I would feel better.

I started going to regular counselling sessions and my doctor increased the dosage of the antidepressants I had been on since the end of my PhD. Counselling was only a band-aid, a way to vent my frustrations and try to work through becoming a functioning human again. The increased medication made my hands shake so much that anything requiring manual dexterity—including handwriting—was off the table. Neither the counselling nor the pills were working.

Despite these worsening problems, I managed a trip to the Rockies to set up preliminary sensors for my Hilda Glacier project. Dave, Tsuga, and I went during the Remembrance Day weekend in 2011 and it was blizzarding and cold when we arrived. We hung temperature sensors in the trees outside the terminal moraine, and Dave climbed over the moraine and into the forefield to mount a sensor on a piece of T-bar metal pounded into the ground. I was excited to be back at Hilda Glacier getting ready for a new research project, but I worried about my state of mind and my ability to do the work. The weather made the drive south to our campsite tricky and slow. We finally arrived at the Mosquito Creek campground and parked in the prime spot for our trailer: right next to the creek and a bit sheltered from the rest of the sites. It was a stereotypical mountain scene: fresh snow on the surrounding peaks, mounds of snow hiding shrubs and clumps of grasses, and steam rising from the creek into the cold air.

The day before we left for our trip, I had found a lump on Tsuga's hind leg. We took him to the clinic when we returned from the field, and the vet diagnosed him with lymphoma. This terrible news came only five months after we'd lost Jasper. It felt like a kick in the stomach after everything we'd already been through. We were devastated and worried helplessly about how much time he had left.

In an attempt to fill the awful void growing inside of me, I decided to get back to writing for the first time in four years, and started a blog. I needed to do something that was just for me, not for work; I also needed a way to connect with the wider world outside my academic bubble. Given that I'd been immersed in science for twelve years, that was what I blogged about. I wrote about the geomorphology of coulees, about trees dying across North America, and about big science and big data. I was relieved to have a writing outlet again, a way to communicate stories about science without revealing the turmoil in my mind.

I had successfully applied for a six-month study leave starting in January 2012. This was a half-sabbatical, which I needed after a gruelling four years at the University of Lethbridge plus two years at the University of Northern British Columbia before that. I proposed a trip to Oregon State University and the H.J. Andrews Experimental Forest to start a new project studying stream temperature. I was conflicted about going, as I didn't know if Tsuga would live long enough for me to see him again. In hindsight, I should just have taken the time to recuperate and work on existing projects that needed to be finished. I could have continued with my Hilda Glacier project instead of putting it off until the summer, and stayed home to be with Tsuga. Instead, I went to Oregon, and flew home when it was time for him to go. The goodbye was gut-wrenching; he'd been a part of our family and our adventures for seven years, and we'd always assumed he'd live to a ripe old age rather than be ravaged by cancer. Losing a canine companion is like losing a limb. I flew back to Oregon, lasting only a week in my grief before I cut my trip short and headed home again.

Two weeks after Tsuga died in February, Dave and I were on the road to get a new puppy. We had been waiting for her since the fall, and had planned for her to be a sister for Tsuga. Sadly, he hadn't lived to meet her and we were still mourning him while preparing a welcoming environment for her. Cedar was a lively black flat-coated retriever, mischievous and energetic, requiring all of our attention and care. We drove from Lethbridge to Vancouver to pick her up, the winding mountain passes across British Columbia still snowy and slick as we travelled through small towns like Kaslo, Cherryville, and Lumby. We took Cedar to Vancouver Island for a week before heading back home, getting acquainted and bonding as a family on the sandy beaches in the early spring sun. She helped us take our minds off the loss of Tsuga, though we never stopped missing him.

✴ By the time we got home from Vancouver Island I was a mess. I was only a few months into my study leave but my problems with research analysis were only getting worse, and public speaking was next to impossible. My brain sometimes wouldn't stop racing and I developed an addiction to sudoku puzzles to try to calm it down. I would methodically work through six puzzles just before bed, trying to use up my excess mental energy in preparation for sleep. When I did manage to sleep, I was startled awake by terrible nightmares. As when Jasper died in June 2011, I was adrift. Once again, I spent hours sitting on our deck, questioning what I was doing. I had no idea how I was going to resume my full work duties when my study leave was over in June.

Eventually I stopped being able to function in my personal life, not just at work. Many things became difficult to do. Yes, I drank in the field and at conferences. Yes, I took on too much during my study leave. Yes, I was stressed from the death of my dog. But there was something more going on.

I was becoming a stranger in my own mind, standing outside of myself, watching how I laboured at almost everything, wondering what caused these changes and why they were paralyzing me. I had bouts of extreme anxiety and difficulty breathing. I was ridiculously nervous talking with even one person. It was hard to hold on to a thought while conversing; conversations stalled because there was absolutely nothing going on in my head, and nothing for me to say. Things that I once took for granted—like concentrating on novels or research papers, tracing character development or following the thread of a logical argument—were completely beyond my cognitive abilities. Noise put me on edge: traffic, people talking, the garbage truck, a lawnmower. Even the stimuli of driving became far too much to handle, making me frustrated and more likely to cause an accident. Decision-making froze me in my tracks, whether it meant deciding what I'd wear that day or at what time I should schedule a doctor's appointment. I wanted to disappear, to just quietly fade away into nothingness.

Earlier that year, Rita and I had been working on the final report for the grant that funded Jared's graduate work. While I was able to write the background and study-site sections, I was stumped when I got to the research results and discussion sections. What *had* we found out about how snow processes responded to climate change and the associated forest disturbance? What was important? Why was it important? What did it tell us? How was it relevant in the real world? I typed in some keywords to build on and sent the document to Rita, hoping she'd fill in the gaps. Even now when I read that report, I spot missteps that I might have avoided if I'd been feeling fully myself.

✶ I had to take a medical leave from my position at the University of Lethbridge. It was one of the most difficult decisions I've ever made. I was ashamed, like I was a failure at my job. I knew this wasn't logical. If I'd had a heart attack or had broken a bone, I would ask for medical leave and not feel one iota of shame. But mental illness is an invisible disability that carries a stigma, whereas physical illness or injury does not.

In March 2012, I went to the dean of arts and science to get permission to take a leave, armed with a letter from my doctor. I was accompanied by Kim, a colleague from the university's faculty association; I'd asked her to attend to take notes and remember what the dean had said in case I didn't. It was eerily similar to when I talked to Martin about putting my PhD thesis on hold. Since we don't talk about mental health in academia, it's hard to bring the subject up—especially if you're the person with the problem. So I didn't bring it up with the dean. I simply said I had a medical condition that required me to take a leave, and I didn't know when I'd be well enough to work again.

The dean was remarkably sensitive and accommodating. Because I was requesting a medical leave partway through my study leave, he said that when I returned to work I'd be allowed to undertake the remainder of that leave. This was a generous offer, and one that I fully intended to take him up on. If I just stuck with the counselling and took my meds, I reasoned, I would improve enough to get back into the fray in no time.

That spring, I received notification from the university that I had been awarded tenure. I also got a letter from NSERC telling me I'd successfully secured a Discovery Grant. Though I'd been striving to reach these goals for five years, they no longer mattered to me, given how I was feeling. It was as though someone else had achieved these milestones, someone who was more capable and well than I was. Academia was finally going my way just as I reached the end of my rope.

I attended the annual conference for my research field in Banff, a conference that I had helped organize. Word had gotten out that I was going on medical leave, so colleagues naturally asked if I was okay and when I might be back. I prevaricated, not wanting to talk about the thing we don't talk about in academia, not wanting to seem weak. Instead, I told them that my doctor was still running some tests, that we still had some things to figure out. Those people who did know the truth were sworn to secrecy.

I switched to a different counsellor, one assigned by the university's benefits provider. I also visited a psychiatrist every two weeks, who tried to put a name to my condition and find a medication that would help. He diagnosed generalized anxiety disorder and major depressive disorder. His approach was to attack the depression with antidepressants of various types, which I tried for six to eight weeks at a time to see if any of them would work. None of them did, and some had terrible side effects. One caused a migraine so intense that I ended up in the emergency room needing intravenous medications to quell it. Another caused such bad stomach and gut upset that I was forced to stay home, close to the washroom. Others had no effect at all, like swallowing a sugar pill and hoping it would cure what ailed me. The psychiatrist said I was part of the 60 per cent of the population who weren't helped by medication. He recommended that I continue with the latest drug cocktail and try to work harder in counselling to make up the shortfall. I called bullshit on that. Counselling wasn't going to cure my anxiety and depression. It would only give me tools to manage it.

Nevertheless, I did as I was told, taking my meds and doing my counselling in a bid to beat this thing and get back to some semblance of normal. I also went ahead with my plans to remove my weather stations from the SRWP sites and bring them back to the lab. The field crew and Janice were kind enough to do the full uninstallation, since I wasn't well enough to participate. I'd test and reconfigure the stations for Hilda Glacier work as soon as I was feeling better. Everything was going to be all right.

Dave and I got a second puppy in the spring of 2013. Cosmo, another black flat-coated retriever, had a forehead that resembled that of a Klingon from *Star Trek*. He was a great playmate for Cedar and they raced around the yard and wrestled in the house together. It lifted my spirits a bit to see them so happy and to watch them learn new things.

I would go for long walks with one dog or the other, wandering the neighbourhood paths like a ghost, searching for peace of mind and a way to calm down. On one of my walks, a colleague who lived around the corner stopped his car and asked how I was doing. He invited me over for coffee, but in my depressed state it wasn't clear what he meant by the invitation. Was he just being friendly? Or did he have some advice to dole out? Did he want the inside scoop about what was wrong with me? Regardless, I didn't take him up on it. I was ashamed of my illness and didn't want to share it with anyone. I didn't want my failure to be reflected back at me.

As my illness dragged on, it became obvious that I wasn't likely to get better and return to my job anytime soon. Dave had always been my rock, but now I relied on him for even basic things like grocery shopping or getting to appointments. I started to feel that I might not get better at all, and wasn't sure that the psychiatrist had made the right diagnosis. I transitioned from a short-term medical leave to a long-term disability leave, at which point we decided that it was time to leave Lethbridge to head back to the coast. It was the one place to which we always retreated to heal and recover. We could always move back if I recovered sufficiently to return to work.

In October 2013 we sold the house, packed up, and drove west to Vancouver Island. We stopped in the Rockies for a week to enjoy the early fall weather and hike in to our favourite spots one more time, including Hilda Glacier. Our last day in the mountains coincided with the season's first snowfall, and the dogs had a blast chasing each other in the fresh powder, racing around full of adolescent energy. I wished I felt the same, but the weight of my illness pressed down on me like a ten-ton rock.

Once back on the island, we rented a house in Black Creek, halfway between Courtenay and Campbell River. It was situated on the back half of a ten-acre parcel, hidden in the trees, with an extensive trail network in the nearby woods. It had one and a half bedrooms—the half bedroom was up a short flight of stairs and located right under the roof. The long, narrow room had dingy fake-wood panelling, a scruffy brown carpet, and clerestory windows that provided a bit of natural light. We painted the panelled walls white and added white moulding to make the room feel brighter.

This became my writing garret, my perch at the top of the house. I had two desks. One was just for journalling, writing by (shaky) hand: a tiger maple antique with turned legs and a small arch in the front to accommodate a seated person. I bought it second-hand from a woman in Comox, who posted it for sale but hadn't even had a chance to empty it out before I came to see it. She slowly removed her personal items and reluctantly took my money, sad to let the desk go; perhaps in losing it, she was losing a dream or a fond memory. I also had a work desk where my desktop computer sat, which was where I wrote my blog posts.

Blogging kept my brain from atrophying as I was sucked down the rabbit hole of my illness. The more time I spent away from academic life, the broader the range of topics I explored, exercising the writing muscles that had deteriorated during my time in Lethbridge. I wrote about the state of Canadian science and science communication, and the experience of women in science. I interviewed environment writers, and participated in a blogging challenge where I wrote a blog post a day for twenty-six days, one for each letter of the alphabet.

Still, it would take over a year before I took control of my illness by openly writing about my mental health, instead of just referring vaguely to "health issues."

✴ Not long after we arrived in Black Creek, I found a family doctor who referred me to a local psychiatrist. Surprisingly, I got an appointment with him only a month later. In January 2014 I was diagnosed with generalized anxiety disorder and bipolar II disorder (BP-II).

I wasn't surprised about the anxiety diagnosis, as it was the same diagnosis the other psychiatrist had made. I'd been anxious since I was a child, always worried that something bad was going to happen or that I'd done something wrong. Those anxieties had coloured my whole life.

The bipolar diagnosis was different, and I was catapulted into the new world of mood disorders, which are more serious than depression and anxiety. BP-II meant cycling between euphoric highs during which I felt unstoppable, to deep depressions during which I felt my world was going to end. This was exactly what I had experienced over the last year: months in a high phase, when I could juggle all my tasks at once, followed by months in a depressive phase, when I could barely drag myself to work. I was currently stuck in a depressive phase, which is why the previous psychiatrist had diagnosed major depressive disorder. But the new psychiatrist said my history of highs and lows, and the resistance of my depression to common antidepressants, made a BP-II diagnosis more plausible.

Apparently, BP-II is harder to treat than BP-I. The latter consists largely of manic episodes that are suppressed by antipsychotic medications, and the patient then goes back to "normal" life until they have another manic episode. With BP-II, however, I experienced depressive periods and intermittent hypomania, which isn't as bad as mania but has some of the same symptoms. The psychiatrist explained that the goal was to stop the hypomania, because it's always followed by a devastating low that also causes cognitive decline. Dealing with the depression without triggering hypomania was tricky, given the medications available. I had to pay close attention to my moods and the warning signs of hypomania so we could stop it before it did more damage.

Not only is BP-II difficult to treat, when combined with anxiety it's even harder. I could attest to the fact that both conditions were excruciating to live with. Just as the last psychiatrist had done, my new psychiatrist started me on a merry-go-round of medications, trying to find ones that would work without unbearable side effects. Some made me sleep for an inordinately long time during the day. Some left me nauseated and heaving into the toilet. Others caused a restlessness so terrible that I wanted to pull my skin off just to stop the sensation of ants crawling all over me.

In the meantime, the university's insurance provider organized a cognitive function test to see whether I was able to go back to work. I found the test difficult and draining, and did it in two sessions rather than the usual single session. It involved tasks like identifying keywords spoken by one person in a recording with someone else talking in the background, or pressing a button every time a specific number was spoken in a recording with music in the background. The results suggested that, unless I experienced a miracle recovery, I wouldn't be going back to my old job ever again; I would stay on long-term disability for the foreseeable future.

I had been forced out of academia by my bipolar diagnosis. I was broken and lost, with no idea how I would move forward from this unexpected condition and the symptoms it caused. If I couldn't go back to my job, what would I do? How would I structure my days? What was my purpose in the world?

While Dave did contract work in dendrochronology for the federal government, I went for long walks in the woods with the dogs, everything winter-wet and dripping: me, the dogs, the trees. Cedar and Cosmo always found the muddiest puddles to play in, and ran up and down the saturated, leaf-covered paths with sticks and other woodland treasures, only half-listening to me when I called them off a particularly nice-smelling slug or a pile of deer poop. There was a small swimming hole on our rented property where I would take them after our walks to get the worst of the mud off them. They loved the freedom of the water and swam with abandon in that small pond. These walks were my lifeline—the quiet time with the dogs was consoling and helped me get out of the house every day.

Some days we'd go to the beach. We'd take a brief forest trail from the road, then follow the beach for a kilometre or two until we walked back up onto the trail and headed towards a beachfront campground and restaurant. Once there, we'd turn around and head back. The dogs loved splashing in the ocean to fetch toys, racing along the sand and leaping over driftwood logs to come back to me so I'd throw the toy again. And again.

I took up photography and practised my skills in the forest and around the property. There was an old car abandoned in the woods, overgrown with blackberry vines and moss, which made a perfect photo subject. The dogs were also good subjects, in the rare moments they stopped running long enough to be photographed. Photography was a way of stilling my mind, to look only at patterns and colours and how they interacted. I also took up knitting, another mind-calmer. The quiet click of the needles as I knit one and purled the next, the slowly growing scarf in my lap as my stitches added up to an actual garment. I tried to do the sudoku puzzles that had calmed my mind in the early stages of my illness, but found I could no longer solve them. I just couldn't figure out the right combinations of numbers to make them work.

My days were mostly the same. Force myself to get up and have breakfast. Take the dogs for a walk. Garden. Play with the camera and look at my pictures. Have lunch. Write in my journal or write part of a blog. Nap. Have dinner. Watch TV and knit. Go to bed.

I was comforted by this predictability, one of the few things that kept me going. Changes in routine caused major anxiety, and keeping each day very much like the last helped me guard against surprises. As Annie Dillard wrote, "A schedule defends from chaos and whim. It is a net for catching days."[1] It wasn't a bad way to spend each day. But it wasn't how I was used to spending my days. My illness was holding me hostage: it controlled me rather than me controlling it. It told me when I needed extra sleep, when I needed to avoid people, when I should adjust my meds and, if I had any energy, when I was able to be sort of normal. There was no way to know which days I'd feel okay versus which days I'd feel terrible, because I hadn't yet found a way to correlate specific activities or events with an associated emotional or mental response. As a scientist, I was used to evaluating cause and effect, but I couldn't do that with my illness. It was inconsistent and impossible to pin down.

That spring our landlords allotted me a small corner of their larger vegetable garden and I grew some of the best vegetables ever. The carrots and beets were big and beautiful, the beans produced prolifically, and both the new and mature potatoes were delicious. The plot was perfect: the soil was rich from having been amended regularly over the years, and there was an unlimited supply of water from the property's pond, which kept everything growing well during the hot, dry summer days. I found it therapeutic to work with my hands in the dirt, hilling potatoes and harvesting beans, weeding and watering and watching the garden grow.

✻ Despite the obvious toll that mental illness took on my life, I couldn't quite shake the feeling that I was a failure. That if I'd just tried harder, I could have stayed in academia. I was crushed that I wasn't able to take on my renewed Hilda Glacier project; I had squandered my opportunity to forge a new path with my science. As someone who had depended on my mind for so much of my life, I was dismayed that it had turned on me and become unreliable. I was scared that it would never work the same way it had when I was a professor. My thinking was slower, clunkier, and less expansive—I had trouble deciphering a simple recipe. Even basic math, like calculating a waiter's tip, was difficult and painfully slow, the numbers sliding from my brain like water through a sieve.

My academic career hadn't just been a job, it had been an identity. I was defined by what I published, the conferences I attended, the grants I received, the students I supervised, the committees I sat on. All of these things combined created a "me" who had been working hard for thirteen years to make a place and a name for herself in academia. Like most academics I knew, I had become my job and it had become me. When I gave it up, I gave up my identity. Who was I, without being immersed in the constant swirling energy of academic life? Who would I be if I was no longer a professor?

Part of my identity was being a scientist. I struggled with existential questions: What did it mean to be a scientist? Did I have to be doing science every day? Thinking about it? Talking about it? Some argue that a scientist by training remains a scientist no matter where their career path leads. Others define a scientist by papers published and students supervised. But what about scientists in industry, who don't publish or supervise students? What about community scientists? If I took photographs and wrote essays, was I still a scientist?

In leaving academia, I also left behind my community. I was used to being among my colleagues at the university and my peers with whom I connected over email or at conferences. I'd gotten to know the administrative assistants in our department and the research technicians in our building. I was on nodding terms with members of other departments, and on a first-name basis with the person in the procurement office who helped me order research equipment. I knew many of the geography and biology grad students by name and had some idea of who each of them was working with. All of that was lost in an instant. I was on my own, and especially lonely given the stigma of mental illness. It wasn't as though I'd broken my arm and had a cast for people to sign. I had an invisible illness that I worried people would scoff at.

Another big challenge was that I had cut off my career in midstride. Having just gotten tenure and a promotion to associate professor, I was on track to achieve the rank of full professor in another five to eight years. I was the vice president of my professional organization and was set to become its first female president the following year. I had initiated the Hilda Glacier project and was pushing my research towards working on mountains and glaciers rather than in the forests around them. I was building a legacy of experienced graduate students who would go on to work in different industries and form a network of expertise across the country.

Suddenly, I had no career to speak of. I had no clear road map, no signposts that pointed out the requirements needed to progress to the next stage. I was completely cut off, the path ahead of me dark and overgrown, the path behind me blocked by a giant wall. I'd lost my identity, my community, and my career, and it seemed that nothing could adequately fill that void.

I was bitter but also grieving terribly; these losses would take years to come to terms with. I found it difficult to not become mired in the dark present—or fixated on the faraway, glittering past—while I painfully tried to reconstruct everything that had been taken from me, step by slow step. I was fragile, and frustrated that life had come to this. It was not what I had imagined back in graduate school, when I was spending eight weeks each summer in a gloriously remote field camp, writing, exploring, and collecting data.

In a bid to maintain my sanity and regain a sense of connection, I signed on for things that kept me peripherally in academic circles. One of those was a blog network called *Science Borealis*, which aggregated all Canadian science blogs on one website. They also had their own blog and a team of volunteer bloggers who were specialists in various subject areas. It was an exciting time for science communication and blogging in Canada, as this emerging field was gaining popularity and support from the scientific and communication communities. It was also attracting an increasingly interested public. I found that volunteering for *Science Borealis* fit around my mental abilities; even just a few hours a week was a solid contribution.

While I still kept up my own blog, in 2014 I started writing blog posts for Canadian Science Publishing on topics directly aimed at research scientists. Some of these posts explored how to deal with information overload from having access to all the papers published in a specific field, or how to network by capitalizing on your academic genealogy: the relationships built between supervisors and students and between supervisors themselves. This arrangement worked well for me: I had long deadlines and was given free rein over what topics to develop, so I wrote when I was able and rested when I needed to.

The liminality of my position was evident to me as I wrote these blog posts. I occupied the dual role of scientist and writer—many readers took my posts seriously because I was writing from a scientist's perspective. But I wasn't wholly one or the other; I was still making that transition, still learning how to combine the two facets of my life. I was becoming a science writer, but doing so in a nontraditional medium.

To make new professional contacts, I turned to social media. I had started a Twitter account in 2011, mostly to follow like-minded scientists and researchers. Now I used it to interact with science writers and communicators. I found a rich community online and made some great connections with fellow science writers. I participated in some of their research projects, blogged about their open science initiatives, and learned about topics like "the science of science communication," and the challenges of being a researcher who moves into the science communication space. During the depressive phase of my bipolar disorder, it helped a bit to have people to "talk" to online, and to engage with their ideas and thoughts instead of just my own.

While I was working hard to build these connections, I was also rebuilding my identity. It was difficult, however, having been on the academic path for so long and despite my early doubts about whether it was what I really wanted. Sharing ideas with my new online community helped me feel like more of a science writer than an academic scientist.

As I learned more about science communication, I recalled Martin asking if that's what I was planning to do after my PhD. He seemed to assume that it was. I had unintentionally proved him right, though it took me seven years to do so. But the more science writing I did, the more I began to lean towards writing craft over science content. My identity shifted from that of a science writer in particular to that of a writer in general—what I'd wanted to be ever since I was a kid. I remembered that my greatest loves were— and always had been—books and writing. I would read any style of good writing, whether that was science writing or a novel. I was still interested in science, but the craft of writing itself became more important to me as the science became harder to wrap my broken brain around.

If I wanted writing to be my focus, it would help to actively participate in the writing community by attending conferences and volunteering for writing organizations, but that wouldn't be easy, given my mental health limitations. I was what people in disability circles call a Spoonie: I had a limited number of spoons of energy each day, and when they were used up I had no reserves to fall back on. So, I attended conferences and took in webinars as I was able. I joined my provincial writers' organization and a group for writers of creative nonfiction, which is my preferred writing style.

Writing gave shape to my new life. Even though I was able to write for only one to two hours a day, I was doing what I was good at and enjoyed. I started reviewing books, interviewing authors, and writing essays about books, reading, and writing. At last, I had made the full shift from being an academic scientist to being a writer of creative nonfiction and popular science.

✳ Knowing that I wouldn't be able to return to work, Dave and I bought a house an hour north of Victoria in the summer of 2014. It had an awkward layout, but was on two and a half acres with a marsh out back—perfect for Cosmo and Cedar, and quiet for me. The dogs had lots of room to run and play and chase rabbits. We threw ourselves wholeheartedly into new home ownership: Dave repainted the interior walls and built a raised-bed vegetable garden complete with a board-and-batten garden shed. I was excited to have my own garden again as a form of outdoor therapy, and hoped I'd have as much success with growing vegetables as I did in Black Creek.

It was hard but rewarding work, transforming the barren yard into a place we loved to spend time in and play with the dogs. In 2015 we got a third dog, Tsilah, who looked a lot like Tsuga with her German shepherd coat, but was wilder and more independent than he had been. Yard work and dogs took my mind off my inability to do the academic work I once enjoyed, and the tangible outcomes of my physical work gave me a sense of accomplishment. This was so different from academia, where the outcomes of your hard work are an exercise in delayed gratification: one year to publish a paper, two years to see a student graduate, four years to get a research grant, and so on.

Working in the garden gave me lots of time to reflect on the career-related choices I'd made. I was angry at myself for not following a writing path earlier, when I was more able. It was like I'd needed the breakdown in my mental health to push me into it, but when I finally got there I couldn't function at the high level I was used to. Did that mean I wasted my time by remaining a scientist for so long? Perhaps not. I added knowledge to my research field, mentored students, and made many researcher friends. When writing about nature or environment-related topics, I mined my own scientific knowledge or knew where to look to find the best information. I relied heavily on Dave to provide valuable feedback on the pieces I wrote. What I learned from fieldwork translated well into writing: be ready and willing to spend time on your own or with very few companions; observe, observe, observe; persevere even when challenges feel insurmountable; prepare for the worst and make the most of the best. It took me years to understand this connection, the distance of time allowing me to see more clearly the trajectory of my life and the linkages between writing and science.

✳ On the mental health front, my psychiatrist and I eventually found a combination of medications that sort of worked, and I had settled into a daily routine that allowed me to function, albeit at a much lower level than before I became ill. But in early 2019 I had a hypomanic episode that put my mind into overdrive and made me feel on top of the world. I wasn't sleeping. I was writing essays in my head at all hours of the day. I was purchasing all sorts of things online. I was pitching freelance pieces left, right, and centre. I was juggling more balls than I could possibly hope to keep in the air. And I loved it. I was alive and excited and "me" again. I didn't want it to end.

This was a bipolar high manifesting itself. I needed to quell it to avoid falling into a deep low afterwards. I took the required medication but had to keep increasing my dose; it just wasn't knocking down the high. Returning to an even keel took far more medication—and time—than the psychiatrist had expected. Despite levelling off somewhat, my mood and energy levels were still higher than they'd been in a long while, and they stayed that way for most of the year.

One important realization came from this high: I needed to be more in charge of my life. I craved a sense of personal agency, something I'd been missing as I was tossed around by the vagaries of my illness and the side effects of the medications. I wanted goals and a series of steps to reach those goals—steps I'd chosen myself to track my progress.

What did "taking charge of my life" mean, in practice? It meant walking the trails around our house again, something I'd done regularly when we first moved in but dropped during my last depressive phase. It meant committing to writing my first book. It meant signing up for the Lake to Lake Marathon.

I had first read about the Lake to Lake Marathon in 2018 and was intrigued. The event took place on southern Vancouver Island, not far from where we lived, and walkers—not just runners—were welcome to participate. The forty-two-kilometre course followed a gravel railbed trail from Shawnigan Lake to Lake Cowichan, crossing several old train trestles along the way. I liked the idea of walking on gravel rather than asphalt and checking out the views from the different trestles. I didn't think about the training so much as I envisioned a lovely walk in the woods and crossing the finish line.

People with bipolar disorder are notorious for promising the world during a high phase. We have a tendency to take on more than we can handle, and that impulse collides with the inability to follow through, leaving us holding the pieces and wondering what went wrong. During that year's high, I committed to several writing assignments. As my high subsided a bit, I ended up having to cancel one and not do as good a job as I'd planned for another. This left me feeling like a terrible person, an unreliable writer who burned bridges by not delivering on what I'd agreed to. At the same time, however, my determination to walk the marathon never left me. But I soon realized there was no way I was going to complete the full marathon distance. Instead, I switched my sights to the half marathon.

I found a half-marathon training program that seemed like a good fit. It involved scheduling only one long walk per week; on other days I'd do either shorter walks at faster speeds or a session of repeated hill climbs. I'd have two rest days each week when I wouldn't train at all. The program was doable given my limitations—most of my daily walks would fit into an hour or three, and I could recharge on the days off. It also allowed me to address any potential bad days by simply shifting my rest days. I knew, however, that training was pretty much all I would be doing—I wouldn't have enough "spoons" to add any other tasks to the mix.

"Once you experience a high, nothing will ever feel as good again," the psychiatrist had warned, and he was right. I was used to being depressed, trapped under a soul-crushing weight that couldn't be lifted. A bipolar high seemed like a gift, even though I knew it was going to end badly and have serious impacts on my mood and brain function. I revelled in that high. It made me feel like a person again, not just a medicated zombie.

In September 2019 I joined the group of athletes at the starting line and walked the twenty-one kilometres to the finish line. I was proud of myself for finishing strongly and having reached my goal. For once, I was able to commit to something in advance and actually do it, instead of having to bow out because I "wasn't feeling good" or "couldn't function well." I received a medal and proudly displayed it on my bulletin board. I had persevered, and I had overcome. A small victory after seven years of hell.

EPILOGUE

THE PANDEMIC YEARS WERE HARD ON US. The high I had ridden for most of 2019 subsided into a deep depression, and I was back to wrestling with my familiar demons. In 2020 we lost Cosmo to a ruptured tumour and my dad to a stroke. In spring 2022 we lost Cedar to cancer. My world was falling apart, and I had no way to put it back together again.

In the fall of 2022, Dave, Tsilah, and I headed to the Rocky Mountains. Dave and I hadn't been there for nine years. We'd gotten into a rut on Vancouver Island, not going anywhere because we had three dogs, because I didn't feel able to travel, and because leaving the island was an insurmountable obstacle that I just didn't have the oomph to overcome. But Tsilah had never been to the mountains despite being seven years old, and with our twentieth wedding anniversary coming up, we decided it was time to return to our favourite places. To manage my anxiety and make things as easy as possible, we planned our trip meticulously, right down to meals we would have and the frozen food we'd take with us. I needed every detail sorted out in advance so I could enjoy the mountains without crashing and burning.

We got up at 4:00 a.m. to catch the first ferry to the mainland, with a goal of making it to the mountains in one day. The last time

Dave and I and Tsilah at Hilda Glacier, Canadian Rockies, September 2022.
(Photo by D. Lewis, used with permission.)

we'd been to the icefield area was when we left Lethbridge for Vancouver Island in fall 2013, and had stopped in the Rockies for a week's holiday before continuing our travels west. On that mid-October trip we had puppy Cosmo and Cedar, and I was trying to function on the latest medication cocktail from the psychiatrist in Lethbridge. We'd gone to Hilda Glacier in part to retrieve the temperature sensors we'd installed the previous winter; I was disheartened that I didn't get to see that project through. We hadn't been back since.

I was looking forward to this trip. I knew it would completely upend my well-established routine and I'd have to sleep for days once we got home. But it would be worth it to go to Hilda Glacier again, to celebrate our anniversary and see what had changed since our last visit. To observe the current size and extent of the glaciers along the Icefields Parkway. To enjoy a week in the mountains, not as a scientist and field researcher but as a writer and person battling mental illness. We would meet up with our friend Mary, who had been with us in the field at John Evans Glacier. Our friendship had lasted more than twenty years; she was the only person we still kept in touch with from our graduate student days.

Our trip coincided with a spell of warm and sunny weather, more like August than the end of September. The larch trees were on full display, just as they had been when we got married. They glowed yellow against the dark-green conifers, flanking the parkway and climbing up the surrounding slopes. The warm weather brought the tourists out in droves, and they filled the trail below our cabin at Johnston Canyon, chattering loudly about the scenery in a mix of different languages.

We visited the Athabasca Glacier, which had retreated and thinned significantly—we were shocked to see the amount of ice lost in nine years. The glacier was completely unfamiliar: our usual landmarks were now several hundred metres beyond the terminus, and a bedrock hump had begun to emerge from beneath the ice itself.

Thanks to an unseasonably warm autumn, the region's glaciers were still actively melting; water was cascading through the proglacial zone. Dave, Mary, and I couldn't cross the streams to hike in to the glaciers adjacent to the Athabasca. Our outing that day was limited to a walk along the snout of the glacier, talking about fieldwork, relationships, and life, catching up like old friends do. I thought back to that long-ago picture of me at two years old, standing on this very glacier. A lot had changed since then.

The next day we hiked in to a local glacier-fed lake with a perimeter trail. Tsilah loved hiking, always making sure she was out in front, leading the way through the scrubby underbrush. I was fine until three-quarters of the way around the lake, when we encountered a section of trail that steepened towards the glacier valley. There, I experienced a surge of anxiety and couldn't decide which way to go next. Dave had to gently guide me to a flat spot where we could sit and watch a nearby stream while we ate lunch and figured out what to do. We ended up finishing our loop around the lake and heading back to the truck, as I didn't feel I could tackle the climb to the glacier. I was discouraged that my insidious disease had overtaken my joy and freedom in hiking, though I was still happy to be in the mountain environment.

On our anniversary, Dave and I hiked in to Hilda Glacier. The familiar trail was somewhat overgrown from lack of use, and we had to pick our way around the occasional fallen tree. We kicked ourselves that we had once let our dogs run free in these woods, never thinking twice about the possibility of them running into a bear or disturbing other wildlife. Tsilah stayed on leash, happy to be the pack leader. With the increase in elevation, my breathing became shallow and laboured and I started to panic, feeling another anxiety attack coming on. Dave talked me down; after a short break and several deep breaths I was ready to continue along the trail.

We climbed up the ice-marginal moraine to find a completely different scene from the last time we'd been there. The graffiti made from rocks was gone, the push moraines were gone, the stagnant ice banks beside which I had taken my measurements were gone, and the winding channel that disappeared into an underground drainage system was gone. All were replaced by a broad, light-grey proglacial floodplain, across which flowed a braided stream that entered the terminal moraine at its midpoint across the valley. The glacier itself had retreated towards the back wall of the valley, becoming a perfect example of a cirque glacier. The stagnant ice banks had shifted up along the north side of the valley, closer to the glacier terminus, where the shadow of the overlying ridge stayed constant throughout the day.

As we ate our lunch and drank champagne at the edge of the proglacial zone, history played out in my mind. My field school friends and I measuring push moraines. Dave and I gauging streamflow. The two of us standing at the top of the moraine near the rock cairn, exchanging vows. All our trips to the glacier with dogs in tow, sharing our love of the mountains with our furry family.

So much had changed since Mary Schäffer's time. And so much had changed for me, since that long-ago field school that had kicked off my scientific career.

If I'd visited this part of the world more regularly, the landscape changes would have been incremental. Almost unnoticeable. But the nine-year gap made them nothing short of monumental. I understood the power of incremental change. Through that same, slow process, I had found my way back to writing. Despite my limitations, I was doing what I wanted to do, far from the challenging environment of being a woman in academia. This trip to the Rockies strengthened my resolve to return more often, to spend time in this special place with my family, to bring the mountains and their snow and ice back into our lives after having been absent so long. And to write about our adventures there.

ACKNOWLEDGEMENTS

MANY THANKS to Michelle Lobkowicz, my editor, for believing in this book after reading the first two chapters, and for shepherding it through the review process. To Cathie Crooks, Duncan Turner, Alan Brownoff, and the rest of the University of Alberta Press team for their dedication, professionalism, high standards, and their enthusiasm for this book. To Mary Lou Roy for a thorough copyedit that greatly improved the manuscript.

This project has been supported by a cadre of writing friends who always believed I could do it: Antonia Malchik, Kimberly Moynahan, Kim Rogers, Melissa Sevigny, and Erin Zimmerman from our #scienceCNF group. Your beta reading and casual chats were invaluable—I know it takes time, something we're all short on these days. Special thanks to Kimberly Moynahan for manuscript editing—I trust your judgment implicitly. Special thanks also to Erin Zimmerman for Monday check-ins and online chats as we both worked towards finishing our manuscripts (only I wasn't dealing with newborn twins at the time). To Melissa Sevigny for all the marketing tips. Thanks to Frances Peck for writerly support and accountability, and for giving me an insider's view of what it's like to be a published Canadian author.

To Michelle Hanson, Shelly Wismath, and Laura Barakeris for beta-reading feedback, and to Jessie Cherry for cheering from the sidelines. To the women's writing groups on Facebook: I learned so much from your posts and tips. I especially appreciated Jennifer Lunden's daily check-in for members—I love seeing what everyone is working on and how life is going for them.

On the science side of things: Dan Smith got me interested in geography and field science during my undergraduate degree, and supported me throughout my career, whether by sharing helicopter flights or meeting for coffee to talk about academia. Martin Sharp guided me on my PhD journey; some days I wish I had attended convocation so we could have walked the stage together. To Rita Winkler, a fellow woman in science, and a mentor, friend, and collaborator: I'll always remember our research trip to Montana, our day of snow surveys at Mason Lake, and my visit to Upper Penticton Creek. Thanks also to Bea Alt and Alison Criscitiello for agreeing to be interviewed for this book. To my students and colleagues from academia: our field experiences were the best part of it all.

Thanks to my parents for supporting my writing since I was a kid. I wish my dad was here to hold my book in his hands. I think he would have liked it.

I reserve my most heartfelt thanks for my family: Dave Lewis and the dogs (Tsuga, Jasper, Cedar, Cosmo, and Tsilah). They've stuck with me through it all, the many moves and field trips, the good times and the illnesses. Dave was a crucial sounding board for this book and was hugely understanding when I used up my limited energy on writing instead of on family things. I couldn't have done any of it without you (especially the maps you created for the book).

∗ The epigraph is from "The Summer Day" by Mary Oliver. Reprinted by the permission of The Charlotte Sheedy Literary Agency as agent for the author. Copyright © 1990, 2006, 2008, 2017 by Mary Oliver with permission of Bill Reichblum.

NOTES

PROLOGUE
1. Borges, "Of Exactitude in Science," in *A Universal History of Infamy*, 131.
2. Beltran et al., "Field Courses Narrow Demographic Achievement Gaps."
3. Clancy et al., "Survey of Academic Field Experiences (SAFE)."
4. Wadman, "Disturbing Allegations of Sexual Harassment."
5. Jahren, "Science's Sexual Assault Problem."
6. Witze, "Three Extraordinary Women Run the Gauntlet of Science."

1 | VIEW FROM THE TOP
1. Scott, *Pushing the Limits*, 69.
2. Smith, *Off the Beaten Track*, 18.
3. University of Alberta Research Support Services, *Alpine Club of Canada*.
4. Parker quoted in Scott, *Pushing the Limits*, 69.
5. Nisbet, *Sources of the River*, 87.
6. Stutfield and Collie, *Climbs and Exploration*, 103.
7. Stutfield and Collie, *Climbs and Exploration*, 107.
8. Pursuit, "How Fast Does the Athabasca Glacier Move?"
9. Carter et al., "Dendroglaciological Investigations at Hilda Creek."

2 | HISTORY AROUND THE CORNER
1. Hammer and Smith, "Sediment Production and Transport."
2. Smith, *Off the Beaten Track*, 60.
3. Currie Love quoted in Beck, *No Ordinary Woman*, 35.
4. Schäffer, *A Hunter of Peace*, 10.

5. Vaux quoted in Skidmore, *This Wild Spirit*, 210.
6. Harris, *Lands of Lost Borders*, 270.
7. Harris, "The Future of Exploration."

3 | PREPARING FOR TAKEOFF
1. Dreier, "Rachel Carson," in *The 100 Greatest Americans of the 20th Century*, 228.

7 | NOT "PAYING ATTENTION"
1. Oliver, "Yes! No!" in *White Pine: Poems and Prose Poems*, 8.
2. Smith, *Off the Beaten Track*, 184.
3. Don Munday quoted in Smith, *Off the Beaten Track*, 163.
4. Don Munday quoted in Smith, *Off the Beaten Track*, 184.
5. Phyllis Munday quoted in Smith, *Off the Beaten Track*, 192.

9 | WOMEN IN SCIENCE
1. Expert Panel on Women in University Research, *Strengthening Canada's Research Capacity*.
2. De Welde and Laursen, "The Glass Obstacle Course," 574.
3. Baker, *Sexism Ed*.

10 | OUTSIDE SCIENCE
1. Dillard, *The Writing Life*, 32.

BIBLIOGRAPHY

Baker, K.J. *Sexism Ed: Essays on Gender and Labor in Academia.* Raven Books, 2018.

Bayliss, R. "Sir John Franklin's Last Arctic Expedition: A Medical Disaster." *Journal of the Royal Society of Medicine* 95, no. 3 (2002): 151–153.

Beattie, O., and J. Geiger. *Frozen in Time: The Fate of the Franklin Expedition.* Greystone Books, 1987.

Beck, J.S. *No Ordinary Woman: The Story of Mary Schäffer Warren.* Rocky Mountain Books, 2001.

Beltran, R.S., E. Marnocha, A. Race, D.A. Croll, G.H. Dayton, and E.S. Zavaleta. "Field Courses Narrow Demographic Achievement Gaps in Ecology and Evolutionary Biology." *Ecology and Evolution* 10, no. 12 (2020): 5184–5196.

Berton, P. *The Arctic Grail: The Quest for the North West Passage and the North Pole 1818–1909.* Anchor Canada, 2001.

Bingham, R.G., P.W. Nienow, M.J. Sharp, and S. Boon. "Subglacial Drainage Processes at a High Arctic Polythermal Valley Glacier." *Journal of Glaciology* 51, no. 172 (2005): 15–24.

Boon, S. "The Altered State of Field Research: Summer Researchers Dodge Bears, Side-Step Crevasses, Long for Indoor Plumbing." *Folio*, University of Alberta, April 17, 2003.

Boon, S. "Studying Glaciers: An Initiation to the North." *Above & Beyond: Canada's Arctic Journal*, July/August 2004.

Boon, S. "Under the Crowsnest Canopy." *Outpost Magazine*, May/June 2012.

Boon, S., and M. Sharp. "The Role of Hydrologically-Driven Ice Fracture in Drainage System Evolution on an Arctic Glacier." *Geophysical Research Letters* 30, no. 18 (2003): 1916. https://doi.org/10.1029/2003GL018034.

Boon, S., M.J. Sharp, and P.W. Nienow. "Impact of an Extreme Melt Event on the Runoff and Hydrology of a High Arctic Glacier." *Hydrological Processes* 17, no. 6 (2003): 1051–1072.

Borges, J.L. "Of Exactitude in Science." In *A Universal History of Infamy*. Translated by N.T. Di Giovanni. Dutton, 1972.

Bridge, K. *A Passion for Mountains: The Lives of Don and Phyllis Munday*. Rocky Mountain Books, 2006.

Bridge, K. *Phyllis Munday: Mountaineer*. Dundurn Press, 2002.

Carey, M., M. Jackson, A. Antonello, and J. Rushing. "Glaciers, Gender, and Science: A Feminist Glaciology Framework for Global Environmental Change Research." *Progress in Human Geography* 40, no. 6 (2016): 770–793.

Carter, R., S. LeRoy, T. Nelson, C.P. Laroque, and D.J. Smith. "Dendroglaciological Investigations at Hilda Creek Rock Glacier, Banff National Park, Canadian Rocky Mountains." *Géographie physique et quaternaire* 53, no. 3 (1999): 365–371.

Cavell, E. *Legacy in Ice: The Vaux Family and the Canadian Alps*. Altitude Publishing, 1983.

Cech, E.A. "The Intersectional Privilege of White Able-Bodied Heterosexual Men in STEM." *Science Advances* 8, no. 24 (2022): eabo1558. https://doi.org/10.1126/sciadv.abo1558.

Chudley, T.R., P. Christoffersenn, S.H. Doyle, T.P.F. Dowling, R. Law, C.M. Schooman, M. Bougamont, and B. Hubbard. "Controls on Water Storage and Drainage in Crevasses on the Greenland Ice Sheet." *Journal of Geophysical Research: Earth Surface* 126, no. 9 (2021): e2021JF006287. https://doi.org/10.1029/2021JF006287.

Cimpian, J.R., T.H. Kim, and Z.T. McDermott. "Understanding Persistent Gender Gaps in STEM." *Science* 368, no. 6497 (2020): 1317–1319.

Clancy, K.B.H., R.G. Nelson, J.N. Rutherford, and K. Hinde. "Survey of Academic Field Experiences (SAFE): Trainees Report Harassment and Assault." *PLoS One* 9, no. 7 (2014): e102172. https://doi.org/10.1371/journal.pone.0102172.

Colwell, R. *A Lab of One's Own: One Woman's Personal Journey Through Sexism in Science*. Simon & Schuster, 2021.

Czajkowski, C. *Cabin at Singing River: Building a Home in the Wilderness*. Camden House Publishing, 1991.

Czajkowski, C. *Diary of a Wilderness Dweller*. Orca Book Publishers, 1996.

Czajkowski, C. *Ginty's Ghost: A Wilderness Dweller's Dream*. Harbour Publishing, 2012.

Czajkowski, C. *Nuk Tessli: The Life of a Wilderness Dweller*. Orca Book Publishers, 1999.

Davis, W. *The Sacred Headwaters: The Fight to Save the Stikine, Skeena, and Nass.* Greystone Books, 2015.

De Welde, K., and S.L. Laursen. "The Glass Obstacle Course: Informal and Formal Barriers for Women PhD Students in STEM Fields." *International Journal of Gender, Science and Technology* 3, no. 3 (2011): 571–595.

Dillard, A. *The Writing Life.* Harper Perennial, 1989.

Dreier, P. "Rachel Carson (1907–1964)." In *The 100 Greatest Americans of the 20th Century: A Social Justice Hall of Fame*, 228–231. Bold Type Books, 2012.

Dunbar, M. "Women in Science: How Much Progress Have We Really Made?" *Science Forum* 6, no. 2 (1973): 13–15.

Elkins-Tanton, L. *A Portrait of the Scientist as a Young Woman: A Memoir.* William Morrow, 2022.

Expert Panel on Women in University Research. *Strengthening Canada's Research Capacity: The Gender Dimension.* Council of Canadian Academies, 2012. https://cca-reports.ca/wp-content/uploads/2018/10/wur_fullreporten.pdf.pdf.

Gill, C. *Eating Dirt: Deep Forests, Big Timber, and Life with the Tree-Planting Tribe.* Greystone Books, 2011.

Glassley, W.E. *A Wilder Time: Notes from a Geologist at the Edge of the Greenland Ice.* Bellevue Literary Press, 2018.

Hammer, K.M., and N.D. Smith. "Sediment Production and Transport in a Proglacial Stream, Hilda Glacier, Alberta, Canada." *Boreas* 12, no. 2 (2008): 91–106.

Harris, K. "The Future of Exploration." *The Walrus*, June 14, 2018. https://thewalrus.ca/the-future-of-exploration/.

Harris, K. *Lands of Lost Borders: A Journey on the Silk Road.* HarperCollins, 2018.

Hulbe, C.L., W. Wang, and S. Ommanney. "Women in Glaciology, a Historical Perspective." *Journal of Glaciology* 56, no. 200 (2010): 944–964.

Jackson, K. *Mean and Lowly Things: Snakes, Science, and Survival in the Congo.* Harvard University Press, 2008.

Jahren, H. *Lab Girl.* Penguin Random House, 2017.

Jahren, H. "Science's Sexual Assault Problem." *New York Times*, September 20, 2014. https://www.nytimes.com/2014/09/20/opinion/science-has-a-sexual-assault-problem.html.

Lear, L. *Rachel Carson: Witness for Nature.* Holt Paperbacks, 1997.

Lowman, M. *The Arbornaut: A Life Discovering the Eighth Continent in the Trees Above Us.* Farrar, Straus and Giroux, 2021.

Munday, D. *The Unknown Mountain.* Expanded edition. Coyote Books, 1993. Originally published in 1948 by Hodder and Stoughton.

Nares, G.S. *Narrative of a Voyage to the Polar Sea During 1875–6 in H.M. Ships "Alert" and "Discovery,"* Vols. I and II. Sampson Low, Marston, Searle, and Rivington, 1878.

Nisbet, J. *Sources of the River: Tracking David Thompson Across Western North America.* Sasquatch Books, 1994.

Oakes, L. *In Search of the Canary Tree: The Story of a Scientist, a Cypress, and a Changing World.* Basic Books, 2018.

Oliver, M. "Yes! No!" In *White Pine: Poems and Prose Poems.* Mariner Books, 1994.

Patton, B., and B. Robinson. *The Canadian Rockies Trail Guide*, 6th ed. Summerthought Publishing, 1994.

Peterson, B. *Dispatches from the End of Ice: Essays.* Trinity University Press, 2019.

Pollack, E. *The Only Woman in the Room: Why Science Is Still a Boys' Club.* Beacon Press, 2015.

Pursuit. "How Fast Does the Athabasca Glacier Move?" Accessed May 12, 2023. https://www.banffjaspercollection.com/attractions/columbia-icefield/stories/how-fast-does-the-athabasca-glacier-move/.

Querengesser, T. "The Cool Calling: Glaciologist Alison Criscitiello Is Redefining the Term Explorer." *Canadian Geographic*, June 18, 2021. https://canadiangeographic.ca/articles/the-cool-calling-glaciologist-alison-criscitiello-is-redefining-the-term-explorer/.

Raymond, S. "A Very Special Piece of Paper." Canadian Museum of History blog, August 16, 2018. https://www.historymuseum.ca/blog/a-very-special-piece-of-paper/.

Schäffer, M.T.S. *A Hunter of Peace: Mary T.S. Schäffer's Old Indian Trails of the Canadian Rockies.* Introduced and edited by E.J. Hart. Whyte Foundation, 1980.

Scott, C. *Pushing the Limits: The Story of Canadian Mountaineering.* Rocky Mountain Books, 2000.

Serreze, M.C. *Brave New Arctic: The Untold Story of the Melting North.* Princeton University Press, 2018.

Sharp, M., and M. Tranter. "Glacier Biogeochemistry." *Geochemical Perspectives* 6, no. 2 (2017): 173–339.

Skidmore, C. *Searching for Mary Schäffer: Women Wilderness Photography.* University of Alberta Press, 2017.

Skidmore, C., ed. *This Wild Spirit: Women in the Rocky Mountains of Canada.* University of Alberta Press, 2006.

Smith, C. *Off the Beaten Track: Women Adventurers and Mountaineers in Western Canada.* Coyote Books, 1989.

Stutfield, H.E.M., and J.N. Collie. *Climbs and Exploration in the Canadian Rockies.* Longmans, Green and Co., 1903.

Tangborn, W.V. "Prediction of Glacier Derived Runoff for Hydroelectric Development." *Geografiska Annaler. Series A, Physical Geography* 66, no. 3 (1984): 257–265.

University of Alberta Research Support Services. *Alpine Club of Canada: Member Survey.* 2017.

Valian, V. *Why So Slow? The Advancement of Women.* MIT Press, 1998.

Wadman, M. "Disturbing Allegations of Sexual Harassment in Antarctica Leveled at Noted Scientist." *Science,* October 6, 2017. https://www.science.org/content/article/disturbing-allegations-sexual-harassment-antarctica-leveled-noted-scientist.

Witze, A. "Three Extraordinary Women Run the Gauntlet of Science—A Documentary." Review of *Picture a Scientist*, a film by S. Shattuck and I. Cheney. *Nature* 583, no. 7814 (July 2, 2020): 25–26.

www.ingramcontent.com/pod-product-compliance
Lightning Source LLC
Chambersburg PA
CBHW020934030825
30515CB00004B/89